Industrial Policies in the Pacific

Industrial Policies in the Pacific

EDITED BY

Gunnar K. Sletmo
and Gavin Boyd

Routledge
Taylor & Francis Group
LONDON AND NEW YORK

First published 1994 by Westview Press, Inc.

Published 2018 by Routledge
52 Vanderbilt Avenue, New York, NY 10017
2 Park Square, Milton Park, Abingdon, Oxon OX14 4RN

Routledge is an imprint of the Taylor & Francis Group, an informa business

Library of Congress Cataloging-in-Publication Data
Industrial policies in the Pacific / [edited by] Gunnar K. Sletmo and Gavin Boyd.
p. cm.
Includes bibliographical references and index.
ISBN 0-8133-1899-8
1. Industrial policy—Asia. 2. Industrial policy—Pacific Area. 3. Industrial policy—Asia, Southeastern. I. Sletmo, Gunnar K. II. Boyd, Gavin.
HC412.I4835 1994
338.99—dc20 94-32806
CIP

ISBN 13: 978-0-367-00891-8 (hbk)
ISBN 13: 978-0-367-15878-1 (pbk)

Contents

Tables and Figures

Tables

Figures

Preface

The Pacific region remains the focus of questions relating to global trends in economic development and cooperation. In a previous book, *Pacific Service Enterprises and Pacific Cooperation*, we analyzed the rapidly developing service industries in the Asia-Pacific region. The present volume raises issues of industrial policy and reform in key Asia-Pacific countries in the context of Pacific regional cooperation.

The team behind this book includes researchers from North America and Asia. This team approach makes it possible to draw on experts with particular country knowledge and experience and at the same time provide an in-depth overview of the vast Asia-Pacific region.

This project, like the previous book on services, was supported by the Center for International Business Studies (CETAI) of l'École des Hautes Études Commerciales (HEC), Montreal. Financial assistance was provided by CETAI, by HEC's Service de la Recherche and by the Omer DeSerres Chair of Commerce.

Gavin Boyd, Associate Member of CETAI, and Gunnar K. Sletmo, Omer DeSerres Professor of Commerce and Member of CETAI, shared the responsibility of editing the papers and producing the final manuscript.

The editors are indebted to a number of people for their help, advice and support. John Zerby, University of New South Wales, Sydney and Robert Lévesque, HEC, Montreal provided comments and useful suggestions. Roseline Dugas produced the final photo-ready manuscript while Geneviève LeBrun coordinated project activities in their final phase. Dorothy McLeod was responsible for the reconciliation of different formats and spelling conventions as well as for proofreading. Lise Corbeil and Francine Lefebvre greatly facilitated administrative tasks.

The editors are indebted to CETAI and its director, André Poirier, for constructive support and encouragement. Alison Auch of Westview Press deserves a special thank you note for her patience and support. Finally, let it be known that this book would not have happened without Gavin Boyd's boundless energy and enthusiasm.

Gunnar K. Sletmo

1

Industrial Policy: Concepts and Theory

Michael P. Ryan

In the past states sought territory, but today they seek the ability to create wealth,[1] and it is produced, more than ever before, by the multinational enterprise, not the domestic corporation. Multinational enterprises possess the intellectual, organizational, and financial capacities to create technology--and information--intensive products and services for the twenty-first century world economy.[2] The technologies and information are globally diffused hence the business enterprises must be globally dispersed. The most sophisticated demand conditions, the most intense firm rivalries, and most efficient suppliers however tend to cluster in different parts of the world. Hence, business enterprises seek demanding, sophisticated consumers wherever they can be found and the knowledgeable and skilled employees wherever they can be found.[3]

Global corporate strategies have been facilitated by the decreasing costs of transportation and communication, by the homogenization of markets, and by the reduction of international trade and investment barriers, yet the world economy, for the general manager of a multinational enterprise, is not a "borderless world" but a globalized yet fragmented world.[4] It is a world economy cleft politically by sovereign states and separated culturally by ethnicities and religions. Hence, managers of multinational enterprises must evolve globally responsive strategies[5] while policymakers shape functional national strategies.[6] States must make their countries inviting locales for multinational enterprises or find their citizens relatively poorer and their power relatively diminished. National power rests today less on defense policy and more on industrial policy.

In this chapter, industrial policy concepts and theory are discussed within a global comparative context. Industrial policy objectives are related to the strategies of multinational enterprises, national industrial policies are reviewed, and their economic and social outcomes are assessed. Some generalizations regarding industrial policy are then presented, with a Pacific focus.

Industrial Policy in a World Economy

Industrial policy is the use by government of state authority and resources to promote the aggregate wealth of a society, maximize efficient use of its resources, among industries and social groups, and enhance the quality of life.[7] Conceptually, industrial policy comprises goals, domains, instruments, structures, capabilities, strategies and outcomes. Goals refer to the value-based outcomes which policymakers articulate. Domains refer to the policy areas, ranging from trade to direct investment to labor, which are the elements of industrial policy. Instruments are diverse means of state power which governments possess to allocate resources and influence the movement of factors of production, for example tariffs, local content rules, and minimum wage regulations. Structure refers to the national political economies in which policymakers operate: the economic system (agriculture, industry, services) and the political system (pluralism, corporatism, statism). Capabilities refer to political potentials to achieve policy goals and to the competitiveness of the economy, which in most countries is high in some sectors and low in others. Strategy refers to the process by which administrative capacities are employed to achieve policy goals. The strategy of industrial policy may be classified along two dimensions--resource allocation (planning and markets) and internationalization (independence and interdependence). Industrial policy strategies intervene in markets, let markets operate without intervention, or involve some mixed strategy, while pursuing an independent or an interdependent course in the world economy, or some mixed strategy. A strategy can be liberal, with regulatory restraints; or it can favor "champion" firms; or it may seek to guide overall capitalist development. Alternatively it may seek to build a socialist command economy, and it may emphasize import substitution or export-led growth. Outcomes refer to the economic and social effects within a country of industrial policy as measured by GDP growth rates, the balance of payments, income distribution, etc.

The presence of multinational enterprises affects the formulation and implementation of industrial policies. Corporate strategies range from domestic to multidomestic to global. Firms compete in one geographic market, or in many geographic markets without organizational integration, or in many geographic markets with organizational integration.[8] Firms with domestic strategies tend to be more protectionist than firms with multidomestic or global strategies.[9] Multidomestic and global firms fear retaliation, which would injure their interests in other parts of the world. Yet, free trade and protection preferences differ even among the multidomestic and global firms, depending upon their competitiveness.[10] Multidomestic and global firms which have lost competitiveness tend to become protectionist. They tend to call for voluntary export restraints, orderly marketing arrangements, and local content rules. They may take secure protected markets at home if they can get them without damage to their foreign market interests.[11]

It is increasingly difficult however to determine the nationality of a multinational enterprise[12] and this poses a challenge for industrial policymakers. Industrial policy strategies which include substantial elements of planning in the allocation of resources must decide what is a "foreign" firm and whether it should receive any benefits. When the European Community decided to offer subsidies to the semiconductor industry under its JESSI initiative it had to decide whether IBM's European subsidiary was a European firm. (Ultimately, the EC did invite IBM to join JESSI.) In another example, the U.S. Department of Commerce, which with the International Trade Commission implements American antidumping law, was confronted with a petition by the American subsidiary of Brother, the Japanese typewriter maker, that Smith-Corona, the American typewriter maker, was dumping in the United States typewriters which it made in Singapore and Malaysia. Turnabout is fair play, for Smith-Corona had frequently charged Brother with dumping in the U.S. market. Since Brother was producing typewriters in Tennessee, which one was the American firm? which firm's interests ought the U.S. government protect? (The Department of Commerce initially rejected the Brother petition but Brother succeeded in getting the decision reversed on appeal to the Court of International Trade.)

The most progressive actors in the world political economy may be the multinational corporations--once feared by developing and industrialized countries as organizations which undermined national interests. The MNCs are subnational and supranational actors, and increasingly want to be free to organize their research and development, finance, production, and marketing across national boundaries. Thus, while many societal groups encourage societal rigidity, MNCs encourage societal flexibility.

Industrial policymakers establish goals for their countries, either possession goals or milieu goals.[13] Possession goals concern the enhancement or preservation of something to which the state attaches value, i.e., a possession such as territory or an industrial sector. Milieu goals require efforts to shape conditions beyond national boundaries, for example through the support of international economic regimes. The possession goals may include economic growth, full employment, commercial competitiveness, aggregate national income, price stability, favorable balance of international payments, resource mobility, equitable income distribution, social stability and harmony, citizenry well-being, enlightenment, moral rectitude, and a safe, clean environment. Milieu goals may include free trade, fair trade, expanding market opportunities, international economic regime maintenance and growth, peace, stability, predictability, friendly diplomatic relations, and a safe, clean environment.[14] Policymakers do not aim to achieve all of these goals, for, depending upon the values of the society and its leaders, some goals may seem more worthy than others. Further, policymakers may find that all of their goals may not be achieved simultaneously and thus order them as short -and long-term goals.

The most basic contrast in industrial policy goals reflects differences in levels of economic development. Regardless of ethnicities, religions and cultural traditions, the societies of the industrialized countries have gone through a shift in their values and attitudes as a product of their growing wealth.[15] In a process akin to Maslow's need hierarchy, a society's attitudes and values change as its most basic needs for food and shelter are met. They come to value decision-making autonomy, free speech, a clean environment, and the like. In turn, their political leaders reflect (or perhaps lead) the popular will. Industrialized countries may be willing to put income equity, quality of life, and a clean environment ahead of the goals of maximizing national income, price stability, and economic growth. Less-developed countries, on the other hand, tend to put first priority on the purely economic goals. The newly industrializing countries perhaps stand on the cusp attitudinally as well as economically.

The basic cleavage caused by level of development does not completely explain differences in industrial policy goals, for political and social traditions and institutions continue to shape state goals. These value systems may be either individualist or communitarian[16]. Perhaps no country values individualism as much as does the United States (even the United Kingdom, mother of liberal thought). Individualism obligates that the rights to property be protected, that commercial competitiveness be ensured, and that the welfare of consumers be the state's foremost goal. Yet, even societies which tend toward individualism (including the United States) veer toward communitarian industrial policies: full employment, social stability and harmony, citizenry well-being. Social democratic institutions in Western Europe, the Confucian cultures of East Asia, and the communist countries hold these possession goals in high regard. Too many governments however aim to maximize the wealth and well-being of a small elite.

Possession goals are emphasized by most states, since they lack power in the world political economy to realize milieu goals. Only the United States has possessed sufficient power to promote free trade, fair trade, open investment, exchangeable currencies, expanding market opportunities, international economic regime maintenance and growth, stability, and (most of the time) peace. These have been the goals of a hegemony.[17] According to neo-classical economic theory, these goals ought to be the milieu goals of all countries. However, experience shows that states often want these goals to be realized while free-riding themselves. The milieu goal of a clean environment is sought most actively by the social democratic states of Northern and Western Europe, while the perceived trade-off between environmentalism and development urges most LDCs to oppose the realization of environmental goals. The same apparent (though perhaps false) trade-off causes the United States and Japan to make environmentalism a less-important milieu goal for their industrial policies.[18]

Industrial policy is composed of many policy domains, including production ownership, import and export, monetary, direct and portfolio investment, competition and antitrust, research and development, tax, intellectual property rights, and labor. The labor policy domain is further associated with education, worker safety, social insurance, and health care. The global trend in the 1980s was away from state ownership and toward privatization of the means of production. The trend in import and export policies was mixed. The GATT Uruguay Round, the North American Free Trade Area, EC92, unilateral East-Asian liberalization, and LDC liberalization were significant movements toward free trade, but an increasing use of voluntary export restraints, orderly marketing arrangements, and antidumping procedures was a contrary trend. Foreign direct investment policy became more liberal in many developing countries, but the United States policy tended to become somewhat restrictive. Monetary policy indicated a sustained trend toward freely floating exchange rates (with reduced capability for managed floating). Intellectual property rights and public financial support of R&D emerged as critical issue areas, while competition (antitrust) and tax policies seem poised to assume similar status. Labor policy took on new importance as demands for higher skill levels increased and as health care costs for employees continued to rise.

The national political economies within which decision-makers operate may be classified according to their political and economic structures. The structure of the polity refers to the process by which authoritative decisions are made, ranging from pluralism to corporatism to statism. The economic structure is the production pattern, including agriculture, industry, and services. The political-economy structure conditions the processes and outcomes of industrial policy strategies.

The structure of a polity refers to the Weberian concept of the state as "a set of organizations invested with the authority to make binding decisions for people and organizations juridically located in a particular territory and to implement these decisions using, if necessary, force."[19] But the "capacity" of the state to achieve its goals may be relatively weak or relatively strong. The following indicators assess its relative strength:

1. Can the state formulate policy goals independent of particular groups within its own society?
2. Can the state change the behavior of specific groups?
3. Can the state directly change the structure of the society in which it operates?[20]

The state in which the answers to all the questions are more or less "no" is a weak state in which societal groups dominate and maintain considerable independence. The state in which the answers to all the questions are more or less "yes" is a strong state. Many states fall between the weak-strong poles.

The United States is the archetype of the weak state. The polity is pluralistic: power is dispersed, decision-making is fragmented, and resources are allocated mainly through markets. The U.S. Constitution provided the basis for a weak state, with limited powers and checks and balances, which grew without major external security threats and with increasing wealth and relative egalitarianism.[21] Contemporary Britain and India are similarly examples of pluralist polities. Mao's China and the pre-perestroika Soviet Union are archetypes of the strong state. The polity is statist: power is centralized, decision-making is hierarchical, and resources are allocated through planning.[22] The socialist states of Eastern Europe, Asia, and Africa are (or were) similarly examples of statist polities. Switzerland and Austria are the archetypes of the state which lies between weak and strong. The polity is corporatist: power is divided among a tight condominium of state bureaucracies, political parties, and centralized and concentrated interest groups, decision-making results from continuous bargaining, and resources are allocated through markets and planning.[23] In Switzerland and Austria, state, management, and labor act cooperatively under an ideology of social partnership linked with a feudal past but challenged by internal political or economic crises and/or external security threats. Most Western and Northern European states, Japan, and many Latin American states are similar examples of corporatist polities, though differences in political structure exist across these countries.

Whether pluralist, corporatist, or statist, a polity shapes its economy:

> Institutions have been devised by human beings to create order and reduce uncertainty in exchange. Together with the standard constraints of economics they define the choice set and therefore determine transaction and production costs and hence the profitability and feasibility of engaging in economic activity. ...Institutions provide the incentive structure of an economy; as that structure evolves, it shapes the direction of economic change towards growth, stagnation, or decline.[24]

The industrial policy strategies of the various polities differ, contributing to differences in economic outcomes. The structure of an economy however constrains the strategies of industrial policy.

The structure of an economy comprises agriculture, industry and services. In 1990 the low-income economies averaged about 31% agricultural production, about 36% industrial production, and about 35% for services.[25] The middle-income economies (GNP per capita between $611 and $7,619) averaged about 12% agricultural production, about 37% industrial production, and about 50% for services. Industrial production exceeded 45% in countries such as Romania, Botswana, Venezuela, and the Republic of Korea. The structure of production in the high-income countries tends to be neglible in agriculture, between one-third and one-half in industry, and between two-thirds and one-half in services.

As countries become wealthier, industry and service production tend to take relatively larger shares. However, even declining shares of production can be exploited by entrenched interest groups, such as in the agriculture and apparel sectors of industrialized countries.

Industrial Policy Strategies and Outcomes

Industrial policy strategies may be classified along two dimensions: resource allocation (markets-planning) and internationalization (independence-interdependence). The resource allocation dimension concerns the means through which goods and services are distributed within society and the means by which society is organized.[26] Markets afford the exchange of goods and services through bilateral offers of benefit; planning directs goods and services within society by hierarchical directives. Every society employs some mix of markets and planning, ranging between free exchange and state intervention. The interna-tionalization dimension concerns the involvement of the society with its milieu.[27] Independence means an autarkic strategy; interdependence means a strategy of mutual dependence with the world political economy.

Policymakers have historically implemented industrial policy strategies which have relied heavily on the their trade policy strategies. These trade strategies have been mercantilist or neo-classical. In the contemporary era, policymakers have articulated and carried out industrial policy strategies which incorporate non-trade policy domains and employ non-trade policy instruments in addition to trade policy. These strategies may be plotted along the markets vs. planning dimension and along the independence vs. interdependence dimension.

Mercantilist policymakers ensure that exports exceed imports, using a predatorily interdependent trade policy. A neo-classical trade strategy assumes that countries ought to produce and trade that which they are comparatively better at producing.[28] Markets should thus be as large as possible and barriers to the free movement of goods and services should be minimal.

Liberal-regulatory industrial policy has been articulated by the United States in the twentieth century. The rationale is that free markets allocate resources efficiently, give producers incentives to produce what the public wants, provide incentives to acquire useful skills, conserve scarce goods by setting their prices high, and maximize aggregate wealth better than non-market alternatives. But it is recognized that markets that treat the weak, incapable, or unlucky indifferently may be unstable, may allow oligopolies or monopolies to exploit consumers, and may permit negative externalities such as water pollution.[29] In general, the government ought not to decide what should be produced and how or by whom; it does not fix prices itself, nor does it control investment or entry on the basis of its own calculations of how much is economically desirable; the government does not specifically control who should be permitted to do what jobs, nor does it specify the permissable dimensions and characteristics of the product."[30] Government ought to be "maintaining the institutions within whose framework the free market can continue to function, enforcing, supplementing, and removing the imperfections of competition--not supplanting it."

In most national discourses, "industrial policy" demands choices along the continuum from markets to planning, and from independence to interdependence. Not in the United States, points out historian Otis Graham.[31] By the end of the Reagan Administration, in American political discourse the very phrase "industrial policy" came to be laden with strategic content. Industrial policy meant "picking winners." It meant a Japanese-style targeting industrial policy. "Industrial policy" came by definition to contradict the magic of the market and put "faceless" bureaucrats in charge of the economy. In truth, American policy toward industry in the post-World War II era has emphasized markets and interdependence, though swerving toward planning and independence. It is time now to restore a more conventional definition to "industrial policy" and to recognize that the US is pursuing an industrial policy, if not always an integrated one.

As markets in America grew from local to regional to national, and as corporate capitalism supplanted proprietary capitalism early in the twentieth century, the federal government expanded its legal reach such that "only the idiot or the powerless goes into the market without a lawyer, and without political clout--something workers learned after most capitalists had."[32] Regulation of business by the state through "enforcing, supplementing, and removing the imperfections of competition," say Theodore Lowi, has gradually expanded as specialized interest groups pressured Congress to write ambiguous laws, administered by ever-expanding, ever-more intrusive executive branch agencies.[33] Business in America, contends James Q. Wilson, is schizophrenically regulated by the Federal Trade Commission, the Antitrust Division of the Department of Commerce, the Food and Drug Administration, the Occupational Safety and Health Administration, the Environmental Protection Agency, the Office for Civil Rights, and scores of other agencies by lawyers who seek to prosecute every act of regulatory noncompliance and by economists who seek to prosecute only anti-competitive acts.[34] Tension between ideological commitments to legalism and liberalism makes American business-government relations more adversarial and conflictual than in legalistic, liberal, and pluralistic Britain.[35]

The emergence in the twentieth century of the U.S.'s growing and increasingly globally competitive corporate capitalism, coupled with a rise toward great power status, gradually turned its trade and direct investment policy from Hamiltonian mercantilist to liberal.[36] American policymakers led the creation of the GATT and the tariff-cutting and new rule creation in the Tokyo Round and Uruguary Round multilateral trade negotiations. The American hegemony believed its interests and those of its allies were served by a liberal, rule-oriented international trade regime, even if its own behavior throughout the post-World War II era included overt protectionism (e.g., steel and apparel orderly marketing arrangements) and covert protectionism (e.g., automobile voluntary export restraints and abuse of antidumping procedures).[37] Due to the structure of the U.S. economy--a competitiveness based upon technology-intensive industries and services--the interdependence dimension of liberal-regulatory industrial policy now recommends that the GATT-based international trade regime expand to cover services trade, intellectual property rights, foreign direct investment, standards harmonization, and competition (antitrust) policy, and become a General Agreement for Everything regarding Commercial Policy.

Throughout the post-war era American firms became multinational enterprises because they were globally competitive and were innovators in the product cyle. The liberal-regulatory strategy accepted either the view of conservative neo-classical realists in business schools that foreign direct investment promoted growth and that inward FDI restrictions were bad or the view of liberal internationalist scholars who recognized that many countries would press for more control over national resources and production.[38] Thus, the American government promoted outward direct investment, protected U.S. MNC interests in foreign countries, and maintained a largely open domestic investment regime. To promote outward FDI, the U.S. government created the Overseas Private Investment Council and the Export-Import Bank and helped set up the World Bank's Multilateral Investment Guarantee Agency, the International Center for Settlement of Investment Disputes, and the International Finance Corporation's Foreign Investment Advisory Service.[39] To protect U.S. MNC interests, the U.S. State Department would unilaterally demand "prompt, adequate, and effective compensation" in the event of expropriations and (unsuccessfully, at least so far) attempt to codify these demands in international law.[40]

During the 1980s the United States became a net importer of foreign direct investment and a number of high-profile Japanese asset purchases in the United States made inward FDI a major issue for Congress and the executive branch.[41] The attempted purchase by Fujitsu of Fairchild's semiconductor equipment manufacturing operation became a lightning rod which led to the Exon-Florio Amendment in the 1988 Omnibus Trade and Competitiveness Act. This requires the Committee on Foreign Investment in the United States to screen out FDI which might put production and technology capabilities important for national security into the control of foreign firms.

The American liberal-regulatory strategy has thus emphasized market-based resource allocation and interdependence. It has aimed to provide general, non-sector specific industrial policies. Nonetheless, the strategy has also extensively intervened in support of sunrise industries critical to American national defense capabilities[42] and has aggressively protected sunset industries from international competition.[43] Altogether, some say, the strategy is tactical, reactive, and short-term; it produces too many lawyers and too few engineers, and squanders resources developing and producing super-weapons and protecting mature industries.[44]

Some observers have recently suggested that liberal-regulatory industrial policy strategy, misunderstanding the significance of institutions for efficient market operation, has neglected the U.S. infrastructure as a source of national advantage. Government policy, it has been argued, should be aimed at improving the skills of American workers through better K-12, community college, and continuing education.[45] These proposals evidence assumptions that the liberal-regulatory strategy continues to promote American interdependence with the world political economy.

National champions strategy: The national champions industrial policy has been implemented by Germany and France. The Ministry of Economics in Germany and the Planning Commission in France aimed to set up national champions which could challenge the most competitive foreign (i.e., American) companies.[46] Both states subsidized R&D and production, but industrial organization initially differed in the two countries: In Germany, Bundesbank-led capital formation occured through the several large private banks which were major stockholders in the giant industrial firms.[47] In France, the Ministry of Finance provided capital through nationalized banks paired with forced mergers of traditionally family-run companies to create national champions. The Germans meanwhile sought interdependence, pressing companies to export, and supported the U.S. drive for a liberal world trade order. The French, on the other hand, sought more independence, limiting access to the national market through import and investment controls and assuring market demand through state intervention. Both the German and French strategies depended on cooperative relations among business, government and labor.

Measured by economic growth and welfare outcomes, the corporatist states outperformed the pluralist states until the 1980s,[48] though the superior growth was likely a product of economic reconstruction and catch-up. European corporatism is better than American pluralism at integrating labor into managerial decision-making and European firms have often been more competitive as a result.[49] The interventionist strategy has achieved considerable success in Germany where firms were encouraged to face the discipline of international competition, but French strategy failed where the firms were largely insulated from global competition. The contrast suggests that interdependence strategies are superior to independence strategies and that resource allocation through planning fails but works if paired with interdependent strategies.

Though not entailed by the national champions strategy, the French, the Germans and other Europeans have promoted regional interdependence. Jean Monnet, the French civil servant who conceived of and first headed the French Planning Commission, articulated a supranational vision of Europe, beginning with the European Coal and Steel Community which evolved into the European Community.[50] Monnet envisioned a "large and dynamic common market," but one guided by planning. Conflict thus developed within Europe between market-oriented supranationalism (favored by the Germans and the Benelux countries) and Monnet's planning-oriented supranationalism. The community orientation became market-oriented supranationalism (except for the Common Agricultural Policy) because the Germans wanted it that way and because planning-oriented supranationalism contradicted de Gaulle's goal of independence.

Excited talk in the EC of a United States of Europe with centralized political decision-making by the turn of the century has been muted by realizations that European nationalism persists. Nevertheless, the EC92 initiative should be seen as an extraordinary element of industrial policy strategy. The harmonization of technical standards through Commission directives and mutual recognition is changing the competitive environment in Europe.[51] Business interests in Europe generally support the harmonization effort because it will rationalize their markets. Yet, it is unclear that the corporatist polities of Europe will tolerate the closing of plants in, say, Germany to re-open them in, say, Spain. It is also unclear whether antitrust policy will be implemented to preserve vigorous competition in Europe or whether subsidies to national champions will continue along side subsidies to supranational champions.[52]

Capitalist developmental strategy has been articulated by the Japanese. It combines central features of the mercantilist, liberal, and import substitution policy strategies. Like the import substitution strategy, the capitalist developmental strategy substitutes imported goods and services with domestically-produced goods and services through import and foreign direct investment restrictions. However, the goods and services are also to be sold in international markets. Like the mercantilist endeavor the strategy aims to ensure that exports exceed imports by a considerable margin and that trade relations are non-reciprocal. Indeed, Japanese inward FDI and import patterns are far outside the norm among the OECD states, and resemble import-substituting India more than an industrialized country.[53]

The capitalist developmental strategy targets key industries for promotion. Japan successfully targeted apparel, steel, shipbuilding, automobiles, machine tools, computers, consumer electronics, semiconductors, and telecommunications,[54] but its targeting of pharmaceuticals, chemicals, and commercial aircraft has (so far, anyway) failed.[55] The Japanese employed import restrictions (quotas and tariffs); subsidies to R&D, production, and exports; investment controls; an undervalued exchange rate; export promotion assistance; government and private procurement preferences; and a competition policy aimed at maintaining vigorous, if oligopolistic, rivalry within market sectors, especially among the *keiretsu* groups. The strategy picks "winner" industries (not winner national champions as in Europe) whose promotion Japanese planners believe will benefit the economy disproportionately to the costs of the promotion itself. As with the national champions strategy in Europe, the Japanese strategy also depends on a polity which is corporatist or perhaps statist, for it must possess the political capacity to intervene rationally, not politically, in the market.

The capitalist developmental industrial policy has created a cottage industry in the American economics profession debating its rationality.[56] Okimoto points out, however, that Japanese industrial policy has had much less to do with the commercial success of Japan's new industries in the 1980s than it did from the 1940s to the 1970s. In short, the capitalist developmental strategy lies between independence and interdependence, between markets and planning. Korea, Taiwan, and Deng's China adopted capitalist developmental industrial policies;[57] other developing countries may be following.

Korea and Taiwan had implemented import-substitution strategies after the end of Japanese colonialism and both were making their transitions away from import substitution by the end of the 1950s. Both were experiencing balance-of-payments problems and were heavily dependent upon U.S. aid and were met with U.S. demands that they wean themselves off of that aid. The results were transitions toward export-led strategies to achieve balance of payments equilibrium and earn foreign exchange for domestic development.[58] The regimes in South Korea and Taiwan faced serious external threats that motivated industrialization of the economy, not predation of it for the benefit of wealthy elites.

These export-led efforts came to mirror in many respects the Japanese strategy because they appealed to many in the powerful state structures in Korea (military, single party rule) and Taiwan (Leninist party rule). In Korea and Taiwan the strategy involved high levels of planning and interdependence, including very high levels of productive investment, more investment in certain key industries than would have occurred without government intervention, and exposure of many industries to international competition.[59] The governments intervened in the markets through land redistribution, financial system controls to put industrial production ahead of consumer spending, price controls, undervalued foreign-exchange rates, wage controls (and union repression), export performance rewards, foreign direct investment controls, foreign technology acquisition, and sector-specific subsidies and export promotion assistance.

Korea and Taiwan are "late industrializers," and successful late industrializers are good learners.[60] They visit international expositions, attend international conferences, visit foreign plants, consult foreign suppliers, hire foreign experts, and beg, borrow, buy, and steal foreign designs. Nevertheless, there have been constrasts. The Korean economy has been dominated by massive, privately held, diversified *chaebol* modeled after Japan's pre-war *zaibatsu*, while Taiwan's economy has been dominated by publicly-held national champions and small, independent firms. The high growth rates in Korea and Taiwan in the 1960s, 1970s, and 1980s were the results of extensive market intervention to create globally competitive firms disciplined by international markets.

Socialist command industrial policy has been implemented in pre-perestroika Soviet Union and Maoist China. The strategy placed the state in control of resource allocation through planning. In order to do so, the state seized nearly complete control of the means of production. Control over resource allocation was used to establish and maintain independence in the world political economy and support considerable military capability. Resource deployment in both states favored agriculture and heavy and energy sectors over light, consumer-oriented industries.[61] The Soviet Union established through its republics and eastern European satellites a largely dyadic and asymmetrical regional economy organized under its control.[62] The policy succeeded in industrializing the Soviet Union and in creating a mighty war machine, but at the expense of consumers. The strategy might have survived had not the Chernobyl disaster and the pace of technological progress in the West delegitimized the Soviet state: it was abandoned by China in 1978 and by the Soviet Union and East European countries by the end of the 1980s.

Compared to the Soviet strategy, the Chinese implemented a more independent policy. Until 1978, China's economic strategy had been classic import substitution: import barriers, foreign exchange controls, and foreign direct investment restrictions.[63] This resulted in chronic poverty, poor infrastructure, a widening technological gap between world standards and Chinese capabilities, and a standard-of-living gap between China and its rapidly industrializing East Asian neighbors. There was a famine with 20-30 million deaths around 1960 and economic, political, and social chaos in the late 1960s and 1970s.[64] Advocates for change within China argued that "socialism" must not mean "egalitarianism on the basis of universal poverty."[65] After a consolidation of power by Deng Xiaoping, the Chinese government announced in December 1978 a new "Open Door" policy to stimulate China's modernization in science and technology. However, the logic of the policy was not liberalization but the adoption of Western technology and the export of manufactured goods.[66] Hence, import barriers would be removed and trade and investment decision-making would be decentralized only when necessary for the strategy. China has adopted the capitalist development industrial strategy says Chalmers Johnson, who first coined the phrase for his study of Japan.[67]

By the end of the 1980s, fundamental economic and political reform was underway throughout Eastern Europe and the Union of Soviet Socialist Republics was itself doomed. The challenge was not only to adopt new industrial strategies but to change the statist, nonmarket economies. Whether they are to become corporatist or pluralist is difficult to say. There is no historical experience of simultaneous economic and political reform. In the West there has been little reason to think about it; in the East there were reasons not to speak about it. It is clear that the transitions are highly unstable and it is likely that neither domestic political groups nor foreign governments will tolerate in these countries Korean or Taiwanese-style statism and that political consensus will be lacking for Japanese-style corporatism.[68] Policymakers are thus concentrating on stabilization, liberalization, and institutionalization.[69]

Import substitution had been advocated by Raul Prebisch and the *dependencia* school of Latin American development economists.[70] The *dependencia* school contended that the developing countries were locked into a relationship in which they were exploited by the industrialized countries. The rich countries extracted raw materials and agricultural commodities from the developing countries for which they paid little and shipped back manufactured goods for which they charged dear. Greater independence was advocated through market intervention (import and FDI restrictions) substituting imported goods and services with domestically produced goods and services. Many developing country governments demanded joint equity and local managerial control of or expropriated the assets of MNCs.

Developing countries presented proposals for restructuring the world political economy at the first United Nations Conference on Trade and Development in 1964. They requested trade preferences for their manufactured goods; commodity price stabilization; resource and technology transfers; reductions in freight and service charges; debt rescheduling and reductions; and a new forum to replace GATT.[71] Becoming the economic strategy mirror of the security strategy of the Non-Aligned-Movement and inspired by the success of OPEC oil cartel in 1973-74, the Group of 77 developing countries used their numbers at the United Nations in 1974 to vote in a Declaration on the Establishment of the New International Economic Order (NIEO). The NIEO contained policy preferences which had been stated since 1964 at UNCTAD and asserted the right to nationalize foreign enterprises, create commodity cartels, and regulate multinational corporations.[72] Having achieved tariff preferences from the industrialized countries in 1970 under GATT auspices (the Generalized System of Preferences),[73] the G-77 went about establishing commodity cartels to improve the prices of the their exports on world markets.[74]

Whether the measure is growth rates, current account balances, or income distribution, the import substitution strategy has performed poorly. The Commodity Common Fund achieved some success stabilizing and raising prices but turned out to be fool's gold, for oil is the only exception to the rule that commodities are substitutable with alternatives.[75] Furthermore, the oil shocks of the 1970s increased the dollar needs of the non-oil producing developing countries and falsely raised the hopes of the oil-producing developing countries.

The commercial banks of the industrialized countries recycled petro-dollars through the developing countries and the outcomes were levels of national debt which became a "debt crisis" in 1982 and subsided to a "debt problem" by the end of that decade. The Group of 77 lacked the power in the world political economy to achieve their New International Economic Order; by the end of the 1980s the NIEO had dropped off the international agenda. Import substitution failed, however, not because of greedy foreign banks or the structure of world power but because the strategy itself was flawed. It depended upon markets which were too small to provide economies of scale, and on demand conditions which were too insulated to produce globally competitive industries. Import substitution often resulted in inefficient production and bad products.

Import substitution may have been the best available response of countries such as Mexico and Brazil to the external economic and political shocks of the Great Depression and World War II.[76] It became politically entrenched through the "triple alliance" of the wealthy, domestic elites, government leaders, and multinational corporations[77] and reinforced through misguided advice from industrialized states, the IMF, and the World Bank. While the strategy was a failure it would take much better governance than that with which most developing countries are accustomed to articulate and implement a new strategy.[78] Apparently only economic and political crisis (in this case, the Debt Crisis) could alter political forces sufficiently to change both strategy and governance. During the 1980s and 1990s, developing countries have been dropping their import substitution strategies in favor of export-led industrial policies. Mexico has acceded to the GATT and negotiated a free-trade agreement with the United States and Canada, liberalizing its trade and investment policies in the process. Latin American governments are liberalizing trade and investment policies and negotiating free-trade agreements in order to create bigger, more efficient markets, thereby attracting more foreign direct investment. India is liberalizing its economy as well; the ASEAN countries have begun to establish a free-trade area and seem to be following the Korea and Taiwan models.

Because states want to encourage more FDI and believe that they competing for it, developing and industrialized countries alike are exploring the utility of investment incentives, including tax abatements, investment credits, subsidized loans, and performance requirements. These inducements affect the potential investor's (1) revenues, (2) cost of inputs, (3) factors of production, and (4) profitability.[79] Some of these may marginally encourage inward FDI, but must be considered in the light of restrictions placed on export subsidies under GATT:[80] The policy direction in the world economy seems be toward multilateral agreement to restrict investment incentives which could lead states into costly and unpleasant bidding wars. When offering incentives, states must insure that their policies are stable and their commitments are credible or MNCs will conclude that the initial bargain will become obsolete.[81] Yet, it must be stressed that the most important reason for FDI in a developing country is a desire to improve a company's position in a growing market. The biggest concerns MNC strategists list when considering an investment are (1) political stability, (2) demands for local control, (3) the guaranteed remittance of earnings, (4) monetary and financial policies (though fluctuating foreign exchange rates are a managable problem), (5) transportation and communication infrastructures, (6) standards of business behavior, (7) import barriers, (8) export quotas, and (9) regulatory factors.[82] Clever incentives tend to matter less than the fundamentals: market opportunities, foreign exchange, infrastructure, and political and legal stability. Indeed, IMF and World Bank structural adjustment programs cannot encourage FDI when the fundamentals are absent and these depend on political capacity. The IMF and the World Bank have come to recognize problems of "governance" in many developing countries.[83]

It is unclear how the new export-led strategies of the developing countries will evolve. The capitalist developmental strategy in Japan produced an astonishing rise to economic superpower status and in Korea and Taiwan an equally astonishing rise to the brink of industrialized country status. The strategy worked because it paired import substitution with export promotion, thus ensuring that domestic firms would compete against the best producers in the world for sales to the most demanding consumers and thereby become globally competitive. The strategy also worked because the U.S. hegemony had created a liberal world trade order and itself imported billions of dollars worth of East Asian manufactured goods. The strategy was possible because it was implemented by states with the political capacity to guide industrial activity. Developing countries aiming to adopt the strategy now confront significant challenges. First, the manufactured goods competition in North America and Europe is intense and protectionism is a persistent threat. Second, free-riding on the GATT regime which was tolerated or even encouraged through the 1970s has given way to aggressive unilateral enforcement of GATT rules by the U.S. government.[84] Third, the political capacities of many developing countries falls considerably short of those in Japan, Korea, and Taiwan. China, Vietnam, and the Southeast Asian states (except the Philippines) are strong enough to implement the strategy; many of the Central and South American, African, and South Asian states are not.

Generalizations and Conclusions

Why do states choose certain industrial policy strategies? They make choices influenced by the structures of their political economies and the goals which they articulate. The countries of the world economy and their industrial policy strategies could be classified around 1980 (on the brink of the Debt Crisis and the great take-off in technological progress in the West) according to Table 1.1. Only the communist countries implemented the planning resource allocation-independence strategy, as their statist polities and autarkic goals suggested it. Mexico, Brazil, India, and many of the developing countries adopted the mixed resource allocation-independence strategy, for their goals of independence from the OECD countries suggested it. Japan, Korea, Taiwan, and France implemented the mixed resource allocation-mixed internationalization strategy, for their corporatist or statist polities and mercantilist goals (in the case of Japan, Korea, and Taiwan) or desire for independent production capabilities (in the case of France) assured that orientation. Germany chose the mixed resource allocation-interdependence strategy, for its corporatist polity and recognition of the benefits of international competition accorded with that orientation. The United States employed the market resource allocation-interdependence strategy, as its pluralist polity and hegemonic status virtually obligated. Several of the cells are empty, suggesting that certain industrial policy strategies are not or cannot be implemented. It is hard to imagine a strategy which combines planning-resource allocation and interdependence or market-resource allocation and independence.

Which industrial policy strategies have worked? Success or failure depended upon a fit between structures, capabilities and goals. The evidence suggests that independence paired with either planning or mixed resource allocation fails. Import substitution and socialist command industrial policy strategies have also failed because of insufficient emphasis on the discipline of international market competition. The LDC and communist countries which implemented these strategies experienced low growth, inadequate production, significant unemployment or under-employment, and balance-of-payments problems. On the other hand, the mixed resource allocation-interdependence and market resource allocation-interdependence strategy have all done moderately well to very well. The liberal-regulatory, national champions, and capitalist developmental strategies have been generally successful in achieving

Table 1.1 Industrial Policy Strategies in the World Economy Circa 1980

	Independence internationalization	Mixed internationalization	Interdependence internationalization
Planning resource allocation	USSR, China, Eastern Europe		
Mixed resource allocation	Mexico, India, many LDCs	Japan, Korea, Taiwan, France	Germany
Markets resource allocation			United States

solid or even high growth rates and generally acceptable unemployment levels in North America, Western Europe, and East Asia. All these strategies succeeded be-cause they took advantage of interdependence and market competition. That France has achieved relatively less than the others reinforces the industrial significance of international competition for domestic firms.

Nevertheless, there is a disturbing trend: in all the industrialized countries growth rates gradually lessened. Mancur Olson has offered his logic of collective action to explain this, suggesting that special interest groups form and collude to redistribute resources to their own members.[85] These "distributional coalitions" accumulate over time, increasing the range and complexity of regulation, and reduce efficiency and aggregate income. Explains Olson:

> Countries whose distributional coalitions have been emasculated or abolished by totalitarian government or foreign occupation should grow relatively quickly after a free and stable legal order is established. This can explain the postwar "economic miracles" in the nations that were defeated in World War II, particularly those in Japan and West Germany. ...In Japan and West Germany, totalitarian governments were followed by Allied occupiers determined to promote institutional change and to ensure that institutional life would start almost anew.

Yet even Japan and Germany have seen their growth rates slow and political divisiveness increase as interest groups have become entrenched. Thus, we return to the capacities of states to implement industrial policy strategies. Peter Evans offers in this regard a helpful concept regarding state-society relations: "embedded autonomy." The meritocratic, effective, Weberian bureaucratic state must be sufficiently autonomous to pursue collective goals, but sufficiently embedded within society to aim for development of the country, not predation by the state.[86]

The puzzle for decision-makers in the 1990s is, which industrial policy strategies are likely to succeed in the years to come? Will the corporatist polities with their mixes of planning and market strategies continue to outperform the pluralist polities with their liberal-regulatory structures and strategies? Will even pluralist polities incorporate more planning in their strategies? Or, put another way, is there a particular strategy of industrial policy or structure of polity which better solves Olson's problem?

Planning-oriented states may find that it is easier to target for their economies the industries or firms which have been shown to be critical for the development of the great industrial powers (apparel, steel, automobiles, machine tools, consumer electronics, computers) than it is to identify industries critical for advanced economic growth in the twenty-first century. "Smart" states may turn out to not be smart enough. An industrial policy of targeting probably may be better suited to compressing economic development during intermediate stages of industrialization than accelerating growth in its higher stages. Further, competition within global markets now makes the nationalism of government targeting anachronistic. Thus, only low -and middle-income states should consider national champions or capitalist developmental strategies and then only those that can boast of the proper "embedded autonomy" politically. Higher income states will find an interdependent, market resource allocation strategy most effective. Industrialized countries should not attempt to target in the way that they have in the past and should themselves move toward interdependence and market resource allocation.

The corporatist industrialized countries of Western Europe and Japan may find the national champion and capitalist developmental strategies difficult to implement in the years to come. Their administrations may lack the autonomy to choose rationally rather than politically. Their political structure, which was an advantage in the post-war catch-up years, may turn out to be a disadvantage in the years to come. American pluralism is probably not compatible with either a national champions or capitalist developmental strategy and these could not be effectively implemented even if desirable. Indeed, the U.S. pluralist polity may in the future be the type with the most political capacity to adapt to changing economic circumstances. Its liberal-regulatory strategy--with some improvements of policy mixes, not strategy--may be the most capable of fostering competitive industries, although this is not anticipated in American political discourse which has been rife with talk about "political gridlock".

The relative political capacity of the pluralist polities is of interest to students of not only the United States and India, but to students of Russia, Brazil and China as well. These countries have been described as suffering from the challenge of scope, of "giantism."[87] Because of their vast populations and territories, all will be pluralist polities in the years to come, I believe. Even statist China will not be able to continue the capitalist developmental strategy for many years longer, for statism is waning and corporatism presumes a centralization and concentration of interest groups which China is unlikely to have even in the near future.

Nevertheless, states in the twenty-first century will likely have ample opportunities to make policies which help them create wealth or which lead to their decline. States should invest in transportation, communication, education, and basic, pre-competitive science and technology research, to attract multinational enterprises. Such enterprises bring the additional intellectual, organizational, and financial capabilities which countries need to continue to grow. Regarding science and technology investment, industrial policymakers should take account of their present national strengths and continue to develop those intellectual resources. Also, regarding science and technology investment, industrial policymakers may find that "portfolio diversification" is an effective strategy, as investment resources are limited.

Among the most critical industrial policy domains in the 1990s and beyond are antitrust/competition and intellectual property rights. With these policy domains states shape the environments which encourage or discourage innovation and promote or inhibit firm competitiveness. The mid-1980s "trade" dispute between the United States and Japan over semiconductors was fundamentally about differing industrial organizations; it was the harbinger commercial dispute for the world economy. Antitrust/competition policy should be near the top of the agenda for industrial policymakers and should be near the top of the agenda in the next round of GATT multilateral trade negotiations. Intellectual property rights has similar significance for competition in the world economy.

In the years to come industrial policy strategy will come down to a choice along the internationalization dimension. An independent strategy will employ import protection, foreign direct investment controls, and continued subsidization of national champions. An interdependent strategy will employ free trade with selective, adjustment-oriented protection under the safeguards policy, open foreign direct investment (with the exception of national security sectors), subsidization of basic science and R&D, and heavy investment in labor (continuous education, health care, social and retirement insurance). Industrial policymakers will find that disturbingly rapid economic change will mean that those who do not aggressively implement interdependent strategies will encounter enormous political pressure to pursue independent strategies.

Notes

1. John Stopford and Susan Strange, *Rival States, Rival Firms: Competition for World Market Shares* (New York: Cambridge University Press, 1991), 1.
2. These are different reasons for global enterprise in the present era than the reasons offered for global enterprise in the previous era. See Theodore H. Moran, "Foreign Expansion as an 'Institutional Necessity' for US Corporate Capitalism: The Search for a Radical Model," *World Politics* (1973): 369-386.
3. Michael E. Porter, "The Competitive Advantage of Nations," *Harvard Business Review* (March-April 1990): 73-93; Bruce Kogut, "Country Capabilities and the Permeability of Borders," *Strategic Management Journal*, 12 (1991): 33-47.
4. Kenichi Ohmae, *The Borderless World: Power and Strategy in the Interlinked Economy* (New York: Harper Collins, 1990); Yves Doz, "International Industries: Fragmentation Versus Globalization," in Bruce Guile and Harvey Brooks, *Technology and Global Industry* (National Academy Press, 1987), 96-118.
5. Gary Hamel and C.K. Prahalad, "Do You Really Have a Global Strategy?" *Harvard Business Review*, reprint #85409; Michael E. Porter (ed.), *Competition in Global Industries* (Boston: Harvard Business School Press, 1986), 96-118; Bruce Kogut, "Designing Global Strategies: Comparative and Competitive Value-Added Chains," *Sloan Management Review* (1983): 15-28.

6. John H. Dunning, "The Global Economy, Domestic Governance, Strategies and Transnational Corporations: Interactions and Policy Implications," *Transnational Corporations*, 1 (December 1992) 3: 7-45.
7. My definition is similar to, but somewhat broader than, the definition of development strategy offered by Gary Gereffi, "Paths of Industrialization," in Gereffi and Donald L. Wyman (eds.), *Manufacturing Miracles: Paths of Industrialization in Latin America and East Asia* (Princeton: Princeton University Press, 1990), 23.
8. Porter, *Competition in Global Industries...*, 17.
9. Helen Milner, *Resisting Protectionism* (Princeton: Princeton University Press, 1988); I.M. Destler and John S. Odell, *Anti-Protection: Changing Forces in United States Trade Politics* (Washington: Institute for International Economics, 1987).
10. John Zysman and Laura Tyson (eds.), *American Industry in International Competition: Government Policies and Corporate Strategies* (Ithaca: Cornell University Press, 1983).
11. Helen Milner and David Yoffie, "Between Free Trade and Protectionism: Strategic Trade Policy and a Theory of Corporate Trade Demands," *International Organization*, 43 (Spring 1989) 2: 239-273.
12. Robert B. Reich, "Who Is Us?" *Harvard Business Review* (January-February 1990) and "Who Is Them?" *Harvard Business Review* (March-April 1991), reprint #91222.
13. Arnold Wolfers, *Discord and Collaboration: Essays on International Politics* (Baltimore: Johns Hopkins University Press, 1962), 73.
14. See generally Myres McDougal and associates, *Studies in World Public Order* (New Haven: Yale University Press, 1960), 17; Stephen Krasner, "State Power and the Structure of International Trade," *World Politics*, 28 (1976): 317-318; I.M. Destler, *Making Foreign Economic Policy* (Washington: Brookings Institution, 1980), 1-18; David Baldwin, *Economic Statecraft* (Princeton: Princeton University Press, 1985).
15. Ronald Inglehart, *Culture Shift in Advanced Industrial Society* (Princeton: Princeton University Press, 1990).
16. George Cabot Lodge, *Comparative Business-Government Relations* (New York: Prentice-Hall, 1990).
17. David Lake, *Power, Protection, and Free Trade : International Sources of U.S. Commercial Policy, 1887-1939* (Ithaca: Cornell University Press, 1988).
18. Andrew Hurrell and Benedict Kingsbury (eds.), *The International Politics of the Environment* (New York: Oxford University Press, 1992).
19. Dietrich Rueschemeyer and Theda Skocpol, "The State and Economic Transformation," in Peter B. Evans, Rueschemeyer, and Skocpol (eds.), *Bringing the State Back In* (New York: Cambridge University Press, 1985), 46.

20. Stephen D. Krasner, "United States Commercial and Monetary Policy: Unravelling the Paradox of External Strength and Internal Weakness," in Peter B. Katzenstein (ed.), *Between Power and Plenty: Foreign Economic Policies of Advanced Industrial States* (Madison: University of Wisconsin Press, 1978) 54.
21. Krasner, "United States Commercial and Monetary Policy..." 61.
22. Ellen Comisso, "State Structures, Political Processes, and Collective Choice in CMEA States," in Ellen Comisso and Laura D'Andrea Tyson (eds.), "Power, Purpose, and Collective Choice: Economic Strategy in Socialist States," *International Organization*, 40 (Spring 1986) 2: 207.
23. Peter J. Katzenstein, *Small States in World Markets: Industrial Policy in Europe* (Ithaca: Cornell University Press, 1985), 32.
24. Douglass C. North, "Institutions," *Journal of Economic Perspectives*, 5 (Winter 1991) 1: 97-112; see also North, *Institutions, Institutional Change and Economic Performance* (New York: Cambridge University Press, 1990).
25. *World Development Report 1992* (Washington: IBRD, 1992), 222-223.
26. Charles E. Lindblom, *Politics and Markets: The World's Political-Economic Systems* (New York: Basic Books, 1977).
27. Robert S. Keohane and Joseph S. Nye, *Power and Interdepedence: World Politics in Transition* (Boston: Little, Brown, 1977).
28. James R. Markusen and James R. Melvin, *The Theory of International Trade* (New York: Harper & Row, 1988).
29. Paul Wonnacott and Ronald Wonnacott, *Economics* (New York: McGraw-Hill, 1979), 60-61.
30. Alfred E. Kahn, *The Economics of Regulation: Principles and Institutions* (Cambridge: MIT Press, 1988).
31. Otis L. Graham, Jr., *Losing Time: The Industrial Policy Debate* (Cambridge: Harvard University Press, 1982).
32. Martin Sklar, *The Corporate Reconstruction of American Capitalism, 1890-1916* (New York: Cambridge University Press, 1988), 88.
33. Theodore J. Lowi, *The End of Liberalism: The Second Republic of the United States* (New York: W.W. Norton, 1979), 125.
34. James Q. Wilson (ed.), *The Politics of Regulation* (New York: Basic Books, 1980).
35. David Vogel, *National Styles of Regulation: Environmental Policy in Great Britain and the United States* (Ithaca: Cornell University Press, 1986).
36. Krasner, "State Power and the Structure of..." 317-347; Lake, *Power, Protection, and Free Trade...*
37. Stephanie Ann Lenway, *The Politics of U.S. International Trade* (Boston: Pitman, 1985).
38. Thomas J. Biersteker, "Assessments of Indigenization: A Critical Review of Six Theoretical Approaches," in *Multinationals, the State, and Control of the Nigerian Economy* (Princeton: Princeton University Press, 1987): 11-51.

39. Clarke N. Ellis, *Foreign Direct Investment and International Capital Flows to Third World Nations: U.S. Policy Considerations*, in Cynthia Day Wallace (ed.), *Foreign Direct Investment in the 1990s* (Boston: Martinus Nijhoff, 1990), 1-27.
40. Charles Lipson, *Standing Guard: Protecting Foreign Capital in the Nineteenth and Twentieth Centuries* (Berkeley: University of California Press, 1985).
41. Edward M. Graham and Paul R. Krugman, *Foreign Direct Investment in the United States* (Washington: Institute for International Economics, 1991).
42. Matthew Evangelista, *Innovation and Arms Race: How the United States and the Soviet Union Develop New Military Technologies* (Ithaca: Cornell University Press, 1988); Herbert F. York and G. Allen Greb, "Military Research and Development: A Postwar History," in Thomas J. Kuehn and Alan L. Porter (eds.), *Science, Technology, and National Policy* (Ithaca: Cornell University Press, 1981), 190-214.
43. Zysman and Tyson, *American Industry in International Competition...*
44. Fernando Fajnzylber, "The United States and Japan as Models of Industrialization," in Gereffi and Wyman, *Manufacturing Matters*, 323-352; Jean-Claude Derian, *America's Struggle for Leadership in Technology* (Cambridge: MIT Press, 1990).
45. Michael L. Dertouzos et al., *Made in America: Regaining the Productive Edge* (Cambridge: MIT Press, 1989); Robert Reich, *The Work of Nations: Preparing Ourselves for 21st-Century Capitalism* (New York: Alfred A. Knopf, 1991).
46. Michael Kreile, "West Germany: The Dynamics of Expansion," in Katzenstein, *Between Power and Plenty...*, 191-224; John Zysman, "The French State in the International Economy," in Katzenstein, *Between Power and Plenty...*, 255-294.
47. Simon Reich, *The Fruits of Fascism: Postwar Prosperity in Historical Perspective* (Ithaca: Cornell University Press, 1990).
48. John R. Freeman, *Democracy and Markets: The Politics of Mixed Economies* (Ithaca: Cornell University Press, 1989).
49. Lowell Turner, *Democracy at Work: Changing World Markets and the Future of Labor Unions* (Ithaca: Cornell University Press, 1991).
50. Stephen George, *Politics and Policy in the European Community* (New York: Oxford University Press, 1985), 4.
51. Alan C. Shapiro, "The Economic Import of Europe 1992," *Journal of Applied Corporate Finance*, 3 (Winter 1991) 4: 25-36; Gary C. Hufbauer, "An Overview," in Hufbauer (ed.), *Europe 1992: An American Perspective* (Washington: Brookings Institution, 1990), 1-64.
52. Douglas E. Rosenthal, "Competition Policy," in Hufbauer, *Europe 1992...*, 293-344; Peter Montagnon, *European Competition Policy* (London: Royal Institute of International Affairs, 1990).

53. Dennis J. Encarnation, *Rivals beyond Trade: America versus Japan in Global Competition* (Ithaca: Cornell University Press, 1992); Edward Lincoln, *Japan's Unequal Trade* (Washington: Brookings Institution, 1990); for a differing view, see any of the numerous papers by Gary Saxonhouse, including his recent "What Does Japanese Trade Structure Tell Us About Japanese Trade Policy?" *Journal of Economic Perspectives*, 7 (Summer 1993) 3: 21-44.
54. Chalmers A. Johnson, *MITI and the Japanese Miracle* (Stanford: Stanford University Press, 1982); Marie Anchordoguy, "A Challenge to Free Trade? Japanese Industrial Targeting in the Computer and Semiconductor Industries," in Kozo Yamamura (ed.), *Japan's Economic Structure* (Seattle: Society for Japanese Studies, 1990); Daniel I. Okimoto, *Between MITI and the Market: Japanese Industrial Policy for High Technology* (Stanford: Stanford University Press, 1989).
55. David Friedman, *Misunderstood Miracle: Industrial Development and Political Change in Japan* (Ithaca: Cornell University Press, 1988).
56. Paul Krugman (ed.), *Strategic Trade Policy and the New International Economics* (Cambridge: MIT Press, 1986).
57. Alice H. Amsden, *Asia's Next Giant: South Korea and Late Industrialization* (New York: Oxford University Press, 1989); Robert Wade, *Governing the Market: Economic Theory and the Role of Government in East Asian Industrialization* (Princeton: Princeton University Press, 1990); Stephan Haggard, *Pathways from the Periphery: The Politics of Growth in the Newly Industrializing Countries* (Ithaca: Cornell University Press, 1990).
58. Haggard, *Pathways from the Periphery...*; Tun-jen Cheng, "Political Regimes and Development Strategies: South Korea and Taiwan," in Gereffi and Wyman, *Manufacturing Miracles...*, 139-178.
59. Wade, *Governing the Market: Economic Theory...*, 26.
60. Alice H. Amsden, *Asia's Next Giant: South Korea and...*, 20.
61. Ellen Commisso, "State Structures, Political Processes...," 195-238.
62. Michael Marrese, "CMEA: Effective but Cumbersome Political Economy," in Commisso and D'Andrea Tyson, "Power, Purpose, and Collective Choice: Economic...," 287-328.
63. Nicholas R. Lardy, *Foreign Trade and Economic Reform in China, 1978-1990* (New York: Cambridge University Press, 1992).
64. Edward Friedman, Paul G. Pickowicz and Mark Selden, *Chinese Village, Socialist State* (New Haven: Yale University Press, 1991).
65. Margaret M. Pearson, *Joint Ventures in the People's Republic of China* (Princeton: Princeton University Press, 1991).
66. Samuel P.S. Ho and Ralph W. Huenemann, *China's Open Door Policy: The Quest for Foreign Technology and Capital* (Vancouver: University of British Columbia Press, 1984).
67. Chalmers Johnson, "The Nonsocialist NICS: East Asia," in Commisso and Tyson, "Power, Purpose, and Collective Choice: Economic...," 559.

68. Joan M. Nelson, "The Politics of Economic Transformation: Is Third World Experience Relevant in Eastern Europe?" *World Politics*, 45 (April 1993): 433-463.
69. Shafiqul Islam and Michael Mandelbaum (eds.), *Making Markets: Economic Transformation in Eastern Europe and the Post-Soviet States* (New York: Council on Foreign Relations, 1993).
70. Raul Prebisch, "Commercial Policy in the Underdeveloped Countries," *American Economic Review*, 49 (May 1959); Stephen S. Krasner, *Structural Conflict: The Third World Against Global Liberalism* (Berkeley: University of California Press, 1985).
71. Michael Zammit Cutajar (ed.), *UNCTAD and the South-North Dialogue: The First Twenty Years* (New York: Pergamon, 1984).
72. Thomas G. Weiss, *Multilateral Development Diplomacy in UNCTAD: The Lessons of Group Negotiations, 1964-1984* (London: Macmillan, 1986).
73. Anindya K. Bhattacharya, "The Influence of the International Secretariat: UNCTAD and Generalized Tariff Preferences," *International Organ-ization*, 30 (1976) 1: 76-90.
74. Robert L. Rothstein, "Regime-Creation by a Coalition of the Weak: Lessons from the NIEO and Integrated Program for Commodities," *International Studies Quarterly*, 28 (1984) 3: 307-328; Jock A. Finlayson and Mark W. Zacher, *Managing International Markets: Developing Countries and the Commodity Trade Regime* (New York: Columbia University Press, 1990).
75. Stephen D. Krasner, "Oil is the Exception," *Foreign Policy*, 14 (1974): 64-85.
76. Haggard, "Mexico and Brazil in Comparative Perspective," in *Pathways from the Periphery...*, 161-190.
77. Peter B. Evans, "Class, State, and Dependence in East Asia: Lessons for Latin Americanists," in Frederic C. Deyo (ed.), *The Political Economy of the New Asian Industrialism* (Ithaca: Cornell University Press, 1987), 203-226; Jeffrey A. Frieden, *Debt, Development, and Democracy: Modern Political Economy and Latin America, 1965-1985* (Princeton: Princeton University Press, 1991).
78. Stephan Haggard and Robert B. Kaufman (eds.), *The Politics of Economic Adjustment* (Princeton: Princeton University Press, 1992); Joan M. Nelson (ed.), *Economic Crisis and Policy Choice: The Politics of Adjustment in the Third World* (Princeton: Princeton University Press, 1990).
79. Stephen Guisinger, "Host-Country Policies to Attract and Control Foreign Investment," in Theodore H. Moran (ed.), *Investing in Development: New Roles of Private Capital* (New Brunswick: Transaction Books, 1986), 157-172.
80. Gary Clyde Hufbauer and Joanna Shelton Erb, *Subsidies in International Trade* (Cambridge: MIT Press, 1984).

81. Guisinger, "Host-Country Policies...," 162; Thomas P. Murtha, "Surviving Industrial Targeting: State Credibility and Public Policy Contingencies in Multinational Subcontracting," *Journal of Law, Economics, and Organization*, 7 (1991) 1: 117-143.
82. Cynthia Day Wallace, "Foreign Direct Investment in the Third World," in Wallace, *Foreign Direct Investment in the 1990s*, 119-147.
83. Carol Lancaster, "Bad Government and Development: The Reason for Low Investment?" *International Economic Insights* (September-October 1991): 20-22.
84. Michael P. Ryan, *Playing by the Rules: USTR, GATT, and American Trade Power in the Pacific* (forthcoming).
85. Mancur Olson, *The Rise and Decline of Nations: Economic Growth, Stagflation, and Social Rigities* (New Haven: Yale University Press, 1982), 74.
86. Peter B. Evans, "Transnational Linkages and the Economic Role of the State: An Analysis of Developing and Industrialized Nations in the Post-World War II Period," in Evans, Rueschemeyer, and Skocpol, *Bringing the State Back In*, 192-226.
87. John P. Lewis, "Some Consequences of Giantism: The Case of India," *World Politics*, 43 (April 1991) e: 367-389.

2

Policy Mixes and Industrial Policies

Gavin Boyd

The internationalization of markets, through the large scale integration and production activities of transnational enterprises, and the trading operations of national firms, presents increasing challenges for governments. Their efforts to promote growth and employment are affected because the evolution and decline of industrial sectors is determined increasingly by the decisions of foreign and often very distant managements. Volumes of international production, with which much intrafirm trade is associated, greatly exceed arm's length exports in the world economy, and shares in those volumes constitute increasing proportions of each "national" product. National administrations compete to attract manufacturing investment by transnational enterprises, and also compete through endeavors to enhance the competitiveness of their exporting firms. Various forms of competitive macromanagement are evolving, and they include industrial policies that differ in commitment, scope, and efficiency.

In the Asia-Pacific region, comprising principally the market economy East Asian and North American states, contrasts in the competitive effects of differing policy mixes have assumed great significance because they have caused strained asymmetries in structural interdependence throughout the area, especially between the U.S. and Japan. These are very prominent in the regional political economy, and are affecting the growth prospects of the industrializing East Asian states. Japanese competitive macromanagement is securing very substantial benefits from a complex imbalanced economic relationship with the U.S. American policymakers are engaging with difficult issues in this asymmetric interdependence, especially because of the domestic significance of large deficits in trade with Japan and of very substantial manufacturing in the U.S. by Japanese firms. Deep Japanese strategic penetration of the American market is not being balanced by U.S. penetration of the Japanese market. An aggressive market-opening trade policy is being implemented by the U.S. administration, and it is taking industrial-policy initiatives to enhance the strengths of American manufacturing firms. These initiatives are intended to help those firms increase their exports, primarily in competition against Japanese enterprises.

In Japan's competitive macromanagement a very functional industrial policy operates within a culturally based tradition of integrative cooperation and mutual responsiveness between managements and technocrats. This ensures cumulative learning on each side, with limited rent seeking. Sustained solidarity building results, with synergistic sharing of analytical and planning functions in intensive consultations between the government and enterprise levels. A high degree of integration in the national political economy is thus maintained, although firms that have been able to gain large shares of foreign markets and then begin overseas production have been able to shape their strategies with considerable self reliance.

The American policy mix, shaped in strongly pluralistic political processes, tends to be less functional in the public interest, notably because of heavy fiscal deficits that contribute to trade imbalances. Relations between the administration and corporate managements are managed distantly, because of a liberal political tradition and pervasive business distrust of government, and because on each side there is much confidence in the efficiency of market forces. Domestic pressures for improved growth however are causing the American policy process to be dominated by concerns that go beyond interest in a liberal approach to structural competitiveness. That would focus almost exclusively on measures to reduce information costs, production costs, transaction costs, and excessive regulation, while improving infrastructures and basic services and aiding fundamental research.

In the industrializing East Asian states policy mixes have interventionist orientations, and are thus in some respects similar to Japan's, but there are major contrasts. The mixes in South Korea and Taiwan express much technocratic rationality, but in Malaysia and even more in Indonesia such rationality is affected by leadership patronage, while in Thailand it is limited by a fragmentation of authority. All of these policy mixes are influenced by incentives to cooperate with a rapidly expanding Japanese corporate presence in East Asia. This corporate presence is larger than a less integrated American one, which is growing at a slower pace, with less support from its home government. Rivalry between the two for control of regional markets has effects determined mainly by the Japanese policy mix. The contests affect the growth prospects of the industrializing East Asian states, but their governments lack the solidarity that would be needed for collective engagement with the challenges posed by Japanese and American policies and corporate strategies.

Competitive Policy Mixes

The general intensification of competition to dominate markets that are being internationalized is causing governments to compete not only through forms of selective trade discrimination but also through measures influencing the evolving patterns of transnational production. Each administration's intent is to increase domestic benefits from the operations of firms that are linking national economies through commerce and international manufacturing. Favorably balanced structural interdependencies are striven for, while endeavors are made to foster industrial growth in line with concepts of desirable national economic systems.[1] The competition between governments expresses and activates economic nationalism, which influences perspectives on the development of each country and its structural interdependencies.

In Japan a major effect of the competition with the U.S. is a strengthening of a long-standing elite consensus for the maintenance of a highly integrated national political economy, in which relational ties cluster firms in industry groups and networks that have active links with the economic ministries. In the U.S. economic nationalism is weaker and has diverging effects on what has been a liberal economic policy orientation. One major effect is acceptance of a rationale for government measures to protect industrial growth against disruptive foreign penetration, and to assist such growth through subsidies and aggressive diplomacy to open foreign markets. About this however there is ambivalence because of beliefs about the efficiency of free-market forces and the deficiencies of bureaucratic structures. Contributions to the policy literature have demonstrated that administrative efforts to enhance industrial development can weaken international competitiveness, but have also argued that East Asian firms have derived unfair competitive advantages from subsidies and other form of assistance provided by their governments.[2]

Issues concerning the mobility of capital complicate the perceived requirements of competitive macromanagement, more for the U.S. than for Japan. These issues are politically much less prominent in the U.S. than those posed by trade imbalances, but have great significance for the development of the national economy. There is a flow of portfolio investment to the high growth East Asian economies. More importantly, production abroad by U.S. firms for foreign markets and the home market is becoming much larger than production at home for export, and is not balanced by foreign production in the U.S. for the host and foreign markets. The building of industrial capacity abroad rather than in the U.S. responds to foreign location advantages and to tax and other incentives which become stronger as U.S. economic growth slackens with that outward direct investment and on account of the effects of heavy government debt.[3] Production abroad by Japanese firms is proportionally less in relation to production in Japan for export and thus has a smaller "hollowing out" effect. The Japanese administration moreover has a significant capacity to influence the evolving balance between domestic and overseas production.[4] Japanese firms retain strong home-country loyalties, while U.S. firms tend to lose their home-country identities.

Competitive pressures in internationalized markets are causing firms to undertake integrated global operations, to maximize the utility of differing location advantages.[5] Most governments thus have to be concerned with the futures of domestic firms threatened by international corporations that have much larger resources.[6] Attention also has to focus on ways of securing the cooperation of national enterprises that have undertaken transnational operations. Commonly recognized requirements are to reduce sectoral disruptions due to continuing relocations of industrial capacity, so as to facilitate stable growth, with suitable balances between manufacturing for export and the service of foreign markets through overseas production.

Acquisitions of global oligopoly power result from the intensifying competition in internationalized markets. While weaker domestic firms are forced into declines, weaker international corporations are also marginalized or are absorbed by more powerful multinationals.[7] In the interdependent policy environments which allow scope for all the competitive activity, larger states have superior leverage on trade and foreign direct investment issues. Use of this leverage of course can be hindered by problems of governance, which for example can be responsible for much indecision, but for all mid-sized and smaller states the tasks of competitive macromanagement are becoming more difficult because of gains in oligopoly power by the stronger multinationals. Most of these firms are based in, or have influence in, the large industrialized democracies that can to considerable degrees impose their preferences in trade and investment dealings with smaller states. Yet it must be stressed that outward direct investment from a large state, because of "hollowing out effects", can contribute to a slowing of growth that increases problems of governance. A smaller but more integrated trading partner enjoying more loyalty from the managements of its firms can thus implement a more functional policy mix, with competitive benefits for its international enterprises. This has been made evident by Japan's macromanagement achievements.[8]

The oligopolistic trend is especially significant in higher technology sectors where large resources are needed in competitive endeavors to make advances in research and development, and to apply those advances through product innovations that secure market gains. The technological rivalry develops principally between very powerful international firms, and causes them to complement that rivalry with strategic alliances. Smaller international firms gradually lose capacities for technological competition, and meanwhile the pattern of higher technology market dominance affects the evolution of mature technology sectors in the various national political economies linked in that pattern of higher technology market dominance. Consideration of projections regarding Japanese corporate involvement in that pattern have motivated U.S.

government efforts in recent years to assist research and development endeavors by American firms.[9]

An effect of the oligopolistic trend is to increase the significance of competition (anti-trust) measures in national policy mixes. For effectiveness in internationalized markets however cooperation between governments is necessary, and is typically lacking. Industrial policy initiatives thus tend to assume greater importance as the oligopolistic consequences of intensifying international competition become more evident. At the same time the functional qualities of each policy mix, determined by its components and their relationships, become more critical: public goods requirements are more demanding as shifts in the competitive advantages of firms alter the markets which they are changing and the national economic structures which they are linking.

Pacific Policy Mixes

The policy mixes of the East Asian and North American market economy states are outcomes of differing policy styles, in which diverse policy communities are involved. These styles reflect primary distinctions in policy analysis between consensual holistically rational decision making and conflicted, reactive, experimental, disjointed decision making. Also reflected are contrasts between formal and informal policy making, and between executive-dominated policy processes and those shaped with much autonomy at the working levels. The Japanese policy style is broadly consensual and holistically rational, and results in informal understandings regarding objectives to be striven for through autonomous working-level operations. The value orientations in the policy process are basically the same as those responsible for relational contracting between Japanese firms and for working-level autonomy within those firms. The American policy style is conflicted, reactive, cybernetic, and formal, with emphasis on top-level directiveness. Policy styles in South Korea and Taiwan have affinities with that in Japan, but that in Indonesia combines strong elements of personal rule with bureaucratic authoritarianism. Policy making in Thailand is conflicted and reactive because of factionalism in its parliamentary system, but policy processes in Malaysia are relatively more consensual and rational, although strongly influenced by leadership communal bias.

The intensifying pressures of competition in world markets set requirements that can be met most effectively by consensual and holistically rational policy making based on working-level autonomy. A consensual process promotes integration in a national political economy and ensures a concerting of energies. Holistically rational decisions are necessary, as structural competitiveness depends on meeting public goods obligations through comprehensive coordination functions that cannot be fulfilled through the pursuit of market gains by individual firms. In the Japanese system a high degree of integration is maintained through multilevel relational cooperation, within and between firms, between firms and representative institutions, and between those institutions and the administration. The efficiency of coordination functions in the pervasive cooperation is made possible through general emphasis on entrusting major responsibilities to the working levels. Between firms relational contracting, especially within industry groups, generates efficiencies that would not be possible if their activities were totally competitive.[10]

A strongly pluralistic policy process, responding cybernetically to vote maximizing opportunities, in effect relies very much on the operations of national firms to cope with the challenges of global competition. If these firms cooperate very little with each other and tend to loose their home-country identities while moving into international operations, the national economy will be adversely affected by losses in the domestic and foreign markets, due to the competitiveness of enterprises operating out of more integrated political economies. As growth slackens and unemployment increases the policy processes will be influenced by pressures to introduce trade barriers for the protection of disrupted industries. Such a sequence in the U.S. has had exceptional dimensions because of the trade effects of heavy and prolonged fiscal deficits. These have evidenced the breadth of legislative distributional compromises necessary to secure budget approval, and have been responsible for very large external debt obligations. To meet those obligations improvements in the balance of payments have been needed, and these have been intended to result from increases in exports, made possible by the technological upgrading of U.S. manufacturing firms. Executive influence on the interest-rate decisions of the Federal Reserve has been exerted to lower the cost of capital for American enterprises, but this has remained higher than Japanese levels, while the options of U.S. firms have been restricted by pressures from shareholders to achieve short-term results.[11]

Highly effective competitive macromanagement in Japan tends to reinforce its elite policy consensus, as this is influenced by neomercantilist ambitions encouraged by the weaker structural competitiveness of the other industrialized democracies. Problems of competitive macromanagement on a liberal basis tend to increase in the U.S. because of the intensification of growth, distributional, and employment issues caused by debt burdens, trade imbalances, and the large-scale development of industrial capacity at foreign locations, together with some flights of capital to such locations. The policy style does not adapt readily to the tasks of engagement with these problems because it is driven by assertions of individual interests that resist aggregation for the common benefit. The representation of corporate interests is fragmented, and this is especially serious because the organizational weaknesses of the major political parties prevent them from harmonizing sectoral and community concerns for the making of policy.[12]

Competitive macromanagement for export-led growth in South Korea and Taiwan has been similar to that in Japan, but under authoritarian direction until the late 1980s. There has been emphasis on maintaining a highly integrated national political economy in each state, for rapid self-reliant outward-oriented industrialization, although with much dependence on imports of capital goods from Japan. Macromanagement in both South Korea and Taiwan has been doubly competitive because the promotion of manufacturing at rising technological levels for the American and European markets has entailed rivalry with Japanese firms as well as with those in the major trading partners, while coping with the disadvantages of limited access to the Japanese market. Each macromanagement process has been long-term oriented and consensual in recent years, but with less autonomous corporate inputs than those in Japan, as administrative guidance from the technocratic level has been more firmly prescriptive. Each policy mix has been distinguished by fiscal discipline--reflecting moderate distributional pressures--that has facilitated subsidiation of investments in plant and machinery.[13]

Policies in the larger members of the Association of Southeast Asian Nations (ASEAN), have been weaker forms of competitive macromanagement, due to lower levels of political development. In Indonesia's system of personal rule and bureaucratic authoritarianism, leadership preferences interacting with technocratic expertise set direction for an industrialization strategy financed mainly by exports of energy resources, primary products, and low technology manufactures. Fiscal policy emphasizes support of the military establishment's virtual monopoly of power, which results in considerable elite involvement in neopatrimonial practices.[14] Thailand's policy mix, shaped by a substantially representative but factionalized administration, fosters industrial growth on a more liberal basis, in a society profoundly influenced by popular struggles against military rule.[15] Malaysia's relatively well-institutionalized representative system expresses a more purposeful commitment to industrialization, which is put into effect with stronger technocratic capabilities, but under rather autocratic leadership, and with bias against the large Chinese community. The Philippines, ranking very low on most criteria of political development, is recovering from the highly destructive maladministration of the Marcos period under a weak representative government implementing liberal economic policies.

Japanese Policy

The Japanese policy mix is basically an expression of administrative-corporate solidarity in support of a well-established macromanagement strategy for superior global competitiveness. This strategy is intended to ensure concerted applications of entrepreneurial and technocratic skills for the building of a very advanced industrial structure and the penetration of foreign markets with high-technology manufactures.

Synergistic interaction between the technocratic and managerial levels has solidarity building effects, although Japanese manufacturing firms have acquired large resources through export ventures and can plan their operations with considerable independence. The interactions between the two levels involve intensive exchanges, which, in conjunction with more extensive ones between firms, overcome problems of informational market failure. Low-risk long-term corporate planning, moreover, is facilitated by the solidarity which develops between managements and in the pattern of technocratic-corporate relations. At the enterprise level a broadly productive balance is maintained between competition and cooperation, with restraints on rent seeking.[16] The entire pattern has remained relatively stable despite fragmentation of the political party system, which resulted in the formation of a coalition government in 1993.[17]

Fiscal discipline has been a major feature of the policy mix. This has been made possible by restraint on distributional demands, due to weak representation of labor interests and the strong influence of senior officials in the Ministry of Finance. The fiscal discipline has held down the costs of government, limiting the diversion of investment funds away from directly productive use, and emphasis on this discipline has remained strong, although it was relaxed in 1993 for expansionary stimulus to overcome a recession. Monetary policy seeks to slow currency appreciation resulting from accumulations of large trade surpluses, while maintaining low inflation. Strong administrative influence over the financial sector aids this policy, and this influence tends to remain effective because the nation's financial managements operate within the culture of the integrated political economy, through relational dealings with Finance Ministry officials and those of the major manufacturing enterprises.[18] Foreign trade policy is tacitly restrictive, in line with the preferences of large national firms dominating the home market, whose informal ties with each other constitute entry barriers.

Industrial policy has evolved from successes in administrative guidance and support of mature and then higher technology manufacturing for export. These successes have facilitated corporate learning for the management of further outward-oriented manufacturing and the development of production operations at foreign locations, especially in the U.S. and the industrializing East Asian states. This learning has involved much acquaintance with broad policy concerns, and the evolution of a pervasive corporate consensus on the functional value of technocratic-managerial consultations, with extensive information sharing, and of administrative sponsorship of cooperative private-sector research and development. The provision of subsidies, originally an important element of industrial policy, has lost significance because of the large resources which Japanese firms have secured through exporting, and because they are advantaged by the lower costs of capital in their home economy. Inward foreign direct investment that might reduce effective protection of the domestic market is hindered by the relational bonds within Japanese industry groups and networks.[19]

The promotion of technological advances by Japanese firms assists a major industrial policy objective--the retention of high value-added manufacturing activities in the home economy. This tends to ensure a functional relationship between exporting and the service of foreign markets through overseas production which reduces the danger of a "hollowing out" of national industrial capacity. Highly integrated management of each major Japanese corporation's overseas operations from centers in the home economy is facilitated by the maintenance of exclusive corporate cultures, and the cooperation of central managements with industrial policy objectives is encouraged by the consultative bonds between technocrats and those managements. The development and sharing of advanced technology, with concerted efforts for rapid application ahead of foreign competitors, which is aided through administrative sponsorship of cooperative research and development, tends to be concentrated in the home economy, and its dynamic centers of innovation profit from the attraction of foreign corporate interest.[20] Technology developed by Japanese firms at their overseas locations is swiftly incorporated into research endeavors at the centers in the home economy.

Japanese policy, with corporate cooperation, thus has a considerable external reach. There is concerted aggressive penetration of foreign markets, especially in the U.S. and other industrialized democracies. This is strategic because of a concentration on high-technology sectors, in which gains then affect mature and low-technology sectors, as well as the service sectors. The capacities of Japanese firms to achieve technologically based market gains tend to become more significant as their successes increase their resources for the support of research and for rapid large-scale applications of new technology. These resources assume collective significance because of the affiliations which link Japanese firms in industry groups and networks operating globally from the home economy.

American Policy

The challenges of competitive macromanagement are more difficult for the U.S. policy process, because of its liberal tradition and strong pluralism, and because it is an exercise of fragmented authority, based on fragmented interest representation. Corporate cooperation, moreover, is limited because of distrust deriving from the intense individualism of the national culture and because home-country loyalties are relativized as firms undertake overseas production. In recent years the tasks of competitive macromanagement have become especially demanding because of the accumulating effects of failures in fiscal management, aggravated by regulatory failures in the financial sector. Restructuring and reorientation of the system of government has not been possible, because of leadership deficiencies, weak aggregating capabilities, and the negative effects of conflicts of interest and opportunism in the legislature.[21] The principal current innovation is an endeavor by the Clinton administration to promote technological upgrading in American firms. This is linked with a politically more visible activist trade policy, to protect domestic enterprises and open foreign markets. This policy is aligned with currents of public opinion disturbed by losses of industrial capacity attributed to competing imports. The politically intractable problem of fiscal indiscipline has more diffuse effects on popular attitudes, and is not a source of imperatives for restraint that could ensure political benefits, on balance, for the executive, because of the strength of distributional pressures.[22]

The inflationary effects of heavy deficit spending necessitate monetary tightening, often in conflict with executive demands for expansionary measures that will increase growth. The formally independent Federal Reserve is sensitive to the interests of financial institutions in maintaining relatively high interest rates, while holding down inflation, and to the interests of the administration in facilitating economic growth through strong consumer demand and the availability of low-cost capital. The financial sector's cooperation is limited, and many financial institutions are operating under severe strains because of risky speculation that followed a deregulatory trend in the 1980s.[23] Serious unresolved issues affect the operations of financial regulatory authorities, and financial institutions are able to invest abroad at higher rates rather than provide low-cost funding for American producers and consumers, while exploiting fluctuations of the dollar in international money markets. There is a significant risk of a financial crisis, due to the weaknesses of numerous banks and savings-and-loan associations, and to the danger of losses of domestic and foreign investor confidence in the national growth potential.[24]

Foreign-trade policy, under pressure from business groups and legislators to reduce persistently large imbalances, shows a strong thrust toward managed commerce, especially in the relationship with Japan. Export promotion is aided by the currency depreciation that results from the large fiscal deficits and the trade deficits, but uncertainties about the future of the economy tend to impose caution on entrepreneurial initiatives related to export ventures. Investment in overseas manufacturing, although more costly because of currency depreciation, is an attractive alternative to exporting, not only because of the importance of foreign location advantages but also because of the prospect of higher taxation and slow growth in the home economy.

The regulatory problems of the financial sector are factors in a larger configuration of issues in competition (antitrust) policy. The deregulatory trend of the 1980s opened the way for intensified competition but facilitated corporate integration strategies that increased degrees of oligopoly power in the manufacturing sector and in service sectors. The scope for tacit collusion by strong firms, for increased market domination, became wider. Indecision on issues of competition policy tends to persist because of the difficulties of securing sufficient legislative cooperation for rationalization of the regulatory agencies and more functional designation of their responsibilities.[25]

The primary policy concerns to promote growth and employment cannot be furthered by more fiscal expansion, as it is widely understood that the present level is becoming unsustainable. There is a consensus that the growth which is hoped for must, to a considerable extent, be export led, with greater protection for domestic firms. Export increases resulting from assistance for technological upgrading by American enterprises will of course be slow, and accordingly much reliance tends to be placed on trade policy activism, to open foreign markets while giving more shelter to the home economy. U.S. international trade leverage however has been reduced in recent years by stresses in relations with the European Community and by dependence on Japanese investor confidence, especially for the support of deficit financing. The incentives for U.S. manufacturing firms to produce abroad for foreign markets, moreover, remain strong.[26]

Industrializing East Asian Policies

Policies in the more advanced industrializing East Asian states--South Korea and Taiwan--are managed at levels of institutional development sufficient for functional processing of representations of interests. They have affinities with Japan because of this and also because their policies are implemented with strong technocratic guidance, responsive to corporate interests, in political cultures based on group and community values. These cultures sustain relatively new democratic systems that became established in high-growth contexts, following decades of successful outward-oriented industrialization under authoritarian regimes. The regional settings in which high growth has continued, however, have been changing in ways that have tended to restrict the scope for self-reliant competitive macromanagement.

South Korea and Taiwan have maintained fiscal and monetary discipline and strong financial regulation while promoting vigorous infrastructure development. A spirit of solidarity in each national political economy has been fostered through intensive government-business consultations, the encouragement of cooperation between national firms, and combinations of administrative guidance and support for vigorous export endeavors. South Korean policies have fostered the growth of very large conglomerates for international competitiveness in higher technology markets, in effect discriminating against smaller and newer enterprises, but in recent years this emphasis has been relaxed. Taiwan has implemented a more liberal policy, facilitating outward-oriented industrial development by a large number of medium-sized firms, notably in the electronics industries. This has been done with great emphasis on self reliance, while South Korea's growth has been financed with considerable dependence on international lending institutions.[27]

Growth strategies in South Korea and Taiwan have been facilitated by access to the U.S. market, but trade surpluses which have been built up have provoked U.S. retaliation. Export diversification has become a basic imperative for each government, and the main trend has been an expansion of sales to the European Community. Meanwhile Taiwan has substantially increased commerce with and direct investment in nearby parts of China. At the same time both South Korea and Taiwan have been able to expand exports to Japan, at rates faster than the growth of their sales to the U.S., with prospects of overtaking those sales during the next few years.[28] Inflows of direct investment from Japan, which are larger and are growing more rapidly than those from the U.S., are increasing asymmetric structural interdependencies which are becoming potent sources of influence on policies in both South Korea and Taiwan.

The larger ASEAN states, with inferior capacities for competitive macromanagement, are implementing growth strategies that tend to result in greater external investment and technological dependence. Transitions to self-reliant outward-oriented industrialization are hindered by elite interests in perpetuating highly protected import-substituting industrial development under diverse forms of official patronage. The development of export-oriented manufacturing tends to depend on the attraction of foreign firms into assembly-type operations. As incoming Japanese firms are more open to joint ventures than American enterprises, a potential benefit from their involvement is that sheltered ASEAN companies that have lacked stimulus to attain international competitiveness may achieve increased efficiencies through collaborative ventures in which Japanese corporations are the dominant partners.

Within ASEAN the most serious institutional deficiencies are in Indonesia, and they are due mainly to strong elements of personal rule in its army-dominated regime: technocratic expertise serves leadership preferences in a very subordinate fashion, corporate policy inputs are weak, autonomous representations of interests are repressed, and elite endeavors to preserve a system of sheltered industrial development encounter virtually no opposition. The policy mix diverts substantial resources to the support of the military establishment and in effect prolongs the country's dependence on exports of primary products and low-technology manufactures.[29] Thailand's less serious government deficiencies and somewhat more substantial technocratic capacities allow more autonomous activity by domestic (Thai and Chinese) firms and foreign enterprises, but as the country's representative administration is factionalized the policy mix represents a shifting assortment of compromises. Heavily protected import-substituting industrialization promoted on a neopatrimonial basis under military regimes has shaped much of the economy, and the internally divided leadership lacks the resolve and capacity to initiate a drive for outward-oriented growth with substantially reduced shelter for domestic firms.[30] As in Indonesia, developmental prospects are affected by continued dependence on exports of primary products and low-technology manufactures.

Malaysia's policy mix has greater developmental significance, in terms of leadership commitments, technocratic capacities, societal cooperation, and substantive content. Progress is being made in a transition to outward-oriented industrialization from import-substituting growth that has been less sheltered than that in Thailand and less influenced by high level political involvement in business activity. Autonomous entrepreneurship by the vigorous resident Chinese however has been restricted by discriminatory measures intended to enhance the economic status of the Malay population.[31] There is considerable openness to foreign direct investment in outward-oriented manufacturing, and the location advantages offered are greater than those in Thailand, especially because of superior infrastructure development and administrative services.

Singapore, the most advanced political economy in ASEAN, implements very liberal policies which emphasize openness to international trade and foreign direct investment. Because of exceptional location advantages for commercial, industrial, and financial activities, foreign corporate involvement in the island's small economy has become very large in relation to local firms. The developmental significance of liberal macromanagement has thus differed from that of the self-reliance practised in South Korea and Taiwan, and that attempted in Malaysia. Very impressive economic growth in Singapore is not encouraging other ASEAN countries to place less emphasis on self reliance, but is causing recognition of Singapore's administrative achievements in providing advanced infrastructure and services. Singapore is at the center of ASEAN's main trade and investment flows, linking Thailand, Malaysia and Indonesia.[32] The Philippines, because of its underdeveloped political economy, is on the periphery of that pattern.

Competing Industrial Policies

Industrial policies, as factors in the macromanagement competition of the Asia-Pacific region, influence corporate activities in conjunction with trade, competition, foreign direct investment, fiscal, monetary, financial, and infrastructure policies. The resulting patterns of market penetration, industrial evolution, and structural interdependence reflect significant contrasts in policy orientations and capacities. Efficiencies in Japanese administrative guidance of and collaboration with national firms are responsible for cumulative increases in competitiveness at the enterprise and national levels. The limited scope of American industrial-policy measures and the intense rivalry between American firms are sources of disadvantages in competitiveness at both levels and thus cause reliance on trade policy, for sheltering and market opening purposes. Industrializing East Asian states have secondary roles in the regional economic competition, primarily because of weaker bargaining resources and smaller involvement in the area's commerce and transnational production. Constraints due to retaliatory capacities set the context for economic rivalry between Japan and the U.S., but in their relations with industrializing East Asian states they exert superior bargaining leverage. Those industrializing states accordingly are challenged to make more intensive use of their resources in striving for greater structural competitiveness, but encounter Japanese and U.S. trade discrimination in their efforts to move into higher stages of export-led growth.

Japanese industrial policy, contributing to market gains by the nation's firms throughout the region, and especially in the U.S., is having significant effects on the evolution of that country's industries and on structural interdependencies in the bilateral relationship.[33] The neomercantilist thrust in Japanese policy is strengthened by the continuing successes, which sustain the broad policy consensus between managements and technocrats. The U.S. administration's efforts to respond to rising Japanese structural competitiveness are hampered by weak solidarity in the national political economy and by institutional fragmentation. Solidarity building is difficult because managerial distrust of government is perpetuated by uncertainties regarding the outcomes of administrative patronage extended to constituency interests. Institutional fragmentation, a well-established feature of the American authority structure, prevents coherent expression of executive purposes, and new agencies planned for the technological upgrading of U.S. firms have to be authorized through generally awkward compromises between groups with diverging and opposing interests.[34] In Japan the broad high-level policy consensus between technocrats and managements is threatened indirectly, to a degree, by the politicization of decision making in the infrastructure ministries and by problems of stability in coalition cabinets. The effects on structural competitiveness, however, are likely to be small.

Industrial policies in South Korea and Taiwan support competition by their national firms against Japanese enterprises for deeper penetration of the U.S. market, but those national firms are tending to be drawn into increasing cooperation with Japanese corporations for wider operations in the U.S., despite difficulties of access to the Japanese market. With the continued strengthening of the Japanese corporate presence in East Asia the decision-makers shaping industrial policy in South Korea and Taiwan have incentives to align with Japanese objectives while endeavoring to maintain self-reliance. Those incentives tend to become more significant because South Korea and Taiwan are especially vulnerable to American pressures on trade and investment issues.

Through intensely self-reliant endeavors and collaboration with Japanese enterprises South Korea and Taiwan can maintain substantial involvement in regional mature and higher technology commerce, with further deepening industrialization. Such outward-oriented advancement however is not becoming feasible for the larger ASEAN states. The deficiencies in their industrial policies, which are not being remedied by progress in political development, are tending to prolong their participation in lower-technology regional trade and their dependence on exports of primary products. The external reach of Japanese industrial policy has increasingly significant effects on the evolution of national firms in the larger ASEAN members, principally because of opportunities which incoming Japanese enterprises provide for subcontracting and for more active association with the integrated Japanese East Asian international production system.[35] The expanding Japanese corporate involvement in ASEAN, together with increasing Japanese influence at the policy level, on the basis of that involvement, is to a considerable extent a result of competition against American firms, but it is also a consequence of rivalry with enterprises in South Korea and Taiwan. Their regional opportunities tend to be restricted by the Japanese gains in ASEAN markets, and an effect of this gradual change is to increase their incentives to associate with, and profit from, the expanding Japanese regional involvement.

The imbalanced processes of Asia-Pacific industrial competition are altering a context in which regional trade liberalization is being promoted by the U.S. and other members of the Asia Pacific Economic Cooperation forum. This is a highly complex interactive process of trade policy competition and collaboration, driven mainly by U.S. efforts to secure reductions in foreign trade barriers through the use of leverage based on the size of the American market. With the lowering of trade barriers regional markets are also intended to become more open through the liberalization of foreign direct investment policies. The U.S.'s bargaining strength tends to be increased while it consolidates its position as the central member of a North America Free Trade Area, but this advantage is offset by Japan's steady acquisition of a dominant role in the structural interdependencies of the Asia-Pacific region. In this regard, it must be reiterated, U.S. trade policy operates under increasing constraints because of dependence on Japanese investor confidence for the financing of fiscal deficits and for stability in the U.S. economy.[36]

The trade barriers of the industrializing East Asian states hinder U.S. firms more than Japanese enterprises. American corporations tend to receive less consideration from administrations in those states because U.S. direct investment in the area is decreasing relative to Japan's, is not matched by similar volumes of economic aid, and has less long-term significance.[37] The integrated pattern of Japanese international production in East Asia moreover is based on a dispersal of specializations that results in much intrafirm trade at transfer prices that reduce the significance of tariffs. Japanese manufacturing within each of the industrializing East Asian states, as it is becoming larger than American manufacturing, is a source of further advantages in coping with their protectionist measures.

The U.S. administration's capacities to evoke positive responses to trade liberalization proposals from the industrializing East Asian states are decreasing as the Japanese presence in their area strengthens. For those states the likely costs of making responses not favored by Japan are rising, and it evidently becomes clearer that the Japanese preference is the development of close informal bilateral ties with each of their administrations that will restrict their dealings with other major trading partners. The responses to U.S. proposals and Japanese preferences are individual choices, as the industrializing East Asian states do not constitute an effective caucus, and are thus influenced by the constraints of weak bargaining power.

In the regional setting the competitive potential of Japanese industrial policy is thus a dominant factor, and it limits the potential of U.S. industrial policy initiatives that could otherwise be significant in a context of regional trade and investment liberalization. The immediately critical area of industrial policy rivalry however is in the bilateral Japan-U.S. relationship, in which the principal contests are between Japanese and U.S. firms for shares of the *American* market. U.S. trade policy activism has not been able to promote competition on a comparable scale in Japan.[38]

Interactions

Changing complex asymmetries in policy interdependence between the U.S. and Japan are being shaped by shifts in structural interdependence and macromanagement capabilities. The U.S. administration endeavors to alter those asymmetries through leverage on trade issues while coping with an adverse trend in structural interdependence and while experiencing macromanagement difficulties. Negotiations develop primarily because of U.S. demands for greater access to the Japanese market and for Japanese fiscal expansion that will raise internal demand, hopefully drawing in more imports. The demands have been made with threats to increase protection of the U.S. market through restraints on imports of Japanese mature -and higher-technology products, and with requests for quantitative increases in U.S. shares of the Japanese market, through the virtual introduction of a system of managed trade. U.S. objectives have been to reduce large Japanese surpluses in bilateral trade and related industrial disruptions and employment losses in the U.S. economy caused by high volume imports from Japan.[39] The pressure applied for greater market access in Japan has amounted to a requirement that the Japanese government enforce sharing of the domestic market through its influence on national business groups, but that the controls of those business groups over the domestic distribution system be reduced, to facilitate market entries by American enterprises. There has been a pervasive political cost, as the U.S. demands have aroused Japanese economic nationalism.

American industrial policy initiatives have minor significance in the strained trading relationship because increases in the competitiveness of U.S. firms depend mainly on their own efforts. Their growth prospects moreover are greatly limited by the high degrees of effective informal protection which shelter the domestic market positions of Japanese enterprises, and by the large scale operations of those enterprises in the U.S. American firms have very little scope for production and marketing in Japan. These aspects of the asymmetric structural interdependence are major sources of demands by U.S. interest groups and legislators for aggressive market-opening diplomacy. Rationales for these demands, in terms of basically complementary interests, have reflected awareness of policy-supported oligopoly power in Japan that has been all the more significant because of funding advantages derived by large Japanese firms from high rates of domestic saving at home, and from the higher costs of capital that have to be accepted by American firms.[40]

Japanese responses have been defensive moves toward incremental accommodation, reflecting a breadth of consensus among business elites in favor of maximizing, within prudent limits, the advantages of the unequal commercial relationship. This focus of interests, with which officials in the Ministry of International Trade and Industry appear to have been identified, has excluded concerns with fundamental problems of interdependent growth in the relationship, and has risked provoking severe U.S. trade retaliation. That danger has assumed more significance with the formation of the North America Free Trade Area (NAFTA), in which the U.S., as the central member, can enlist Mexican and Canadian support for its interests in the Pacific. Yet it must be stressed that, while resorting to trade-policy activism, the U.S. administration has to seek Japanese monetary and financial cooperation. Japanese investor confidence has become vital for the stability of the U.S. economy. There is a constant need to secure collaboration that will slow falls in the value of the U.S. dollar, and to develop understandings and goodwill that will help management of a possible economic crisis in the U.S. Monetary expansion is becoming less useful for the management of such a crisis. While it may threaten because of government and corporate debt burdens it may be precipitated or worsened by disposals of excess dollar reserves by European banks as their Community advances toward monetary union.[41]

With the formation of NAFTA the industrializing East Asian states have become more important in the external dimension of Japan's industrial policy. There is a clear imperative to increase support for corporate activities linking those states with the Japanese economy and thus effecting favorable change in the incentives influencing their foreign economic policies. There has been a rapid expansion of Japanese exports to those states over the past half decade, and these now roughly equal the volume going to the U.S., which has been increasing at a relatively slow pace. Of these states only the ASEAN members have some capacity for collective bargaining on trade and foreign direct investment issues, but they have shown little political will to collaborate with each other. As their economic ties with Japan become stronger they compete against each other to attract Japanese direct investment and official aid. Interests in this investment and aid, and in economic links with the U.S. and Europe, largely account for the lack of attention given in the resource-rich ASEAN states to trade liberalization within their association, and to opportunities for industrial cooperation within that grouping.[42]

Issues

The complex configuration of issues in the Asia-Pacific pattern of interactions has resulted principally from the U.S.'s difficulties of adjustment to Japan's structural competitiveness while failing to maintain fiscal discipline and experiencing movements of industrial capacity to foreign locations. Japan's structural competitiveness has been superior mainly because of the solidarity building and guidance functions of its industrial policy, and the informal entry barriers associated with that policy. The U.S.'s fiscal problems have been politically intractable, and the liberal industrial policy which it has been evolving has not engaged with the problem of achieving a functional balance between manufacturing for export and production abroad for foreign markets and the home market. The costs of these macromanagement deficiencies have been losses of structural competitiveness.[43] Imperatives for adjustment have become increasingly urgent, but the dynamics of the American system have generated pressures to externalize the costs through leverage on Japan to accept considerable managed trade and to resort to fiscal expansion.

The limited scope of the U.S.'s evolving liberal industrial policy has raised questions about the advancement of industrial objectives through competition policy and foreign direct investment policy, as well as trade policy. Competition (antitrust) policy enforcement was relaxed during the 1980s to facilitate mergers and acquisitions that enabled U.S. firms to become larger and acquire greater resources for competitive international operations.[44] Meanwhile in the mid 1980s the U.S., under the Structural Impediments Initiative, demanded stronger enforcement of Japan's competition policy, which was considered to be too relaxed. U.S. foreign direct investment policy has remained liberal, despite efforts by legislative groups to impose limits on the production of Japanese automobiles in the United States. Trade policy activism to further industrial objectives, through sheltering and market-opening endeavors, has contributed very little to improvements in U.S. structural competitiveness. There is considerable support for the view that it could be more effective, however, and it engages the administration's attention because domestically it can be politically rewarding. The problem of industrial "hollowing out" through corporate emphasis on developing industrial capacity abroad defies engagement because of the focus of managerial loyalties on the interests of their firms, discerned in the context of intensifying global competition. The high volume of overseas production in relation to exports from the U.S. has great significance for the overall trade balance, and the balance of payments, as well as the management of monetary policy. Executive interest in this ratio however tends to be discouraged by the complexity of the issue, the prospect of legislative obstruction, and the probability of general corporate opposition.[45]

Elite perceptions of policy choices in Japan, it must be stressed, have been strongly influenced by the demonstrated achievements of relational task-oriented interactions between technocrats and managements and by rises in economic nationalism provoked by public U.S. pressures that have disregarded the status concerns of their administrations. A shift to a liberal industrial policy, with reduced technocratic-managerial consultations and responsiveness, would require a virtually impossible consensus, in conflict with the pervasive normative emphasis on relational exchanges between the two levels. Imperatives to raise the nation's superior structural competitiveness to even higher degrees are clearly recognized, and are seen to depend on maintaining established applications of integration logic above the corporate level, to internalize interactions that would amount to arm's length political contracting in a pluralistic state.

Economic rationality in Japanese macromanagement thus seems to demand trade concessions to the U.S. while industrial policy remains active and wide ranging, on a solidarity-building basis. The political feasibility of trade concessions however remains low, because of the strong representation of manufacturing and trading interests and because of general business reluctance to allow foreign influence on the development of consumer tastes. Recognition of the U.S.'s macromanagement problems, moreover, evidently encourages hopes that its bargaining strength will diminish, over time, and that accordingly concessions can be delayed. Such expectations undoubtedly have considerable significance in Japan's highly consensual policy processes, as these tend to inhibit assertions of leadership in the public interest. In this regard there is a problem of advanced political development which affects the overall utility of the level of integration achieved in the political economy. The micro-level efficiency of administrative guidance is not directly affected, but the higher order choices of trade policy, which have industrial policy implications, do not evoke holistically rational responses.[46] The incremental decisions made on these tend to be outcomes of external pressures that enable advocates of change, including technocrats, to present rationales more persuasive than would otherwise be possible.

For managements of American firms the problems of access to the Japanese market, and the difficulties of competing against the integrated Japanese corporate presence in the industrializing East Asian states, tend to make alternative market and location advantages more attractive. Europe remains the favored location of U.S. investment in manufacturing and services, and surpluses in U.S. trade with the European Community offset roughly a third of the deficits in U.S. trade with Japan. Direct investment in and exports to the Community are encouraged by the integration of the Community market, the strong competitive positions already occupied by U.S. firms in that market, and the relative weaknesses of many European enterprises. U.S. exports to the Community are twice as large as those to Japan, and U.S. production in the Community for its market is approximately four times greater than the volume of U.S. exports to the Community.[47]

The general orientation of corporate interest influences geographic priorities in U.S. policy making, and, thus, the evolving liberal industrial policy. Because of the superior competitiveness of U.S. firms in the large European market there is no perceived rationale for industrial policy activism to enhance that competitiveness. Japanese rivalry in the European market, although increasing, is on a modest scale, and major European Community members support protectionist measures directed against Japan. Very slow growth in the European Community, however, and its difficulties in forming an economic union, are obligating long-term U.S. corporate and government planning in which industrial policy issues will be prominent.

Policy options for industrializing East Asian states are being gradually restricted by the growth of their asymmetric structural interdependence with Japan, and by the absence of American corporate involvement in their area that would offer sufficient alternative possibilities for collaboration. European trade and transnational production activities are on a smaller scale and have been contracting because of Japanese and American competition.[48] Policy processes in the industrializing East Asian states are not being aided significantly by consultations between their administrations that could overcome informational problems regarding potentials for cooperation with each other. Opportunities for industrial cooperation within ASEAN and between ASEAN, South Korea, and Taiwan, are not being explored. This neglect, it must be stressed, results in failures to attain urgently needed collective improvements in structural competitiveness. Meanwhile a progressive decline in national bargaining strengths continues, because of relatively weaker growth, the lack of political will to work together on regional trade issues, and the continuing expansion of the integrated Japanese-East Asian production system.

Notes

1. John H. Dunning, "Governments, Economic Organization, and International Competitiveness," in Lars-Gunnar Mattsson and Bengt Stymne (eds.), *Corporate and Industry Strategies for Europe* (Amsterdam: Elsevier, 1991), 41-74.
2. Roger G. Noll, "Structural Policies in the United States," in Samuel Kernell (ed.), *Parallel Politics: Economic Policymaking in Japan and the United States* (Washington: Brookings, 1991), 230-280; and Laura D'Andrea Tyson, *Who's Bashing Whom? Trade Conflict in High Technology Industries* (Washington: Institute for International Economics, 1992).
3. The incentives include opportunities for reduced tax exposure through the reinvestment of profits earned abroad and the use of transfer pricing on intrafirm shipments. See James Hines and Glenn Hubbard, *Coming Home to America: Divident Repatriations by U.S. Multinationals* (Cambridge: National Bureau of Economic Research Working Paper 2931, 1989).
4. Gavin Boyd, *Corporate Planning and Policy Planning in the Pacific*, (London: Pinter, and New York: St Martin's Press, 1993), ch. 7.
5. *World Investment Report, 1993: Transnational Corporations and Integrated International Production* (New York: United Nations Conference on Trade and Development, Program on Transnational Corporations, 1993).
6. The implications for developing states are discussed in John Stopford and Susan Strange, *Rival States, Rival Firms: Competition for World Market Shares* (Cambridge: Cambridge University Press, 1991).
7. Ibid.
8. Boyd, *Corporate Planning and Policy...*
9. Tyson, *Who's Bashing Whom? Trade Conflict...*
10. W. Carl Kester, "Industry Groups as Systems of Contractual Governance," *Oxford Review of Economic Policy*, 8 (Autumn 1992) 3: 24-44; and Boyd, *Corporate Planning and Policy Planning...*
11. Michael T. Jacobs, *Short Term America* (Boston: Harvard Business School Press, 1991).
12. Boyd, *Corporate Planning and Policy Planning...*, ch. 8.
13. Tun-jen Cheng, "Political Regimes and Development Strategies: South Korea and Taiwan," in Gary Gereffi and Donald L. Wyman (eds.), *Manufacturing Miracles: Paths of Industrialization in Latin America and East Asia* (Princeton: Princeton University Press, 1990), 139-178.
14. For a review of the Indonesian political economy, see R. William Liddle, "Indonesia's Democratic Past and Future," *Comparative Politics*, 24 (July 1992) 4: 443-462.
15. Somrudee Nicro, "Thailand's NIC Democracy: Studying from General Elections," *Pacific Affairs*, 66 (Summer 1993) 2: 167-182.

16. William Case, "Semi-Democracy in Malaysia: Withstanding the Pressures for Regime Change," *Pacific Affairs*, 66 (Summer 1993) 2: 183-205.
17. Boyd, *Corporate Planning and Policy Planning...*, ch. 7.
18. Ibid.
19. Kester, "Industry Groups as Systems of..."; and Dennis J. Encarnation, "A Common Evolution? A Comparison of United States and Japanese Transnational Corporations," *Transnational Corporations*, 2 (February 1993) 1: 7-32.
20. David C. Mowery and David J. Teece, "Japan's Growing Capabilities in Industrial Technology: Implications for U.S. Managers and Policymakers," *California Management Review*, 35 (Winter 1993) 3: 9-34.
21. *Journal of Law, Economics and Organization*, 6, Special Issue, 1990, Symposium on U.S. Political Institutions.
22. Mathew D. McCubbins, "Party Politics, Divided Government, and Budget Deficits," in Kernell, *Parallel Politics: Economic Policymaking...*, 83-118.
23. Martin Feldstein (ed.), *The Risk of Economic Crisis* (Chicago: University of Chicago Press, 1991).
24. Ibid.
25. Lawrence J. White, "Competition Policy in the United States: An Overview," *Oxford Review of Economic Policy*, 9 (Summer 1993) 2: 133-153.
26. Boyd, *Corporate Planning and Policy Planning...*, ch. 8; and John A. Cantwell and Francesca Sanna-Randaccio, "Multinationality and Firm Growth," *Review of World Economics*, 129 (1993) 2: 275-299.
27. Cheng, "Political Regimes and Development Strategies..."
28. *Direction of International Trade Statistics Yearbook, 1993* (Washington: International Monetary Fund, 1993).
29. Liddle, "Indenosia's Democratic Past..."; and Andrew J. MacIntyre, "Indonesia, Thailand, and the Northeast Asia Connection," in R. Higgott, R. Leaver, and J. Ravenhill (eds.), *Pacific Economic Relations in the 1990s* (Boulder, Lynne Rienner, 1993), 250-270.
30. Ibid.; and Nicro, "Thailand's NIC Democracy: Studying..."
31. Case, "Semi-Democracy in Malaysia..."; and *The Developing Economies*, XXIX (December 1991) 4, Symposium on Malaysia's New Economic Policy.
32. Garry Rodan,"Reconstructing Divisions of Labour: Singapore's New Regional Emphasis," in Higgott, Leaver, and Ravenhill, *Pacific Economic Relations in...*, 223-249.
33. C. Fred Bergsten and Marcus Noland, *Reconcilable Differences? United States-Japan Economic Conflict* (Washington: Institute for International Economics, 1993); and Tyson, *Who's Bashing Whom? Trade...*
34. *Journal of Law, Economics, and Organization*, 6, Special Issue, 1990...

35. *World Investment Report 1991: The Triad In Foreign Direct Investment* (New York: United Nations Center on Transnational Corporations, 1991), 44-52; and *Sustaining Rapid Development in East Asia and the Pacific* (Washington: World Bank, 1993), 48-49.
36. See comments on the fragility of the U.S. financial system in Feldstein, *The Risk of Economic...*
37. World Bank, cited.
38. Encarnation, "A Common Evolution? A Comparison..."
39. Bergsten and Noland, *Reconcilable Differences?...*
40. Tyson, *Who's Bashing Whom? Trade...*; and Jacobs, *Short Term America...*
41. Louis W. Pauly, "The Politics of European Monetary Union: National Strategies, International Implications," *International Journal*, XLVII (Winter 1991-1992) 1: 93-111.
42. On the evolution of cooperation within ASEAN, see Hans C. Blomqvist, "ASEAN as a Model for Third World Regional Economic Cooperation?" *ASEAN Economic Bulletin*, 10 (July 1993) 1: 52-67.
43. On these losses, see Bergsten and Noland, *Reconcilable Differences?...*; Tyson, *Who's Bashing Whom? Trade Conflict...*; and Richard R. Nelson and Gavin Wright, "The Rise and Fall of American Technological Leadership: The Postwar Era in Historical Perspective," *Journal of Economic Literature*, XXX (December 1992) 4: 1931-1964.
44. White, "Competition Policy in the United States..."
45. On the complexity of the problem, see DeAnne Julius, *Global Companies and Public Policy* (London: Royal Institute of International Affairs, 1990). For details of the U.S. direct investment position abroad in 1992, see *Survey of Current Business*, 73 (July 1993) 7: 88-124.
46. On the decisional problem, see Kent Calder, "Japanese Foreign Economic Policy Formation: Explaining the Reactive State," *World Politics*, XL (July 1988) 4: 517-541.
47. *Survey of Current Business*, 73 (July 1993) 7; and *Direction of International Trade Statistics Yearbook 1993* (Washington: International Monetary Fund, 1993).
48. On the problems of European competitiveness, see Kirtsy S. Hughes, "Trade Performance of the Main EC Economies Relative to the USA and Japan in 1992-Sensitive Sectors," *Journal of Common Market Studies*, XXX (December 1992) 4: 437-454.

3

The Funding of Pacific Industries

J. Colin Dodds

As other chapters in this book have illustrated (Noland 1990; Sletmo and Boyd 1993; the World Bank 1993), the economic growth achieved in the Asia-Pacific region and in particular the Dynamic Asian Economics (DAEs) has been caused by a coming together of a number of factors. These include the rapid accumulation of physical and human capital, relative macroeconomic stability with low fiscal deficits and moderate inflation rates, and pervasive but tailored government intervention: intervention which, for the changing environment of the 1990s, is increasingly called into question (World Bank 1983; Leipziger and Petri 1993). The policy reforms instituted by many governments have had a broad base and have not followed a uniform structure. Rather, they have been in line with an increased emphasis on the supply side of the economy. Their aim has been to increase the impact of market forces and promote higher domestic saving, while achieving a more effective utilization of the saving and facilitating greater access to international capital markets via Foreign Direct Investment (FDI; Akhter 1993) and portfolio investment. The greater flexibility of markets, including foreign exchange markets, and the cross-border mobility of capital are now reinforcing each other and leading to greater macroeconomic stability, including the ability to withstand external economic shocks.

The impressive and relatively recent sustained growth rates in the region, particularly in Japan, East Asia and China, have been unparalleled in history and are not explained in terms of the "classical" literature on growth (Schumpeter 1942; Kuznets 1971). Development is a difficult process and as Patel (1993) has argued, development economists little understand the dynamics of a growth process that has been achieved with a capital output ratio of about 3:1.[1] This has led not only to a decisive transformation in the economic structure of these countries, but to an increasingly integrated regional pattern of trade (intratrade now accounts for 44% of exports and 51% of imports; Hill and Phillips 1993) and large-scale intra-FDI--not just from Japan but from the DAEs to China, Indonesia, Malaysia and Thailand.

Japan has led the high-growth process in the region (Francks 1991; Matsumoto 1991) and Hong Kong, Singapore (traditional trading centers and now regional financial centers), Taiwan and Korea have followed and have been particularly successful in their export-oriented development strategies. More recently, other countries in the region have adopted significant structural reforms (Streeten 1988; Aziz 1990). China,[2] Malaysia, Thailand, Indonesia and even the Philippines are following in this "ladder of development" with other potential emerging countries such as Vietnam poised to join the virtuous cycle of growth--a cycle seemingly out of the grasp of countries in other parts of the world (Stiglitz 1993, for a discussion of the success of East Asia compared to that of other countries). The growth projections for China in particular are startling, with the Word Bank (1993) estimating that China has the potential by the year 2000 to be the third largest market for export growth after the two trading blocs of the EC and NAFTA. Indeed, the Chinese economy *ceteris paribus* could be the most important growth force in the region, with overseas Chinese communities contributing capital, technology and marketing expertise.

Japan continues to play a pivotal role in a shifting process of regional, corporate and financial integration. The yen is being used increasingly in the region as reported in surveys of FDI (Ozawa 1991), trade invoicing, the denomination of loans and reserve holdings (Tavlas and Osek 1992). Japan's persistent trade and current account asymmetries derive from international differences in saving and investment. Japan traditionally has had a high level of national saving and a net outflow of capital to the rest of the world ($119 billion in 1992), yet a net import of portfolio investment, an issue considered in the next section. The potential for the emergence of a yen bloc remains (Frankel 1992; Bowles and MacLean 1992), although the dollar is still dominant (Helleiner 1992; Frankel and Chinn 1993). These trends have to be set in a context of increasing but imbalanced macro- and micro-economic integration (Goldstein et al. 1992) as well as increasing globalization and integration of the world financial system (Stockman 1988; FRBNY 1987, 1988; Campbell and Hamao 1992; Dodds 1989, 1993). The integration brings with it increased systemic risks, particularly in securities markets (OECD 1991).

This chapter focuses on industrial funding in countries of the region. It illustrates how funding sources have changed, particularly with the increasing trend of cross-border capital flows--both FDI and portfolio. The former brings with it the transfer and diffusion of technology and management. As Wei (1993) has demonstrated, these factors were critical to the growth in China in the late 1980s and remain so today. Meanwhile, with the increases in portfolio investment, the agency issues change corporate governance relationships. The volume of securitized flows is reaching unprecedented levels, offering borrowers (and investors) a range of financial instruments. Questions about financial mixes and lower costs of capital as competitive levers are discussed. With the growth in the region the Asian borrowers, particularly Japan, China and the East Asian countries are now active in accessing private market financing with both bond and equity issues. The Pacific financial services industry meanwhile is evolving in the context of increased financial interdependencies. Domestic financial markets (OECD 1993) are becoming more adaptive and international, and segmentation is giving way to greater integration and convergence. The impact of these on Multinational Enterprises (MNEs) and on policymakers (Langford and Brownsey 1988) is reviewed later in the chapter.

Development Finance

The relatively open trade regimes in the region contrast sharply with closed financial sectors. The financial markets of many countries have remained underdeveloped. Governments have relied heavily on state-owned banks and other financial institutions to mobilize saving and allocate it for development. To achieve this, they used controls and administrative guidance. Markets, *per se*, have not played a significant role in the mobilization and allocation of funds. However, governments are now taking steps to broaden and deepen their financial markets and, as with their trade policies, are contributing to the development of a more outward, private-sector environment. To achieve this, they need sound institutional frameworks within which financial markets can operate. To assist in this process of liberalization, the Asian Development Bank has played an important role (Tarumiza 1993).

The policy issues in development finance are controversial. Some recent literature (see chapters in Giovannini, 1993) is skeptical about the role of financial markets in the development process. Fundamental questions of the desirability of financial liberalization and its sequencing remain. (Park 1993, for a discussion in respect of South Korea and Taiwan.) The role of foreign capital in development and the interconnections of monetary and fiscal policies, financial markets and financial flows, including those cross-border, are also still very much debated. Villegas (1990), however, provides a cogent argument to support the importance of foreign borrowing to growth in the region. Of particular concern to some commentators (Stiglitz 1993) is the fact that liberalization policies often focus on secondary markets and therefore ignore primary markets which raise and allocate capital.

In contradistinction to this, there is an increasing body of "old" and new literature which is linking the critical role that the financial sector and financial markets can play in economic development. (See, for example, Cameron 1967; Collier and Mayer 1989; Goldsmith 1969; McKinnon 1973, 1991; Shaw 1973; Townsend 1983; Gertler 1988; Greenwood and Jovanovic 1989; Benciverga and Smith 1991; Chandravarkar 1992; Roubini and Sala-i-Martin 1992; Saint-Paul

1992; and Mayer and Vives 1993.) In particular, recent papers by King and Levine (1992 and 1993) find a dominant role for financial intermediaries in the organization of industry and show that measures of the scale and efficiency of financial intermediation are robustly correlated with economic growth. Indeed, we can summarize the two rather polar views in Figure 3.1.

The diversification of investors' portfolios is likely to facilitate the continuing growth of cross-border investment both outward and inward. Together with the access to offshore financing for investment, there is a consequential effect on domestic financial markets with the need for new financial instruments as well as the inevitable impact of global risk factors on the regional market (Brown and Otsuki 1993). Cross-border trade in capital has an immediate production and income effect (Economic Council of Canada 1990). Cole (1993), Svensson (1987), Persson and Stockman (1988), and Schadler et al. (1993) have shown that there are gains from the trade in international financial markets analogous to those from trade in goods. New questions and challenges are thus emerging as the financial systems of countries in the region change at an unprecedented rate.

Figure 3.1 The Two Views of the Linkage Between Financial Intermediation and Productivity

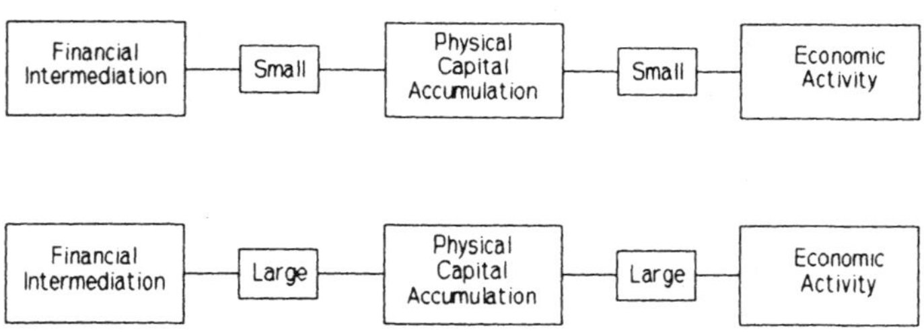

Source: King and Levine (1993), Figure 6.1 and 6.2, p. 160 and p. 163.

The Growth--Funding Linkage

Countries in the Asia-Pacific region differ markedly in size, natural and human environments, culture, socio-politico economic characteristics, and positions in the global environment when they commenced dynamic growth. The literature illustrates that there are a number of "common" elements that these countries share (World Bank 1993 and other chapters in this book). However, it is recognized that following strains associated with growth and others caused by external shocks, country-specific structural adjustment policies have been necessary to meet particular national needs including the retention and development of comparative advantages.

While the purpose of this chapter is to examine the funding aspects of the growth process, the caveat has to be made that fixed investment is not a sufficient condition for growth.[3] The effectiveness with which funds are utilized is critical to the growth process. We cannot, therefore, unequivocally argue that capital formation is the engine of growth. Krugman (1993), utilizing both neo-classical and new growth theories of Lucas (1988) and Romer (1986), which give a greater role to the effect of government policies on growth, argues that even large inflows of capital may not make a significant impact on the rate of growth; indeed, they may exacerbate development problems. Certainly, the expansion of bank syndicated sovereign lending in the period 1972-1981 did not lead to any significant sustained development in the receiving countries.

For the countries of East Asia, capital investment has provided the impetus to growth. In recent years the import of capital has not only led to further growth (for example, Korea borrowed heavily and invested in export-oriented industries) but has confirmed the confidence of both the receiving country and the investing country. It has also given some governments, particularly those engaged in structural adjustment policies, the catalyst to growth and the necessary time to bring about change without effecting domestic production, consumption and investment decisions. However, access to foreign exchange to service the borrowing is essential and the export promotion strategy of countries in the region has assisted this (Villegas 1990).

The increasing liberalization of economies with privatization programmes and reforms in the financial sector (Conti and Hamani 1993; Gentle 1993) permit market forces to work, provide competition for funds, and increase the productive use of investment (Cheng 1988; Pelkmans and Wagner 1990; Tseng and Corker 1991). However, there are many differences among financial markets, including their regulatory regimes.

Table 3.1 provides data on the growth rates of GDP in the East Asian countries, which (apart from the "special case" of the Philippines, which negotiated a further debt restructuring package in 1993) confirm the dynamism of their economies.

Table 3.1 Real GDP Growth in Selected Asian Countries and the NIEs

	1981-86 Average	1987	1988	1989	1990	1991	1992	Per Capita 1981-91 Average
Asia	6.6	7.8	8.9	5.5	5.8	5.7	6.9	5.0
China	10.5	10.2	11.1	3.8	4.8	7.7	12.8	7.3
Indonesia	4.3	4.9	5.8	7.5	7.4	6.4	5.9	3.3
Malaysia	3.9	5.3	9.1	8.6	9.8	8.7	8.0	3.4
Philippines	-1.3	4.8	6.2	5.9	2.7	-0.7	0.0	-0.9
Thailand	5.4	9.5	13.2	12.0	10.0	8.2	7.4	5.7
NIEs[a]	7.5	12.1	9.5	6.3	6.8	7.1	5.3	6.6

[a] For South Korea the data for 1989-91 were 6.8%, 90.% and 8.6% respectively.

Source: B.I.S. 1992 and 1993 Annual Reports and IMF World Economic Outlook, May 1992.

A dominant theme in the growth process of countries in the region has been the high saving rates (Dooley et al. 1987; Aghevli et al. 1990), particularly domestic saving as illustrated in Table 3.2.[4] These data confirm the importance of a domestic financial system to generate saving and this is the case even for those countries that have been very successful in attracting foreign investment. They illustrate that saving rates in East Asia are higher on average than all other developing countries and have increased in the past twenty years in contrast to the constant level for *all* developing countries. South Korea is a country where domestic saving increased from 23% in the 1970's to 38% by 1988; although this is still lower than that of Singapore with a rate of over 40%. Part of this difference is due to the debt-servicing constraint. In the Asia-Pacific region,[5] however, the only countries with a large debt overhang are the Philippines and

Table 3.2 Developing Countries--Saving (in % GDP)

	1971-93	1971-75	1976-81	1982-86	1987-90	1991-93*
Asia						
Total saving	28.4	26.3	27.8	28.3	30.6	30.4
Domestic saving	27.5	25.3	27.0	27.0	30.0	29.5
Foreign saving	0.9	1.0	0.8	1.3	0.5	0.9
All Developing Countries						
Total saving	25.6	24.7	26.9	24.6	25.7	25.9
Domestic saving	24.3	23.9	25.4	22.6	24.9	24.5
Foreign saving	1.3	0.8	1.5	2.0	0.9	1.3

Source: Table 15, IMF (1993), p. 77.

Vietnam and it is not surprising then to see the lower growth for the Philippines as reported in Table 3.1.

Households are responsible for the major part of the domestic saving. With changes in regulations, financial innovation, and greater sophistication on the part of the participants, the household sector is now more sensitive to yield, transaction costs, and liquidity. As a result, there are now a wider array of financial instruments, and the availability of higher returns to savers has mobilized new savings. The increased institutionalization of saving will lead to more active portfolio strategies, increased international diversification, and put further pressure on the integration of financial markets. It will also have an impact on corporate governance issues as these investors acquire a greater share of the outstanding holdings, although this is not yet as apparent as it has become in North America (for example, Por 1993) and the U.K. However, if the emergence of institutional investors continues within a country and cross-border, then the issue of how to exercise and control the responsibility that comes from this ownership will arise--as it will for the cross-ownership by banks of Japanese firms and the corporate interlocking in the *keiretsu*.

The data series available and empirical studies[6] on the determinants of household saving are generally weak. However, data compiled by Honohan and Atiyas (1993) for thirteen developing countries (and for four countries in the region), although for a relatively short period, are quite instructive and are given in Table 3.3. They confirm the importance of households as a surplus sector and one which does more to increase the availability for capital to the business sector (a deficit sector) than FDI.

Another recent study by Schmidt-Hebbel et al. (1992) presents evidence for ten developing countries four of which also are from the Asia-Pacific region: Korea, Philippines, Taiwan and Thailand. They confirm the central role of income and wealth to saving and argue that countries should adopt structural adjustment policies to stimulate growth and move their economies from low resource utilization to ones in which saving and growth are mutually reinforcing. To obtain the benefits of economies of scale trade is essential, and, with the move away from primary commodities, countries in the region have cushioned to some extent the effects of a decline in the terms of trade. The shift from agriculture, particularly small-scale, to manufacturing and increasingly to services has occurred, though dependence on primary produced exports is still apparent, notably in Indonesia, where dependence on oil will remain for a long time.

An examination of Table 3.4 confirms by a series of indicators the economic performance of the region. What is particularly striking are the data for investment which show an increase over the period from an already high level attained in the 1980s. Once more there are variations, so for investment South Korea is at 35% of its GDP, ahead of the average of 30.7% (1988-1993).

Table 3.3 Self-financing Ratios--Country Averages

	Household	Business	Government	Sample Years
China	2.26	0.63	1.07	1982-86
Korea	2.07	0.42	1.38	1980-85
Malaysia	6.95	0.54	-0.08	1980, 1985-86
Thailand	2.94	0.58	-0.04	1980-83
Average (13 countries)	2.36	0.55	0.84	

Source: Honohan and Atiyas (1993), Table 2, p. 668.

Table 3.4 Economic Performance of Asia

	1971-93	1971-75	1976-81	1982-87	1988-93	1994-98 projections
Asia :						
Growth	6.5	5.6	5.9	7.3	7.1	6.9
Growth per capita[a]	4.6	3.8	3.8	5.3	5.3	5.2
Investment (% GDP)	27.9	24.9	27.0	28.3	30.7	31.3
Export volume (% change)	10.7	10.2	11.0	10.1	11.3	11.3
Total factor productivity[b]	2.6	2.7	1.9	2.8	3.2	--

[a] real GDP

[b] Total factor productivity is calculated as the residual after taking into account the contribution of capital and labor to growth of potential GDP.

Source: IMF (1993) Table 12, p. 70.

With more market forces at work, successful firms retain profits and can attract more external capital. They can undertake more R&D, invest more and grow further. Mei and Foresi (1993), utilizing a data set from Hayashi and Inone (1991), found that the interaction of firms in similar business helps explain cross-sectional differences in investment. Firms that have lost ground to their competition in a given business cluster increase investment to match the competition. This, however, has been difficult for European firms. A recent survey (Lawrence, 1993) has indicated that a shortage of capital caused by eroded balance sheets and difficult conditions in both the short -and long-term markets is hindering expansion. Weaknesses in the corporate structure in Japan moreover, are now reducing investment.

As Stiglitz (1993) has argued, capital can embody different levels of technology and the investment may have greater synergies (positive and negative) and lead to more learning--particularly if capital investment is associated with an increase in infrastructure investment, for example, education--something that is found in many countries in the region. With the liberalization of trade policies and macroeconomic stability, the climate for foreign investment in the region has improved significantly, and with financial sector reforms, has led to significant cross-border capital flows. However, reference back to Table 3.2 indicates the relatively small percentage of saving attributed to foreign inflow; less than 1% of GDP for the Asia region as a whole. This does conceal great variations. For South Korea in 1991, foreign saving was only 0.4%, for China, Indonesia and Thailand: 1.2%, 1.3% and 2.2% respectively. The significant outlier was Malaysia: 7.4% of GDP.

The degree to which international capital flows can contribute to the productive investments and growth of a country is a matter of increasing interest. Earlier studies by Feldstein and Horioka (1980) and Dooley et al. (1987) have provided some evidence on the elasticity of international capital flows. A more recent study by Honohan and Atiyas (1993) examines the elasticity of these flows across the standard four sectors of the flow of funds matrix. The study finds that for a sample of 17 developing countries (6 of which are from the Asia-Pacific region) after a fall in foreign saving (or government lending), the shortfall is not made up by the household sector and produces a decline in investment. With the growth of cross-border capital flows, there is a potential for greater volatility in the economy, and the consequential need for risk management instruments is apparent as markets move beyond static to dynamic efficiency, with high rates of product and process innovation.

Table 3.5 Capital Flows--Developing Countries in Asia

	1971-76	1977-81	1982-88	1989-92	1991	1992
FDI	8.9	8.9	13.2	22.7	24.1	22.7
Portfolio equity	--	--	--	3.9	1.6	7.5
Bonds	0.7	1.4	5.2	3.9	4.2	6.5
Commercial Bank Loans	21.3	30.9	31.5	23.0	25.5	14.7
Suppliers and Export Credit	9.2	11.9	10.2	10.9	8.8	19.6
Official Loans	42.2	36.0	32.7	29.8	29.8	24.5
Grants	17.7	10.8	7.2	5.7	6.0	4.6
Total in US$ (billions)	10.5	24.6	43.3	73.8	73.7	92.8
Total in constant US$ (billions)	19.8	25.7	40.8	59.8	59.0	73.4

Source: IMF (1993), Table 15, p. 77.

As indicated earlier, the supply of capital investment is only a necessary condition and the decision to invest simultaneously requires a financing decision. Table 3.5 sets out data in capital flows for the developing countries in the Asia region. They confirm that the new pattern of private external flows is radically different from that of the 1970s and early 1980s. Commercial bank loans, which dominated this earlier period, have been replaced by FDI and portfolio flows (equity and bonds) and they respond to many of the same factors that attract them to a country. From the point of view of FDI, this has brought with it technology and the need for human resource development. This has led to stronger domestic competition and easier access to foreign markets, and changed the risk profile of firms in the region, as risk is borne by both domestic and foreign investors.

Japan and the NIEs remain the main source of FDI in Asia, but foreign investment is mainly supplementing new domestic capital formation. Investment flows have shifted from the extractive and manufacturing sectors to services such as telecommunications, transportation and banking. Policy changes have improved access to foreign exchange for imported inputs and have increased freedom to remit dividends and profits. Transparent regulatory and legal regimes with equal treatment of foreigners and domestic investors have also been adopted.

The inflow of capital, both FDI and portfolio, given that both sources are volatile, does raise concerns over the consequences for domestic macroeconomic stability (Schadler et al. 1993). Nevertheless, its potential for developing growth and trade is apparent in the region: China is a clear example (Wei 1993). The open-door policy adopted by China has led to a rapid increase over the 1980s of FDI to the level of $7 billion in 1992. More significant is the fact that this has played a major role in facilitating the growth of trade. Hong Kong has accounted for about 50% of the FDI and has emerged as a service-oriented economy. Hong Kong has also received significant investment from China, cementing perhaps the mutually beneficial relationship that exists prior to unification in 1997.

The emerging markets in the region have attracted[7] investment both direct and via mutual funds, but the receiving countries have to possess financial markets that can absorb the investment as well as give a measure of protection to the investors. Indeed, investors' concerns about the economic and political fundamentals of a country and the need to provide adequate disclosure of information and liquidity are paramount issues. These aspects will be reviewed later in the chapter. Of course, households in the region, increasingly looking to diversify their portfolios, will seek cross-border outlets and firms and will search out new alternatives, including those overseas.

Internationalization of Financial Markets and Cross-border Capital Mobility

Financial markets in a competitive setting can improve efficiency and alleviate informational asymmetries between lenders and borrowers. Financial sector liberalization has thus played an important role in increasing private saving and cross-border capital flows in the region, although the liberalization has been a consequence rather than a cause of the development. Policy shifts in line with this logic have commenced at different times. The relatively free and full-service offshore regional financial centers of Hong Kong and Singapore in particular, but not excluding Australia and New Zealand (Orden and Fisher 1993), have been well in advance of many Asia-Pacific countries, including Japan, which have been under comprehensive regulation. There have been credit-allocation controls, interest-rate restrictions, rigid segmentation of financial markets, capital mobility controls, limited scope in financial markets, and taxes on financial institutions. Entry by foreign banks and foreign investors has also been limited.

In earlier periods financial repression did not reduce growth because governments were generally able to provide macroeconomic stability and allocate funds to growth sectors (Park 1993, for a discussion on South Korea and Taiwan). However, as Cheng and Glick (1988) illustrate, many countries that have relied on these policies have now recognized that in a changed global marketplace, such repression can lead to inefficiencies and sub-optimal resource allocation. Steps were made to remove administrative controls, credit-allocation mechanisms and segmentation, and to encourage the introduction of new markets, with more openness to foreign financial institutions and investors. Malaysia and the Philippines, for example, have taken significant steps to deregulate since the 1970s. South Korea commenced this liberalization process in the 1980s and in 1992 finally opened up its securities markets to offshore investors. Table 3.6 sets out the stock market capitalization for some East Asian countries with comparisons to Japan, U.K. and the U.S. The emergence of stock markets in the region is apparent with Malaysia being the largest (outside of Hong Kong, South Korea and Singapore). In China we have the beginnings of a stock market (Sun et al. 1992). With increased institutionalization of savings (mutual funds, pension funds and insurance companies; Dailey and Motola 1992) and pressures to increase returns and reduce risks, emerging markets have assumed a new importance. The low correlation between the major market indices and the emerging equity markets gives a motivation for portfolio diversification (Walter 1993; Mullin 1993).

To avoid destabilizing capital flows, reform of the financial sector requires the coordination of exchange-rate policy. Exchange rates have failed to track differences in relative price levels (Goodhart 1989). So it is not surprising that Frankel (1989) and Kasman and Pigott (1988) have indicated that the proximate

Table 3.6 Stock Market Capitalization in Selected Countries (Billion US$)

	1985	1986	1987	1988	1989	1990	1991	1992
Asia								
Indonesia	117	81	68	253	2,254	8,081	6,823	12,038
Korea	7,381	13,924	32,905	94,238	140,946	110,594	96,373	107,448
Malaysia	16,229	15,065	18,531	23,318	39,842	48,611	58,627	94,004
Philippines	669	2,008	2,948	4,280	11,965	5,927	10,197	13,794
Thailand	1,856	2,878	5,485	8,811	25,648	23,896	35,815	58,259
Industrial Countries (1,000 billion US$)								
Japan	979	1,842	2,803	3,907	4,393	2,918	3,131	2,332
United Kingdom	328	440	681	771	827	868	1,003	915
United States	2,325	2,637	2,589	2,794	3,506	3,090	4,180	4,023

Source: Goldstein et al. (1993), Part II, Table 22, p. 102.

sources of interest-rate divergences among countries are currency factors, particularly those associated with the difficulty of predicting future exchange rates and the risks of the currency denomination of securities. However, interest-rate linkages have strengthened over the period 1982-1992 (Frankel and Chinn 1993; Hutchison and Singh 1993).

These changes have to be set in the context of a fundamentally altered structure of financial markets, particularly with the explosive growth of Over the Counter (OTC) and exchange-traded financial derivatives (Remolona 1993) to permit the hedging of price risk and to increase the liquidity of the claims in the underlying markets.[8] We can now start to think of a single internationalized financial service industry. In the U.S., U.K., Australia, New Zealand and to a lesser extent, Tokyo and other financial centers, is a system that incorporates "old" and "new" elements of financial contracting.

With cross-border mobility of capital and financial innovation (Merton 1992; Finnerty 1992), domestic capital markets are being increasingly integrated and market driven at the international level. The result is increased efficiency of the use of saving, particularly by the corporate sector. In a well-developed financial system, there are many markets featuring a broadness and depth of coverage. Many Asia-Pacific financial markets are now expanding the range of instruments for investors and lenders. With the capital mobility referred to earlier and the provision of risk-management instruments, investors and borrowers can take advantage of financial services in the other countries. The growth of the availability and volume of trades of futures and options contracts in Japan, Singapore, Australia and New Zealand is a further illustration of this. Regulatory controls vary by country, but the pressures for convergence are such that what is emerging is a seamless global system with financial instruments and credit traded on a 24-hour basis and price established by world supply and demand. There is a potential for a global equilibrium of exchange and interest rates and inflation.

Walter (1992), Dodds (1993) and White (1993) have illustrated how financial systems are converging towards a stylized system. This implies major changes for banks: increasingly, there is a move away from institutional financial intermediation to one which is market-transaction based. Table 3.7 illustrates this for the U.S., Japan and Germany; countries that have had quite different financial systems (Zysman 1983). The implications for countries in the region are important. In the past, East Asian countries have relied heavily on bank borrowing with little recourse to the issue of either domestic and/or international bonds, notes and equities. This is changing rapidly as the segmentation that existed in financial markets and across countries is disappearing and increasingly securities displace bank assets and liabilities. A role for the traditional bank-customer relationship will remain, but the trend toward a disintermediated, liquid and securitized structure will proceed. Increased competition will enforce this and cause increased use of offshore financing.

Table 3.8 illustrates this trend for developing countries in the region. What emerges is the difference in the extent to which different countries utilize offshore markets. This usage requires credit agencies to rate borrowers. Table 3.9 sets out the most recent ratings for some of the countries in the region. Likewise, these ratings are useful to firms contemplating FDI.

Table 3.7 Germany, Japan and the United States: Indicators of Relative Importance of Banks in Financial Activities of Corporations and Households

	Bank Deposits as a Proportion of Corporate Financial Assets	Bank Deposits as a Proportion of Household Financial Assets	Bank Loans as a Proportion of Corporate Liabilities
Germany			
1980	57.7	60.5	63.1
1985	51.1	54.5	60.9
1990	43.8	48.9	61.3
Japan			
1980	78.9	64.4	67.4
1985	77.8	58.5	67.4
1990	46.5	53.2	58.8
United States			
1980	17.8	23.1	33.0
1985	21.5	23.4	29.2
1990	18.8	21.3	25.4

Source: Goldstein et al. (1992), Table 1, p. 3.

The trend to securitization and disintermediation is a challenge; it will bring about fundamental shifts in lender-borrower-state relationships. At the same time, cross-border acquisitions and mergers will increase in the region, implying changes in corporate governance (Jensen 1993; Roe 1993). Table 3.10 illustrates the destinations of these and the importance of North America and the EC. Japan, by virtue of the high percentage of stocks held by financial institutions and non-financial firms, 43.5% and 24.5% respectively in 1987, can prevent hostile cross-border acquisitions. Germany, too, has some insulation from hostile bids with the larger number of private firm and bank stockholdings (Edwards and Fischer 1994). Inevitably, Japan and other countries in the region will experience pressure for more foreign ownership and this will reinforce the corporate, regional and financial integration and convergence. Government channeling of bank loans to targeted sectors which has resulted in high leverage rates will change, as will the domination of financial sectors by government-

Table 3.8 International Bond and Equity Issues by Countries in Asia (Million US$)

	BONDS				EQUITIES		
	1989	1990	1991	1992	1990	1991	1992
China	--	--	115	1335	--	11	1049
Hong Kong	193	66	100	185	--	--	1250
Indonesia	175	80	369	493	633	168	262
Malaysia	425	--	--	--	--	--	382
Korea	258	1105	2111	3330	40	200	150
Singapore	--	105	--	--	214	125	272
Taiwan	100	--	160	60	--	--	543
Thailand	--	--	17	612	100	194	145
Philippines	NA	NA	NA	NA	53	159	392

Source: Goldstein et al. (1993), Part II, Tables 11 and 12, pp. 51 and 53.

Table 3.9 Credit Ratings of Selected Countries in the Asia-Pacific Region

	Moodys	Standard and Poors	ECU Risk Ratings[a]
South Korea	A1	A+	20
Thailand	A2	A-	35
Malaysia	A3	A	30
Hong Kong	A3	A	15
China	Baa1	BBB	30
Indonesia	--	BBB-	40

[a] The lower number indicates lower risk.

Source: *The Economist*, 25 September 1993, Table 10, p. 19.

Table 3.10 Destination of Cross-border Mergers and Acquisitions (Billions US$)

	Targets in					
	United States[a]	Japan	United Kingdom	Continental Europe	Rest of World	Total
1986	29.02	--	5.91	3.15	1.11	39.20
1987	52.18	0.02	7.12	10.22	1.31	70.86
1988	68.39	0.10	15.80	15.21	10.07	109.56
1989	59.68	0.11	28.05	24.20	5.43	117.48
1990	44.80	--	24.40	43.96	15.26	128.41
1991 (first half)	9.43	0.07	7.10	16.32	3.77	36.70

[a] Data for North America.

Source: Goldstein et al. (1992), Table A19, p. 65.

owned financial institutions. Relationships between family-owned companies and the state will change as these companies issue more marketable securities, and as these are increasingly held by offshore investors. The latter will demand increased disclosure. The close customer-bank relationship in Japan will change as the corporate sector issues more marketable securities. Significant changes which have begun in the funding of Japanese industry, with a greater emphasis on international-market financing, particularly by equity issues, will continue.

Capital Structure and Cost of Capital

The search for an optimal capital structure has been a central theme in corporate finance, particularly after the seminal Modigliani Miller (1958) irrelevance article which was cast in a taxless, frictionless world. With these assumptions removed, the financing mix can make a difference as financing instruments vary in their incentives, including tax and risk characteristics. There are many competing theories of capital structure (for example, Remolona 1990; Myers 1993) and it is a matter of record that capital structures vary across countries as Table 3.11 indicates for the period 1982-1987.

Yet, there remains a puzzle despite a wealth of literature (Myers 1984). While the data computed from flow-of-funds accounts confirm the historical dichotomy between the "high" leverage countries, including Japan, and the "low" leverage countries of the U.S. and U.K.,[9] the table also illustrates that leverage in the U.S. has increased, while all other countries have seen a decline. Utilizing another data set obtained at the firm level and which covered larger firms (1,095 U.S. and 1,287 Japanese), Remolona found that once again the

Table 3.11 Book Value Debt/Asset Ratios--Non-financial Firms

	1982	1983	1984	1985	1986	1987
France	69.2	70.7	76.6	73.3	71.0	70.2
Germany	62.0	60.9	59.7	58.6	57.1	NA
Italy	70.4	68.2	67.5	67.0	67.3	66.9
Japan	73.4	73.2	72.6	71.5	70.5	70.1
U.K.	47.9	47.6	48.1	47.6	46.6	NA
U.S.	NA	39.4	40.6	42.2	43.3	44.3

Source: Remolona (1990), Table 1, p. 72.

U.S. emerged as increasing its leverage by the issuing of longer-term debt to finance stock repurchases of nearly $100 billion a year. As the data in Table 3.11 are based on book values, they do not reflect the swings in market prices of debt and equity. Table 3.12 sets out data for the ratio of the book value of debt and the market value of equity. Although this is not a perfect measure, it illustrates a convergence of leverage rates.

U.S. rates would have been even higher if the equity prices had not risen over the period. For Japan, Remolona found that the decline in leverage had occurred through a reduction in short-term debt as well as an increase in equity prices. Table 3.16, later in this section, will illustrate a significant increase in the use of equity financing and this provides another explanation. These trends raise interesting issues as to why there are cross-country variations in leverage ratios at a time when financial markets are increasingly integrated. John et al. (1993) develop a forceful argument that debt can provide an engine of innovation by virtue of the creation of new methods of production and innovation and this is perhaps an explanation of the policies adopted by U.S. firms, particularly in the latter part of the 1980s. However, as Remolona et al. (1993) have reported, there has now been a sharp reversal in the U.S. toward

Table 3.12 Debt/Equity Ratios for U.S. and Japanese Non-financial Firms

	U.S.	Japan
1985	66.9	132.7
1986	66.6	100.7
1987	73.0	65.9
1988	73.7	60.1
1989	66.5	54.8
1990	77.1	65.8

Note: The ratio is computed from the book value of debt (both short and long) to the market value of equity.

Source: Poterba (1991), Table 5, p. 28.

debt with a fundamental restructuring occurring in 1991-1992. They find a significant trend toward strengthening corporate balance sheets with the issue of more equity and with lower interest rates, bond calls and bond sales.

If we examine the sources and uses of funds of companies in the 1980s in Table 3.13, we find that internal sources are the major contributors with the exception of Australia (34.6%). The differences for the other four countries are significant, ranging from 63.2% for Japan to 104.6% for Germany. For external financing, Japan is a heavy user of short-term debt, including bank debt, and U.S. long-term debt. On the uses of funds, a major difference is the importance of dividends in the U.K. and U.S.--a result of their more capital market-price oriented financial systems and the "stickiness" of dividends. The uses of funds by U.S. companies appear to follow the Pecking Order Theory (Myers and Majluf 1984) that, with sticky dividends and a preference for internal financing, firms will only seek external finance to invest in projects with expected positive Net Present Values (NPVs). In choosing the financing instrument to use, the Pecking Order Theory argues that firms move down the range of instruments by risk, choosing those that are less risky first--bonds, then moving through to convertibles with equity as a last resort. Remolona (1990), in testing the hypothesis, found supporting evidence for the U.S. and other countries, including Japan.

Of critical importance to countries is whether their capital structure and cost of capital inhibits or enhances their competitive position and growth (Pecaut 1993, for a critique of the high cost of capital in Canada). In this section we

Table 3.13 Sources and Uses of Funds in Five Countries
(Averages over the period, % of total sources)

	Australia 1984-87	Germany 1983-87	Japan 1984-88	United Kingdom 1983-88	United States 1983-86
Sources					
Internal cash flow	34.6	104.6	63.2	82.5	77.7
External finance	65.4	-4.6	36.8	17.5	22.3
Short-term debt	16.5	-9.4	22.2	-9.3	5.3
Long-term debt	39.0	2.3	10.7	9.4	15.4
Equity	9.8	2.6	3.9	17.4	1.9
Uses					
Investment	121.4	92.6	99.3	83.3	73.8
Dividends	13.1	9.5	6.2	15.3	23.5
Residual	-34.4	-2.1	-5.5	1.4	2.7

Note: Short-term debt includes accounts payable. Investment includes fixed capital, inventory stocks, acquisitions, and financial assets.

Source: Remolona (1990), Table 3, p. 38.

focus on Japan as it is a major global economy whose policies are being emulated in many other countries of the region (Aggarwal and Agmon 1990). The issues of higher leverage rates in Japan and the concept of "cheap" capital relative to "dear" capital have been around for many years and have led to demands for counter policy action by the U.S. Earlier papers by the Semiconductor Industry Association (SIA 1983) and Hatsopoulos (1983) found a large cost of capital advantage for Japanese firms compared to the U.S. Baldwin (1986) provided a critique of these studies indicating major methodological weaknesses and he found overall no significant difference--a result subsequently supported by Ando and Auerbach (1988a). But the same authors, using a larger sample (Ando and Auerbach 1988b), did find a major difference--6% on a before tax basis. The existence of a differential has also found support by Corbett (1987) and McCauley and Zimmer (1989) with strong dissent from Hodder (1991). In Table 3.14 we present estimates that are representative of a range of methodologies used to calculate the cost of capital.

Although these studies use different methodologies, they all point to a lower cost of capital for Japan compared to the U.S. We present a full set of data from the McCauley and Zimmer study in Table 3.15 which covers types of projects and lives and compares the cost for four countries for the period of 1977-1988. The data take into account investment tax credits, depreciation provisions and corporate tax. The differential is consistently present, whatever type of capital investment is considered and for the range of 3-40 year project life. We could go further and break out the overall cost of capital into debt and equity and we would find that the differential is present for both. However, as

Table 3.14 Estimated Costs of Capital--Japan and U.S.

Study	Year	U.S. %	Japan %
A. Hatsopoulos-Brooks	1980	14.1	4.0
(1987)	1985	9.7	3.8
B. McCauley-Zimmer	1980	11.5	8.8
(1989)	1988	11.2	7.2
C. Bernheim-Shoven	1980	18.7	11.0
(1989)	1988	11.1	4.1

Notes: For the Hatsopoulos-Brooks (1987) study, their estimate is derived from the suitable growth netted for the average of cost of capital for all types of capital; for McCauley-Zimmer (1987), the cost of capital for an industrial plant with a twenty-year life was used; and for Bernheim-Shoven (1989), it was the cost of capital of an industrial plant. These last two studies both used adjusted earnings-price ratios.

Source: Poterba (1991), Table 7, p. 3.

Table 3.15 Cost of Capital for Various Projects

	1977	1978	1979	1980	1981	1982	1983	1984	1985	1986	1987	1988
Equipment and machinery with physical life of 20 years												
United States	11.2	11.7	11.2	11.5	13.5	11.5	10.6	11.3	11.1	9.1	10.2	11.2
Japan	5.9	6.9	7.6	8.8	8.8	8.5	8.8	8.4	8.3	7.8	7.0	7.2
Germany	7.7	7.3	7.5	8.6	8.8	7.8	7.0	7.2	7.1	6.9	7.0	7.0
United Kingdom	8.8	10.8	9.8	12.7	10.3	10.7	10.8	9.3	9.4	7.8	8.2	9.2
Factory with physical life of 40 years												
United States	10.0	10.4	8.9	9.3	10.1	12.4	10.8	12.8	12.6	9.3	9.0	10.2
Japan	2.8	4.2	5.1	6.2	6.8	6.6	7.0	6.3	6.1	5.8	4.8	5.0
Germany	5.5	5.5	5.6	7.0	7.4	6.3	5.4	5.7	5.5	5.2	5.4	5.4
United Kingdom	6.7	9.9	7.8	12.2	7.7	8.7	8.8	7.6	8.3	6.1	6.6	7.9
Research and development project with 10 year pay-off lag												
United States	12.5	12.9	11.9	12.4	8.3	18.4	15.2	20.3	20.2	16.8	18.2	20.3
Japan	3.9	5.7	6.5	7.3	8.0	8.3	8.7	7.7	9.2	9.4	8.4	8.7
Germany	13.4	13.8	13.3	15.6	15.7	14.7	13.9	14.6	13.9	13.2	14.4	14.8
United Kingdom	18.2	28.4	21.1	33.4	24.2	29.5	29.2	24.4	25.4	18.9	20.6	23.7
Expensed item with physical life of 3 years												
United States	39.5	40.6	42.4	43.3	38.5	40.5	39.3	39.6	39.1	36.7	39.4	40.4
Japan	35.0	35.1	35.4	36.4	36.1	36.0	36.0	35.7	35.6	35.3	34.8	34.9
Germany	34.7	34.7	34.7	35.4	35.6	35.1	34.7	34.8	34.8	34.6	34.7	34.8
United Kingdom	39.4	40.6	41.4	42.5	40.5	40.0	39.6	38.4	37.7	36.1	37.0	37.4
Land												
United States	10.5	11.1	8.6	9.6	12.6	15.3	12.5	16.1	15.8	10.4	9.3	10.6
Japan	-5.6	1.3	3.2	4.4	7.0	7.8	8.4	6.6	6.0	6.5	4.8	5.4
Germany	3.1	3.7	3.0	5.5	5.6	4.6	3.7	4.6	3.8	3.0	4.3	4.7
United Kingdom	6.8	14.2	9.6	17.8	11.7	14.6	12.5	9.7	9.2	5.4	6.2	7.7

Source: McCauley and Zimmer (1989).

Poterba (1991) has indicated there has been shift in the reasons for the differential. In the early 1980s with higher debt-equity ratios and the lower cost of debt, Japan had an advantage. With the increasing integration of financial markets as discussed in the previous section of this paper, these costs are now converging and the reason for the maintenance of the cost differential is due to lower costs of equity. Nevertheless, firms in Japan still use bank finance and Zimmer and McCauley (1991) estimate that Japanese banks have a lower cost of capital which can be passed on to borrowers, particularly at the wholesale level. Although Japanese firms are now financing extensively on a cross-border basis as Table 3.16 will indicate, the overall cost of equity capital is still lower for Japanese firms compared to those in the U.S. and the differential has *increased* since the late 1980s.

The issue of a lower cost of capital is by no means clear cut and there are many other contributing factors which can give a country such as Japan a competitive lever. This can be particularly important in R&D and industries with high-technology components. Certainly the higher leverage and lower cost of capital found in the earlier studies gave Japan a strategic advantage. Japanese firms could take the longer view. However, corporate governance structures have also assisted. Japan relies heavily on a closely knit network of reciprocity of trade and ownership. As earlier chapters and Nakatani (1984) have illustrated, the *keiretsu* is a prime illustration of this network where a group-owned bank acts as a "Main Bank". This ensures a stable source of financing over the business cycles and, by reducing the financial-distress potential of high leverage rates, it has had the effect of reinforcing the lower cost of capital. The banks have also been able to bring about corporate reorganization when necessary by the "Main Banks" voluntarily subordinating their debt to that of other lending banks. Akai Electric, a member of the Mitsubishi Group, is an example of a significant restructuring which was brought about quickly and effectively in 1985 (Kester 1991). This case also illustrated that such "interventions are directed from the start at searching for an optimal means of governing transactions among all the interacting stockholders rather than resolving first and possibly too late the competing aims of stockholders holding entirely different sets of claims." (Kester 1991: 103.)

Kato and Schallheim (1993), in a study of private equity placings, found the *keiretsu* are beneficial to stockholders. They reduce the agency costs of investors as well as the direct monitoring costs of banks. Lichtenberg and Pushner (1992) found similar results for the investors of firms where banks were inside stockholders. Hostile takeovers are rare, thus reinforcing a strategic longer-term investment strategy on the part of firms. Although the *keiretsu* include only a part of the total number of businesses in Japan, many of their members are larger firms and they account for a quarter of the total sales in Japan (Kester 1991).

Table 3.16 Sources of Finance for Japanese Companies (¥ billion)

	Domestic			External		
Fiscal	Shares	Convertibles (cum-warrants)	Straight Bonds	Shares	Convertibles (cum-warrants)	Straight Bonds
1984	815	1,615 (3)	720	49	1,661 (434)	1,135
1985	651	1,641 (55)	944	11	1,814 (866)	1,439
1986	632	3,572 (104)	980	1	2,478 (1,993)	1,639
1987	2,084	5,055 (0)	915	39	4,516 (3,439)	824
1988	4,564	6,995 (0)	749	17	6,049 (4,982)	843
1989	7,560	8,537 (915)	729	336	10,009 (8,270)	1,120
1990	447	1,306 395)	2,006	0	3,172 (2,652)	2,805
Total	16,783	28,721 (1,472)	7,043	453	29,699 (22,636)	9,805
Total Equity Securities:		46,976 (87.0% of total)			52,788 (83.3% of total)	
Total Domestic		54,019		Total External:	62,593	

Source: Smith, R.C. (1993), p. 13.

Kester (1991) argues that the *keiretsu*, as it embodies the networking of firms and banks, produces a corporate governance system that gives a member firm independence of ownership and control, but with information sharing and selective interaction by stockholders--particularly the "Main Bank" which can re-engineer a firm to face a new set of economic circumstances. However, as we have indicated earlier in this section, the sources of finance for Japanese companies have changed quite dramatically in recent years. In Table 3.16 for the period 1984-1990 external sources of finance outstrip domestic and there is a heavy concentration on equity whether the financing is domestic or external. This confirms the reduction in leverage found in Table 3.12. The data illustrate that Japanese companies have come to favor the issue of convertible bonds with warrants, though the 1990 data are instructive as they indicate a move back to bonds[10]--a trend continued since then in striking contrast to moves in the U.S. to issue more equity! Many investors have detached the warrants from the bonds and trade them separately as a way of trading the underlying equities. Although the majority are still held by Japanese investors, enough have been purchased by offshore investors to develop a market in Japanese equities outside of Japan. This had led to the demand for further innovation in the option markets.

The move to offshore financing is a result of several factors. The deregulation that was stressed in earlier sections of the chapter has been a very potent force on the development of Japanese financial markets and institutions. With Japanese companies able to borrow overseas, they have also been able to relend in Japan. This has led to rapid increase in the liquidity available for domestic investment. The large increase in the value of the yen has further encouraged the borrowing overseas in foreign currencies and then swapping into the yen.

Conclusion

The Asia-Pacific region has emerged as a major dynamic economic force with large internal and external flows of capital, traded goods and services. The growth rates are a matter of record and the financial sector has played a major role in providing the funds for investment--often with guided state direction. Although we have pointed to high saving and its effective use by firms in East Asia as the potent cause of growth, we cannot ignore a range of subsidiary factors. These include higher leverage rates in Japan, for example, and lower costs of capital. The latter have permitted firms to make major strategic investments in R&D and growth industries and countries to build their infrastructure, including education. Despite methodological difficulties encountered in comparing costs of capital on an international basis, the evidence strongly suggests that there has been a differential in favor of Japan. Originally in both bonds and equities, it now persists for equity capital. In recent years leverage rates have been reduced in Japan and increased in the U.S. to produce a rough convergence.

With largely closed domestic financial systems until the mid-1980s and beyond, governments could enforce credit-allocation controls and interest-rate repression. However, the reform of financial systems to remove distortions and inefficiencies are now viewed as critical elements in growth strategies. Indeed, regulatory and administrative controls are viewed as drags on future growth. As a result, with deregulation and more openness, market forces are driving financial markets. This is posing challenges to policymakers as they attempt to sustain growth and balance-of-payments viability. Without the direct policy instruments they possessed previously, they now have to use monetary policy, which requires the existence of a developed money market.

Developments in financial systems are leading to a more effective resource allocation and innovation. For the household sector, this has encouraged further saving, a wider choice of instruments and higher returns. For the corporate sector, firms now have a wider range of financing instruments, including those for risk transformation. As a result, we are witnessing a significant increase in cross-border capital mobility. With the removal of market segmentation in financial systems and the relaxation of regulations (in some countries) on the ownership of financial firms, there is an increased blurring of the distinction between financial and non-financial enterprises.

FDI has played an important, but subsidiary, role (with the exception of Malaysia and China where it has been more dominant) in the growth of countries in the region. The use of offshore financing by firms is occurring--particularly bonds, but increasingly equities. The increased interest in the emerging financial markets of the region by offshore investors has led to significant portfolio flows. It is likely this will continue. With the high savings rates in the region and with increased institutionalization of the savings, as the financial sector broadens and deepens, we are likely to see more intraregion portfolio flows and outflows from the region with greater cross-border FDI.

This chapter has discussed the funding of industries in the context of the internationalization of financial systems. Market forces are now playing a catalytic role as security markets increase their share of financing with the growth of securitized lending. This implies major changes for the corporate governance system in many countries and in state-corporate relationships. The privatization and wider share ownership that results and the increased discretion of firms in global financing challenge traditional bank-customer relationships in many countries, and in particular the *keiretsu* in Japan. Indeed, the problems currently faced by corporate Japan at the time of writing (early 1994) could lead to a fundamental restructuring and reorganization of the elaborate supporting network of relationships which has proved so successful in the past.

With the increased integration of financial markets, the convergence of interest rates, and an increased convergence of financial systems to a "stylized" market-driven system, firms will have to compete more openly for financing, including cross-border. This could lead to hostile bids and a weakening of the cross-ownership in many countries. Policymakers are having to adapt to changing macroeconomic policy instruments, requirements for greater coordination with other countries, and the need for different regulatory regimes. We can see this, for example, in terms of the Bank for International Settlements (BIS) Capital Adequacy Standards which have been put in place to develop a more coordinated global response to the systemic risks faced by banks in the internationalized financial markets.

Japan, despite its current economic and political problems, will continue to dominate the region with Singapore and Hong Kong in subsidiary roles. The developing financial centers will complete the cluster around Tokyo. However, we cannot ignore China which has experienced almost an explosive growth rate. This has been assisted by in-flows of FDI. With the increased openness of its economy and developing financial system[11] and its relationship with other countries in the region, it has the potential to be a dominant economic force. It will have to focus, as Japan has, on less intervention and more on information sharing, coordination and indirect, functional support. This is a strategy some other countries will also have to adopt, including South Korea (Leipziger and Petri 1993).

Notes

1. The United Nations (1951) concluded that the capital needs of the developing countries implied a capital/output ratio of 9:1 on a net and 12:1 on a gross basis, see S.J. Patel, "East Asia's Explosive Development: Its Relevance to Theories and Strategies," Working Paper No. 93.5, International Development Studies, Saint Mary's University, Halifax, 1993.

2. R.E. Feinberg, J. Echeverri-Gent, and F. Müller, "Economic Reform in Three Giants," *U.S.-Third World Policy Perspectives*, 14 (1990), Washington Overseas Development Council; M.W. Bell, H.E. Khor, and K. Kochkar, China at the Threshold of a Market Economy," Occasional Paper 107, (Washington: International Monetary Fund, 1993); and M.I. Blejer, "China: Prolonged Reforms and the Weakening of Fiscal Control," ch. 13, in V. Tanzi (ed.) *Transition to Market: Studies in Fiscal Reform* (Washington: International Monetary Fund, 1993), for a coverage of the market reform process in China.

3. The recent study by M. Blomström, R.E. Lipsey, and M. Zejan, "Is Fixed Investment the Key to Economic Growth?" Working Paper No. 4436, N.B.E.R. (August 1993), for the period 1965-1985 utilized a sample of over 100 countries and they found that although high rates of growth accompany the rapid growth in per capita income, increases in growth preceded increases in rates of capital formation. Furthermore, many of the socialist countries were saving and high capital accumulation rates were offset by inefficiencies in resource allocation, see R.I. McKinnon, "Macroeconomic Control in Liberalizing Socialist Economics: Asian and European Parallels," ch. 8, in A. Giovannini (ed.), *Finance and Development: Issues and Experience*, Centre for Economic Policy Research (Cambridge University Press, 1993).

4. The use of "all Asia data" tends to conceal important variations.

5. A.F. Mohammed, "Contrasting External Debt Experience: Asia and Latin America," ch. 3, in P. Streeten, "Beyond Adjustment: The Asian Experience," (Washington: International Monetary Fund, 1988), contrasts the external debt experience of Asia with Latin America. In the case of East Asia, he finds that it has been the export sector which has permitted debt-servicing rates to decline despite earlier heavy indebtedness by Indonesia and South Korea and increased borrowing by the corporate sector in recent years.

6. For a coverage of recent studies that survey the estimation of saving behavior in developing countries see, for example, A. Deaton, "Saving in Developing Countries: Theory and Review," Proceedings of the World Bank Annual Conference in Development Economics (Washington: World Bank, 1989); and M. Gersovitz, "Saving and Development," *Handbook of Development Economics*, H. Chenery and T.N. Srinivasan (eds.), 1 (New York: North Holland, 1988).
7. There is also an increased interest in empirical financial research in the region. See, for example, W.T. Ziemba, W. Bailey, and Y. Hamao (eds.), *Japanese Financial Market Research*, Elseview Science Publisher, B.V., 1991; and S.G. Rhee, and R.P. Chang (eds.), *Pacific-Basin Capital Markets Research*, I-II (New York: North Holland, 1991).
8. As M. Goldstein, and D. Folkerts-Landau, "International Capital Markets: Part I, Developments, Prospects and Policy Issues, April; Part II, Systemic Issues in International Finance, August" (Washington: International Monetary Fund, 1993) argue, financial derivatives "permit the separation and unbundling of risk, the pricing of its separate components (credit risk, liquidity risk, market risk), and the redistribution of risks to those best able to manage them. As a result, borrowers and lenders can change the risk characteristics of securities, e.g. currency denomination or interest rate structure (floating or fixed, caps) or to create completely new risk positions." p. 23.
9. A dichotomy largely explained by difference in financial systems.
10. Developments in the bond markets (see M. Okuda, and S. James, "The Japanese Bond Market," ch. 3, in D.H. Gowland (ed.), *International Bond Markets* (London: Routledge, 1990)) have led to significant innovation and the greater use of interest-rate swaps.
11. For a coverage of the development of financial markets in China, see C.R. Dipchand, J.C. Dodds, P. McGraw, and K. Chen, "Emerging Trends in China's Financial Sector," *Asia-Pacific Journal of Management*, 8 (April 1991) 1: 35-54.

References

Aggarwal, R., and T. Agmon. 1990. "International Success of Developing Country Firms." *Management International Review*. Vol. 30, No. 2: 163-180.

Aghevli, B.B., J.M Boughton, and others. 1990. "The Role of National Saving in the World Economy: Recent Trends and Prospects." Occasional Paper 67. IMF (March).

Akhter, S.M. 1993. "Foreign Direct Investments in Developing Countries: The Openness Hypothesis and Policy Implications." *International Trade Journal.* Vol. VII, No. 6: 655-672.

Ando, A., and A. J. Auerbach. 1988a. "The Cost of Capital in the United States and Japan: A Comparison." *Journal of the Japanese and International Economics."* Vol. 2: 134-50.

______. 1988b. "The Corporate Cost of Capital in Japan and the United States: A Comparison." In J.B. Shoven, (ed.) *Government Policy Toward Industry in the United States and Japan.* Cambridge: Cambridge University Press.

Aziz, G.A. 1990. *Strategies for Structural Adjustment: The Experience of Southeast Asia.* Washington: International Monetary Fund, Bank Negara, Malaysia.

Baldwin, C.Y. 1986. "Competing for Capital in a Global Environment." In M.E. Porter (ed.) *Competition in Global Industries.* Boston: Harvard University Press.

Bell, M.W., H.E. Khor, and K. Kochkar. 1993. China at the Threshold of a Market Economy." Occasional Paper 107. Washington: International Monetary Fund.

Benciverga, V.R., and B.D. Smith. 1991. "Financial Intermediation and Endogenous Growth." *Review of Economic Studies.* 58: 195-209.

Bernheim, B. D., and J.B. Shoven. 1987. "Taxation and the Cost of Capital: An International Comparison." In C.E. Walker and M.A. Bloomfield, (eds.) *The Consumption Tax: A Better Alternative?* Cambridge, Massachusetts: Ballinger Publishing.

B.I.S. 1992 and 1993. Annual Report, June, Bank for International Settlements, Basle.

Blejer, M.I. 1993. "China: Prolonged Reforms and the Weakening of Fiscal Control." Chapter 13 in V. Tanzi (1993) (ed.) *Transition to Market: Studies in Fiscal Reform.* Washington: International Monetary Fund.

Blomström, M., R.E. Lipsey, and M. Zejan. 1993. "Is Fixed Investment the Key to Economic Growth?" Working Paper No. 4436. N.B.E.R. (August).

Bowles, P., and B. MacLean. 1992. "A Yen Bloc in East Asia? Towards a Political-Economic Evaluation of the Question." ISA Conference, Atlanta, March.

Brown, S.J., and T. Otsuki. 1993. "Risk Premia in Pacific Basin Capital Markets." Working Paper S-93-26. New York University, Salomon Center.

Cameron, R. 1967. *Banking in the Early Stages of Industrialization.* New York: Oxford University Press.

Campbell, J.Y., and Y. Hamao. 1992. "Predictable Stock Returns in the United States and Japan: A Study of Long-Term Capital Market Integration." *Journal of Finance.* Vol. XLVII, No. 1, March: 43-69.

Chandravarkar, A. 1992. "Of Finance and Development." *World Development.* 20: 133-142.

Cheng, H.S. 1988. *Monetary Policy in Pacific Basin Countries.* Boston: Kluwer Academic Publishers.

Cheng, H.S., and R. Glick. 1988. *Capital Mobility and Monetary Policy: Australia, Japan and New Zeland.* Chapter 4, in Cheng.

Chowdury, A., and I. Iyanatul. 1993. *The Newly Industrializing Economics of East Asia.* New York: Routledge.

Cole, H.L. 1993. "The Macroeconomic Effects of World Trade in Financial Assets." *Federal Reserve Bank of Minneapolis Quarterly Review.* Summer: 12-21.

Collier, P., and C. Mayer. 1989. "The Assessment: Financial Liberalization, Financial Systems and Economic Growth." *Oxford Review of Economic Policy.* Vol. 5, No. 4: 1-12.

Conti, V., and R. Hamani. 1993. (eds.) *Financial Markets' Liberalization and the Role of Banks.* Cambridge: Cambridge University Press.

Corbett, J. 1987. "International Perspectives on Financing: Evidence from Japan." *Oxford Review of Economic Policy.* Vol. 3, No. 4: 30-55.

Dailey, L.M., and J. Motola. 1992. "Foreign Investments of Pension Funds in Six Countries." Washington: IMF, 1992, 53-61.

Deaton, A. 1989. "Saving in Developing Countries: Theory and Review." Proceedings of the World Bank Annual Conference in Development Economics. Washington: World Bank.

Dipchand, C.R., J.C. Dodds, P. McGraw, and K. Chen. 1991. "Emerging Trends in China's Financial Sector." *Asia-Pacific Journal of Management.* Vol. 8, No. 1, April: 35-54.

Dodds, J.C. 1990. "Emerging Financial Centres in the Pacific." Chapter 8 in *The Pacific Rim: Investment Development and Trade.* Second Revised Edition, P. Nemetz, University of British Columbia Press.

_______. 1993. "Pacific Financial Services." Chapter 4 in Sletmo and Boyd, *Pacific Service Enterprise...*

Dooley, M., J. Frankel, and D. Mathieson. 1987. "International Capital Mobility: What do the Saving - Investment Correlations Tell Us?" Staff Papers. IMF, Vol. 34 (September): 503-530.

Economic Council of Canada. 1990. *Globalization in Canada's Financial Markets.* Ottawa.

Economist. 1993. "A Survey of Third World Markets." London, 25th September.

Edwards, J., and K. Fischer. 1994. *Banks, Finance and Investment in Germany.* Cambridge: Cambridge University Press.

Feinberg, R.E., J. Echeverri-Gent, and F. Müller. 1990. "Economic Reform in Three Giants." *U.S.-Third World Policy Perspectives.* No. 14, Washington Overseas Development Council.

Feldstein, M.S., and C. Horioka. 1980. "Domestic Saving and International Capital Flows." *Economic Journal.* Vol. 90: 314-329.

Finnerty, J.D. 1992. "An Overview of Corporate Securities Innovation." *Continental Bank Journal of Applied Corporate Finance.* Winter, Vol. 4, No. 4: 23-39.

Francks, P. 1991. *Japanese Economic Development: Theory and Practice.* New York: Routledge.

Frankel, J.A. 1989. "International Financial Integration. Relations Among Interest Rates and Exchange Rates, and Monetary Indicators in International Financial Integration and U.S. Monetary Policy." A Colloquium sponsored by the Federal Reserve Bank of New York, October.

______. 1992. "Is Japan Creating a Yen Bloc in East Asia and the Pacific?" National Bureau of Economic Research. Working Paper No. 4050.

Frankel, J.A., and M.D. Chinn. 1993. "Financial Links Around the Pacific Rim: 1982-1992." Working Paper No PB93-08. Center for Pacific Basin Monetary and Economics Studies, Economic Research Department, Federal Reserve Bank of San Francisco.

FRBNY. 1987. "A Perspective on the Globalization of Financial Markets and Institutions." Spring, Vol. 12, No. 1: 1-9.

______. 1988. "Strengthening International Economic Policy Co-ordination." *The Quarterly Review.* Autumn, Vol. 13, No. 3: 18-27.

Gentle, C.J.S. 1993. *The Financial Services Industry.* Aldershot, Avebury.

Gersovitz, M. 1988. "Saving and Development." *Handbook of Development Economics.* (eds.) H. Chenery and T.N. Srinivasan. Vol. 1. New York. North Holland.

Gertler, M. 1988. "Financial Structure and Aggregate Economic Activity: An Overview." *Journal of Money, Credit and Banking.* 20: 647-664.

Ghate, P. 1992. *Informal Finance: Some Findings from Asia.* Hong Kong Asian Development Bank and Oxford University Press.

Giovannini, A. 1993. (ed.) *Finance and Development: Issues and Experience.* Centre for Economic Policy Research. Cambridge University Press.

Goldsmith, R. 1969. *Financial Structure and Development.* New Haven: Yale University Press.

Goldstein, M., and D. Folkerts-Landau. 1993. "International Capital Markets: Part I, Developments, Prospects and Policy Issues, April; Part II, Systemic Issues in International Finance." August. Washington: International Monetary Fund.

Goldstein, M., P. Isard, P.R. Masson, and M.P. Taylor. 1992. "Policy Issues in the Evolving International Monetary System." Occasional Paper 96. Washington: International Monetary Fund.

Goodhart, C. 1989. "The Conduct of Monetary Policy." *Economic Journal.* June, Vol. 99: 293-346.

Greenwood, J., and B. Jovanovic. 1989. "Financial Developments and Growth and the Distribution of Income." NBER. Working Paper No. 3189.

Hatsopoulos, G.N. 1983. "High Cost of Capital: Handicap of American Industry." Study sponsored by the American Business Conference and Thermo Electron Corporation (April).

Hatsopoulos, G.N., and S.N. Brooks. 1987. "The Cost of Capital in the United States and Japan." Mimeograph, November. Harvard University. Kennedy School of Government.

Hayashi, F., and T. Inone. 1991. "The Relation Between Firm Growth and Q with Multiple Capital Goods: Theory and Evidence from Panel Data on Japanese Firms." *Economatrica.* Vol. 59: 731-753.

Helleiner, E. 1992. "Japan and the Changing Global Financial System." *International Journal.* XLVII, Spring: 420-444.

Hill, H., and P. Phillips. 1993. "Trade is a Two-way Exchange: Rising Import Penetration in East Asia's Export Economies." *World Economy.* Vol. 16, No. 6 (November): 687-697.

Hodder, J.E. 1991. "The Cost of Capital for Industrial Firms in the U.S. and Japan." In Ziemba et al., *Japanese Financial Market...*

Honohan, P., and I. Atiyas. 1993. "Intersectoral Financial Flows in Developing Countries." *Economic Journal.* Vol. 103, No. 418 (May): 666-679.

Hutchison, M.M., and N. Singh. 1993. "Long-Term International Capital Mobility: New Evidence from Equilibrium Real Interest Rate Linkages." Pacific Basin Working Paper Series, PB 93-06. Federal Reserve Bank of San Francisco.

IMF. 1992. "Private Market Financing for Developing Countries." World Economic and Financial Survey (December). Washington.

______. 1992. "Report on the Measurement of International Capital Flows." Washington: International Monetary Fund (December).

______. 1993. *World Economic Outlook.* October. Washington: International Monetary Fund.

Jensen, M. 1993. "The Modern Industrial Revolution, Exit and the Failure of Internal Control Systems." *Journal of Finance.* Papers and Proceedings. July: 831-880.

John, K., D. Madan, and B. Soubra. 1993. "Debt as an Engine of Creative Innovation." Working Paper S-93-37. New York University Salomon Centre.

Kasman, B., and C.A. Pigott. 1988. "Interest Rate Divergences Among the Major Industrial Nations." *Federal Reserve Bank of New York Quarterly Review.* Vol. 13, No. 3, Autumn: 28-44.

Kato, K., and J.S. Schallheim. 1993. "Private Equity Financings in Japan and Corporate Grouping (Keiretsu)." *Pacific Basin Finance Journal.* Vol. 1: 287-307.

Kester, W.C. 1991. "Japanese Corporate Governance and the Conservation of Value in Financial Distress." *Journal of Applied Corporate Finance.* Summer, Vol. 4, No. 2: 98-104.

King, R.G., and R. Levine. 1992. "Financial Indicators of Growth in a Cross-Section of Countries." PRE Working Paper, No 819. The World Bank.

______. 1993. "Financial Intermediation and Economic Development." Chapter 6, in Mayer and Vives, *Capital Markets and Financial...*

Krugman, P. 1993. "International Finance and Economic Development." Chapter 2, in Giovannini, *Finance and Development: Issues...*

Kuznets, S. 1971. *Economic Growth of Nations: Total Output and Production Structure.* Cambridge: Harvard University Press.

Langford, J.S., and K.L. Brownsey. 1988. (eds.) *The Changing Shape of Government in the Asia-Pacific Region.* Halifax: Institute for Research on Public Policy.

Lawrence, R. 1993. *European Business Survey.* London.

Leipziger, Don, and P.A. Petri. 1993. *Korean Industrial Policy: Legacies of the Past and Directions for the Future.* East Asia and Pacific Region Series. World Bank Finances' Paper # 197. Washington: World Bank.

Lichtenberg, F., and G. Pushner. 1992. "Ownership Structure and Corporate Performance in Japan." N.B.E.R. Working Paper No. 4092.

Lucas, R.E. 1988. "On the Mechanics of Economic Development." *Journal of Monetary Economics.* 22: 3-42.

Matsumoto, K. 1991. *The Rise of the Japanese Corporate System.* New York: Routledge.

Mayer, C., and X. Vives. 1993. (eds.) *Capital Markets and Financial Intermediation.* Centre for Economic Policy Research. Cambridge: Cambridge University Press.

McCauley, R.N., and S. Zimmer. 1989. "Explaining International Differences in the Cost of Capital." *Federal Reserve Bank of New York Quarterly Review.* Summer, Vol. 14, No. 2: 7-28.

McKinnon, R.I. 1993. "Macroeconomic Control in Liberalizing Socialist Economics: Asian and European Parallels." Chapter 8, in Giovannini, *Finance and Development: Issues...*

McKinnon, R. 1973. *Money and Capital in Economic Development.* Washington Bookings Institute.

______. 1991. *The Order of Economic Liberalization, Financial Control in the Transition to a Market Economy.* Baltimore and London: John Hopkins University Press.

Mei, J.P., and S. Foresi. 1993. "Interaction in Investment Among Rival Japanese Firms." Working Paper S-93-30. New York University, Salomon Center.

Merton, R.C. 1992. "Financial Innovation and Economic Performance." *Continental Bank Journal of Applied Corporate Finance.* Winter, Vol. 4, No. 4: 12-22.

Modigliani, F., and M. Miller. 1958. "The Cost of Capital, Corporation Finance and the Theory of Investment." *American Economic Review.* June, Vol. 48, No. 3: 261-297.

Mohammed, A.F. 1988. "Contrasting External Debt Experience: Asia and Latin America." Chapter 3, in Streeten, "Beyond Adjustment: The Asian..."

Mullin, J. 1993. "Emerging Equity Markets in the Global Economy." *Federal Reserve Bank of New York Quarterly Review.* Summer: 54-83.

Myers, S.C., and N.S. Majluf. 1984. "Corporate Financing and Investment Decisions When Firms Have Information Investors do Not Have." *Journal of Financial Economics.* Vol. 13: 187-221.

Myers, S.C. 1984. "The Capital Structure Puzzle." *Journal of Finance.* July, Vol. 39: 575-592.

______. 1993. "Still Searching for Optimal Capital Structure." *Continental Bank Journal of Applied Corporate Finance.* Spring, Vol. 6, No. 1: 4-14.

Nakatani, I. 1984. "The Economic Role of Financial Corporate Grouping." In M. Aoki (ed.). *The Economic Analysis of the Japanese Firm.* Elsevier North-Holland Science Publisher B.V.

Noland, M. 1990. *Pacific Basin Developing Countries: Prospects for the Future.* Washington: Institute for International Economics.

OECD. 1991. *Systemic Risks in Securities Markets.* Paris: Organization for Economic Co-operation and Development.

______. 1993. *Emerging Bond Markets in the Dynamic Asian Economies.* Paris: Organization for Economic Co-operation and Development.

Okuda, M., and S. James. 1990. "The Japanese Bond Market." Chapter 3, in D.H. Gowland (ed.). *International Bond Markets.* London: Routledge.

Orden, D., and L.A. Fisher. 1993. "Financial Deregulation and the Dynamics of Money, Prices and Outputs in New Zealand and Australia." *Journal of Money Credit and Banking.* Vol. 25, May: 273-292.

Ozawa, T. 1991. "Japan in a New Phase of Multi-nationalism and Industrial Upgrading: Functional Integration of Trade, Growth and FDI." *Journal of World Trade.* 43-60.

Park, Y.C. 1993. "The Role of Finance in Economic Development in South Korea and Taiwan." Chapter 6, in Giovannini, *Finance and Development...*

Patel, S.J. 1993. "East Asia's Explosive Development: Its Relevance to Theories and Strategies." Working Paper No. 93.5. International Development Studies, Saint Mary's University. Halifax.

Pecaut, D. 1993. "Canada's High Cost of Capital: A Barrier to Investing for the Future." *Canadian Investment Review*. Summer: 9-20.

Pelkmans, J., and N. Wagner. 1990. *Privatization and Deregulation in Asean and the EC: Making Markets More Effective*. Singapore, Asean Economic Research Unit, Institute of South-East Asian Studies.

Persson, T., and A.C. Stockman. 1988. *Theory of International Financial Markets*. Mimeographed. University of Rochester.

Por, J. 1993. "A New Approach to Corporate Governance." *Canadian Investment Review*. Summer, Vol. VI, No. 2: 33-38.

Poterba, J.M. 1991. "Comparing the Cost of Capital in the United States and Japan: A Survey of Methods." *Federal Reserve Bank of New York Quarterly Review*. Winter, Vol. 15, No. 3-4: 20-32.

Remolona, E.M. 1990. "Understanding International Differences in Leverage Trends." *Federal Reserve Bulletin of New York*. Spring: 31-42.

______. 1992. "The Recent Growth of Financial Derivative Markets." *Federal Reserve Bank of New York Quarterly Review*. Winter: 28-43.

Remolona, E.M., R. N. McCauley, J.S. Ruud, and F. Iacono. 1993. "Corporate Refinancing in the 1990's." *Federal Reserve Bank of New York Quarterly Review*. Winter, 1992/93: 1-27.

Rhee, S.G., and R.P. Chang. 1991. (eds.) *Pacific-Basin Capital Markets Research*. Vols. I and II. New York: North Holland.

Roe, M. 1993. "Some Differences in Corporate Structure in Germany, Japan and the United States." *Yale Law Journal*. June, Vol. 102, No. 8: 1927-2037.

Romer, P. 1986. "Increasing Returns and Long-Run Growth." *Journal of Political Economy*. 94: 1002-1037.

Rose, P.S. 1991. *Japanese Banking and Investments in the United States*. New York: Quorum.

Roubini, N., and X. Sala-i-Martin. 1991. "Financial Development, the Trade Regime and Economic Growth." N.B.E.R. Working Paper 3876. Cambridge: National Bureau of Economic Research.

Saint-Paul, G. 1992. "Technological Choice, Financial Markets and Economic Development." *European Economic Review*. 36: 763-781.

Schadler, S., M. Carkovic, A. Bennett, and R. Kahn. 1993. "Recent Experience with Surges in Capital Inflows." Occasional Paper. Washington: International Monetary Fund.

Schmidt-Hebbel, K., S.B. Webband, and G. Corsetti. 1992. "Household Saving in Developing Countries: First Cross-Country Evidence." *World Bank Economic Review*. September, Vol. 6, No. 3: 529-547.

Schumpeter, J.A. 1942. *Capitalism, Socialism and Democracy*. New York: Harper and Brothers.

Shaw, E.S. 1973. *Financial Deepening in Economic Development*. New York: Oxford University Press.

S.I.A. 1980. "U.S. and Japanese Semiconductor Industries: A Financial Comparison." Report prepared by Chase Financial Policy for the Semiconductor Industry Association. June.

Sletmo, G.K., and G. Boyd. 1993. *Pacific Service Enterprises and Pacific Cooperation.* Boulder: Westview Press.

Smith, R.C. 1993. "Why Japanese Companies Finance Abroad." Working Paper S-93-2. New York University, Salomon Center.

Stiglitz, J.E. 1993. Overview, Chapter 11, in Giovannini, *Finance and Development: Issues...*, 343-353.

Stockman, A.C. 1988. "On the Roles of International Financial Markets and Relevance for Economic Policy." *Journal of Money, Credit and Banking.* August, Vol. 20, No. 3: 531-549.

Streeten, P. 1988. "Beyond Adjustment: The Asian Experience." Washington: International Monetary Fund.

Sun B., G. Aiguo, and L. Soener. 1992. "PRC's Emerging Capital Markets: A Case Study of the Shanghai and Shenzhen Stock Markets." RVB Research Papers. Vol. XII, No. 2, December, 17-21.

Svensson, L.E.O. 1987. "Trade in Risky Assets." Institute for International Economic Studies. Stockholm. Working Paper No. 391.

Tarumiza, K. 1993. "Fostering Investor Confidence in the Asian and Pacific Capital Markets." *Pacific Basin Finance Journal.* May, Vol. 1, No. 2: 105-110.

Tavlas, G.S., and Y. Ozeki. 1992. "The Internationalization of Currencies: An Appraisal of the Japanese Yen." Occasional Paper No. 90. January. Washington: International Monetary Fund.

Torre de la, A., and N.R. Kelly. 1992. "Regional Trade Arrangements." Occasional Paper No. 93. March. Washington: International Monetary Fund.

Townsend, R. 1983. "Financial Structure and Economic Activity." *American Economic Review.* December.

Trivoli, G.W., and P.A. Herbig. 1993. "Investment Strategies and Activities of Leading U.S. Multinational Firms in East Asian Markets: An Empirical Study." *International Trade Journal.* Vol. VII, No. 6: 673-701.

Tseng, W., and R. Corker. 1991. "Financial Liberalization, Money Demand and Monetary Policy in Asian Countries." Occasional Paper No. 84. July. Washington: International Monetary Fund.

United Nations. 1951. *Report of the Expert Group on the Measures for Economic Development of Underdeveloped Regions.* New York: United Nations.

Villegas, B.M. 1990. "Economic Adjustment, Financing and Growth in Southeast Asia During the 1980's." In Aziz, *Strategies for Structural...*

Vittas, D. 1993. (ed.) *Financial Regulations Changing the Rules of the Game*. Economic Development Institute, Development Studies. World Bank, Washington.

Walter, I. 1992. "A Framework for the Optimum Structure of Financial Systems." Working Paper S-92-47. New York University, Salomon Centre.

______. 1993. "Emerging Equity Markets: Tapping into Global Investment Flows." *ASEAN Economic Bulletin*. July: 1-19.

Wei, S.J. 1993. "Open Door Policy and China's Rapid Growth in Evidence From City Level Data." Mimeograph. NBER East Asian Seminar, June, San Francisco.

White, L.J. 1993. "Competition Versus Harmonization: An Overview of International Regulation of Financial Services." Working Paper S-93-58. New York University Salomon Center.

World Bank. 1993. *The East Asian Miracle: Economic Growth and Public Policy*. Washington.

Ziemba, W.T., W. Bailey, and Y. Hamao. 1991. (eds.) *Japanese Financial Market Research*. Elseview Science Publisher. B.V.

Zimmer, J.A., and R.N. McCauley. 1991. "Bank Cost of Capital and International Competition." *Federal Reserve Bank of New York Quarterly Review*. Winter, Vol. 15, No. 3-4: 33-59.

Zysman, J. 1983. *Governments, Markets and Growth: Financial Systems and the Politics of Industrial Change*. Ithica: Cornell University Press.

4

Pacific Industrial Policies and Corporate Strategies

Gavin Boyd

In the Pacific as in other regions diverse forms of reciprocal causality operate between industrial policies and corporate strategies, with contrasts sharper than those in Europe. The most notable are between the extensive functional technocratic-managerial interactions in Japan and the more restricted and less productive ones in the U.S. The Japanese system of mutually supportive dealings between technocratic and managerial levels is comprehensive, sustaining diversified growth in an integrated national political economy and facilitating acquisitions of shares in foreign markets by firms operating out of that economy. In the U.S., the administration, observing a tradition of aloofness from industry and commerce, relates distantly to enterprises, and these operate without the benefits of industry group affiliations. The pressures of competition in world markets and of domestic political competition tend to incline the U.S. administration toward closer relations with firms, but their managements are influenced by long-standing distrust of government authority. Hopes of reducing exposure to the home economy's regulatory measures and taxation influence the motivations of managements, causing them to seek opportunities to develop overseas operations.

In the U.S. intensive policy-oriented studies of the Japanese system have led to some recognition that U.S. firms, while continuing to relate distantly to their national administration, would benefit from the formation of systems of implicit contracting like the Japanese industry groups.[1] Literature advocating such arrangements has stressed the potential efficiency effects, without suggesting the adoption of an industrial policy. A larger stream of literature considering proposals for the introduction of an industrial policy has generally avoided suggesting the establishment of Japanese-style industry groups, and has evidenced doubts about the capacity of the American system of government to manage an industrial policy.[2]

The Japanese experience has indicated that potentials for productive interaction between technocrats and managements depend on mutual responsiveness, based on complementary task orientations and the social organization of trust at a relatively high level. The shared intent is to enhance national growth and employment by increasing gains from domestic and foreign trade through specialization, economies of scale and scope, and technological advances, with overall coordination achieved through a balance between competition and cooperation. Problems of market failure at home are thus to be overcome, while functional alignment is to develop between industrial policy and corporate strategy, through mutual learning and socialization, with informal accountability. Intensive information sharing pervades the interactions, with positive effects for firms, that is with respect to long-range planning, transaction costs, business confidence, and the acquisition of frontier technology.[3]

The technocratic-corporate cooperation may weaken if Japanese firms and industry groups become more assertive and independent in response to a fragmentation of authority under coalition governments. This possibility has been evident since the Liberal Democratic Party's loss of its parliamentary majority in 1993. The established pattern of collaboration however may be strengthened in some respects by shared antipathies toward the U.S., caused by U.S. pressures for increased market access and greater managed trade. American policy is strongly influenced by domestic sentiment in favor of "aggressive unilateralism" to achieve more balanced commerce with trading partners enjoying surpluses.[4] U.S. firms endeavoring to consolidate their positions in their home market and to increase exports to Japan tend to support demands for strong leverage against that country. Concerns about losses of international competitiveness influence the managements of these and other American enterprises, and are factors in their endeavors to move into, or to expand, their overseas operations. Their overseas production in effect substitutes for exports, adversely affecting the trade balance, but production in Japan is made difficult by cost problems and informal barriers, and accordingly a common objective is to serve that market through exports.

For the industrializing East Asian states, Japanese-American rivalry at the corporate and government levels presents major challenges. Large efficient Japanese and American firms, especially in the high-technology high-volume industries, are gaining more and more strength in the regional markets, while contributing more and more substantially to the linking of these through trade and transnational production. Smaller and less competitive firms are being driven into declines, while the less industrialized states in which many of those firms are based are increasingly disadvantaged in bargaining over trade and direct investment issues with Japan, the U.S., and the European Community members. There is a major asymmetry in this trend, as Japanese regional market power is becoming stronger than that of the U.S. National firms in the industrializing East Asian states, while threatened in many cases with cumulative losses of strength in their domestic markets, and in some foreign markets, are being attracted toward collaboration with Japanese enterprises, rather than with U.S. firms.[5] The collaboration entails increasing dependence--more than is often necessary in cooperation with American enterprises.

Technocratic-Corporate Relations

Interactions between administrations and firms in the industrial policy and related areas that have productive effects for each side can establish stable patterns of cooperation in which principles and norms are internalized. Alternatively, unpatterned competitive and conflictual interactions can perpetuate adversarial systems that add to the incentives for corporations to move, if possible, into extensive overseas operations, especially to escape regulatory exposure and gain increased bargaining power.

On the technocratic side, policy styles, communities, and orientations, together with levels of institutional development, determine capacities for and influence commitments to cooperation with firms. A moral, cultural, and institutional basis for productive technocratic engagement with corporations can support the development of industry groups and networks with complementary strategies that can serve overall requirements for national economic growth. Where vote-maximizing political-exchange concerns dominate the political style technocratic capacities and commitments tend to be subordinated to leadership interests in extending favors to selected industries. Such favors tend to rely more and more on subsidies and forms of trade protection that induce reliance on such aid. Vicious circles develop in which sheltered industries lose international competitiveness because of the softening of budget constraints, the protection against external challenges, and the diversion of managerial energies into lobbying. Value orientations in such a system meanwhile tend to be responsible for a fragmentation of industrial interests, preventing the formation of strong peak business associations. Very large firms, operating individually, tend to dominate the lobbying processes, thus securing administrative favors that assist the consolidation of their domestic market positions. This happens even while those large firms may be losing international competitiveness, and may be challenged in their home economies by foreign investment in competing ventures.[6]

In a manipulative and adversarial system of technocratic-managerial interactions, perceived needs for technological cooperation tend to assume special significance because of lags behind the advances of foreign firms benefiting from the efficiencies of solidarity based industrial policies and the supportive relational contracting of industry groups. Administrative efforts to promote technological advances and sharing in the basically non-cooperative context however tend to be ineffective because of the priorities given to vote-maximizing arrangements and managerial interests in such arrangements. Endeavors to ensure that national firms will be advantaged while foreign competitors will be excluded moreover tend to be thwarted because the managements of those enterprises have incentives to develop strategic alliances and other links with the foreign firms, and to be open to equity arrangements with such firms.[7]

Managerial needs for comprehensive information processing and sharing in the increasingly complex regional and global environments are met more effectively when a solidarity based industrial policy interacts with industry groups and networks. The increasing complexities of markets that are being internationalized, and of advances in frontier technology, as well as of national industrial, competition, trade, and foreign direct investment policies, pose vast informational problems for managements, and it is becoming more and more important for them to learn about the current and long-term planning of other firms in the same and related sectors. This is especially necessary because very large and rising volumes of investment are required to introduce advanced technology into manufacturing for global markets. Relational rather than strategic information sharing, horizontally, vertically, and between the technocratic and corporate levels, becomes more and more desirable.[8] There is a vital parallel imperative for extensive cooperation between firms, to complement their competition against each other, in the interests of collective efficiency, as has been illustrated by the productive effects of a pervasive balance between competition and cooperation in the Japanese industry groups, and between those groups.[9]

The scope and utility of information sharing between technocrats and managements depend on the strength of shared commitments to complementary tasks. Continuity in structures and processes is essential, on the government side and in the corporations and industry groups. If industry structures are being frequently changed by mergers and acquisitions, and migrations of management personnel, the necessary building of trust will not be possible. Changes on the technocratic side, moreover, occasioned by shifts of power and switches of high-level preferences, will also hinder the growth of confidence in the value of interactions between the two levels.

The qualities of informational exchanges between administrations and corporations are primary determinants of the system-building potentials of the differing components of industrial policies and of corporate activities directed at the technocratic level. Socialization processes are activated by the values, principles, and norms manifested or discredited by each side. Degrees of understanding about opportunities for cooperation can be attained, or may not be reached. Productive interdependence may evolve, or relationships may be mainly adversarial. For firms, political action costs and transaction costs can be affected. For national administrations, the priorities accorded to public goods and political exchange concerns can be altered as the prospective outcomes of dialogue with managements appear to change.

The Japanese administration and Japanese firms can anticipate substantial continuity in their patterns of interaction because of the confidence building and active cooperation which develops out of their information sharing. Relatively high degrees of rapport have evolved regarding the utility of the informational exchanges, the value of administrative guidance based on capacities for macro planning, and the efficiency effects of all aspects of the entire system of relational contracting for national growth and for insulation against the disruptive effects of foreign penetration through imports and inward direct investment. There are no deeply divisive issues which threaten to disturb the consensus on policy and industrial organization.[10] The principal task identified in foreign economic policy is how to adapt, with collective efficiency, to American demands for more balanced structural interdependence.

In the U.S. questions about government-business cooperation remain divisive, in a context of manipulative and adversarial interactions, in which problems of governance are being aggravated by failures in macromanagement. Issues of market efficiency are assuming large dimensions because the substantial openness of the American economy and its lack of relational systems of contractual governance entail vulnerability to negative externalities resulting from foreign penetrations through commerce and transnational production. Adaptation is difficult not only because of excessive competition and inadequate corporate cooperation but also because of strong managerial interest in production abroad rather than in the home economy and in foreign sourcing for the domestic market. The market failure problems identified in proposals for an industrial policy concern the large investments required for commercial applications of advanced technology and the costs of frontier research and development necessary for international competition: substantial subsidies are proposed because the resources of many firms are inadequate.[11]

Of the industrializing East Asian states South Korea and Taiwan derive major advantages from technocratic-corporate interactive patterns that have affinities with the Japanese system. These make possible cooperative engagement with problems of enhancing efficiencies in their domestic markets, while restricting external penetration of those markets. The tasks of increasingly competitive involvement in regional and global markets however strain the capacities of these systems of technocratic-managerial interaction, as numerous Japanese and American firms have larger resources to support struggles for dominance in the Pacific and in the world economy. The bargaining strengths of the South Korean and Taiwan administrations are not adequate for the maintenance of substantial protection of their internal markets through resistance to Japanese and U.S. trade and direct investment proposals.[12]

In the larger members of the Association of South East Asian Nations (ASEAN) forms of government-business interaction tend to be dominated by elements of personal rule, which can be responsible for arbitrary policy preferences and neopatrimonial practices. Domestic low -and mature-technology firms, enjoying sheltered positions in protected national markets, are under managements dependent on official favor and vulnerable to exploitation by corrupt figures in the ruling elites. Less-favored firms endeavoring to maintain their independence are seriously disadvantaged. Imperatives to promote outward-oriented industrialization are understood in varying degrees by leaderships and bureaucrats, but elite subjective preferences are mostly opposed to substantial reductions of the levels of protection given to favored domestic firms.[13] There is considerable reliance on Japanese, U.S., and European direct investment for the development of manufacturing for export, and this is attracted mainly into assembly-type operations. Information sharing between the administrations and the managements of domestic firms contributes little to policy learning, as managerial dependence on leadership goodwill tends to obligate much deference.

Administrative Capacities and Orientations

An industrial policy assumes system-building potential primarily in so far as it can signify integrative intent and capacity, through affirmations of values and principles. Commitments to limited government can be consistent with integrative intent, but a comprehensive industrial policy can give greater expression to such intent, unless vote-maximizing concerns become evident. The scope of an industrial policy and the integrative intent manifested of course have significance in the context of an entire policy mix. The most important aspect of such a mix, for many managements, may be the combination of fiscal and monetary policies, because of their effects on general economic conditions and on the political business cycle. These effects may encourage capital flight, or may inspire confidence that efficient macromanagement will contribute to stable and balanced growth. For the latter effect the implementation of an industrial policy can be a crucial factor, especially if it arouses managerial confidence in technocratic efforts to evolve policy communities open to corporate interests in the service of public goods.

Within a policy mix, the components of an industrial policy express the administration's attributes, that is through information sharing, consultations about corporate planning, administrative guidance, the provision of subsidies, and the use of industrially related trade, competition, and foreign direct investment measures. There may also be interventions, imposing solutions to perceived issues of industrial structuring. A common theme in literature on industrial policies is that governments in the European Community and more advanced Third World states have been learning to work with the strategies of firms instead of attempting to control market forces. But with this learning there has been increasing recognition of the potential utility of discriminatory trade measures that can shelter domestic firms while these engage in competitive penetration of foreign markets.[14] Administrative pressure on such firms to ensure rising export performance, it has been appreciated, can be effective.

Problems of governance can affect the system-building potential of an industrial policy. Modest initiatives in that policy area have been generally unsuccessful in the U.S. because of the divisive effects of pluralistic pressures, a fragmentation of authority in the administrative structure, and inadequate leadership by overloaded executives.[15] Problems of governance in Japan have been much more manageable, because of the efficiency effects of synergistic interactions between technocrats and managements, and the capacities of industrial groups and associations to aggregate corporate interests, as well as to contribute to policy learning in line with requirements for the development of an optimally competitive national economic structure. In the larger states of the Association of South East Asian Nations issues of political development are reflected in the patterns of government-business relations that preserve inefficient import-substituting industrialization, and the continuation of those patterns evidences deficiencies in leadership qualities, institutional development, and decision processes.

Advanced political development can facilitate the making and implementation of an industrial policy oriented toward integrative cooperation with firms, in the public interest. This can help to meet their requirements for information about markets, new technologies, and policies, thus facilitating their planning while reducing the risks of entrepreneurial choices. The cooperation fostered between firms meanwhile can reduce their transactions costs. Their production costs can also be lowered, through efficiencies made possible by technological advances that become more feasible because of the collaboration between the technocratic and managerial levels as well as because of the related growth of operational links between firms.

Macromanagement made possible by advanced political development can therefore cope with market deficiencies cited in rationales for industrial policies. Investments in Research and Development that individual firms would be reluctant to make on a scale necessary for international competitiveness can become feasible through technocratically encouraged cooperation and subsidies. The funding of Research and Development and the introduction of advanced technology in line with competitive imperatives that do not evoke adequate market responses however can proceed with a narrow focus on problems of market efficiency and failure.[16] As national economies are linked increasingly by commerce and transnational production there can be elements of failure in the *internationalized* markets.

Externalities assume special significance as markets are increasingly linked because the large-scale cross-investment between major industrialized democracies involves relocations of industrial capacity and contributes to considerable deindustrialization. The growth effects that might be expected because of the manufacturing investment are not evident. Of course tax burdens, monetary tightening, and losses of business confidence can hinder growth, but in the U.S. negative externalities resulting from inward and outward manufacturing investment have evidently been substantial.[17] Such externalities have been modest for Japan, as a highly integrated political economy experiencing relatively little foreign corporate penetration, and the adaptive capacities of that economy have not been strained. In the United States relational contracting within industry groups could reduce the scale of the disruptions in sectors and communities, but the question of an industrial policy and foreign direct investment policy responsibility also demands consideration.[18] For the industrializing East Asian states, meanwhile, negative externalities that can offset the benefits of Japanese, U.S., and European direct investment constitute industrial policy problems. These are caused mainly by the shifting of foreign manufacturing operations in response to changes in perceived location advantages, including labor costs.

International oligopoly power tends to increase as smaller and less competitive firms are driven into declines while the large flows of foreign direct investment into manufacturing continue. The growth of this power in high-technology sectors increases barriers to entry and has extensive cross-sectoral effects in the industrializing East Asian states, especially the less integrated and less advanced ones in ASEAN, whose dependence on exports of commodities and low-technology manufactures is in effect prolonged. In the U.S. oligopolistic domination of high-technology sectors also grows but changes as Japanese firms increase their penetration through direct investment in manufacturing. Industrial policy, competition policy, and foreign direct investment policy issues are evident. Tacit collusion, against which there is no anti-trust enforcement, is an important method of expanding oligopoly power.[19] The basis of domestic market strength is significant for U.S. industrial policy concerns, but competition policy, in the areas in which enforcement is threatened, including horizontal integration, has inhibiting effects, and thus can hinder gains in international competitiveness. In the Japanese system national oligopoly power as a market efficiency problem has an exceptional context, because of the combinations of cooperative and competitive activity in the industry groups, and the openness of those groups to emerging firms seeking opportunities within their relational settings.

Public goods, insufficiently provided by the activities of firms, demand attention in conjunction with the problems of oligopoly power and externalities. As the internationalization of markets continues, with the contrasts noted between Japan and the U.S., public goods issues become linked across national boundaries. As matters for industrial policy these continue to be seen as domestic questions, notably concerning needs to promote investments in technology which firms are not motivated to undertake, but the ongoing internationalization obligates wider perspectives. The public goods of orderly and stable growth in contexts of high structural interdependence can be provided to a considerable extent through the diversified balances between competitive and cooperative activity within industry groups and networks. If such balances do not develop, tasks for industrial policy can be envisaged. These may be made more manageable through a restrictive foreign direct investment policy, with discriminating openness to inward direct investment from states willing to cooperate in the management of interdependencies.

The high degree of integration in the Japanese political economy limits the challenges posed by the internationalization of public-goods issues and facilitates adaptation to those challenges, but on a neomercantilist basis. The management of industrial policy can be directed toward orderly integration of modest volumes of inward direct investment into the national pattern of manufacturing and trading.[20] In the U.S. however the greater openness of the national economy and the lack of structures for corporate cooperation make the challenges of internationalized public-goods issues quite formidable. The American economy does not function with the degree of dynamic equilibrium attained in Japan, but with considerable disruption and deindustrialization, associated with numerous destabilizing acquisitions and mergers as well as with foreign penetration through commerce and direct investment. The public good of orderly growth is difficult to attain, mainly because intercorporate relations are almost exclusively competitive. An important function for industrial policy may thus be seen, but it would have to be considered with reference to external trade and foreign direct investment issues. The public-good deficiency clearly requires regulatory foreign trade and foreign direct investment measures, but it is linked with international public-goods deficiencies, in part because of high-volume international production by American corporations. Problems of orderly growth in the U.S. are connected with problems of orderly growth in countries hosting large American manufacturing firms.[21]

For the industrializing East Asian states orderly growth has become a very asymmetrically internationalized issue, due to dependence on Japanese, American, and European direct investment and on access to advanced-country markets. Weak bargaining power restricts the scope for international initiative by these industrializing states, and in effect adds to the importance of their industrial policies, to the extent that these can be functional in the national interest. The internationalization of public-goods issues for these states meanwhile increases the potential significance of their capacities for regional economic cooperation, through which their collective efforts could result in the evolution of *common* industrial policies. In the larger context of their relations with the U.S., Japan and the European states, questions of cooperation for generally harmonized realization of mutual gains from trade and international production await initiatives which for the present cannot be anticipated. In the U.S. the major unresolved public-goods issues are seen to have external ramifications mainly with respect to Japan, and these tend to limit interest in cooperation with industrializing states.[22] In Japan macromanagement successes achieved through the promotion of orderly national growth have tended to strengthen economic nationalism, causing this to dominate perspectives on relations with the industrializing East Asian neighbors.

Information problems assume vast dimensions as markets are internationalized: information costs rise for firms engaged in international operations, but also for domestic firms contending with foreign penetration of their economies. For the purposes of Japanese industrial policy the expanding international information requirements are met rather effectively by the sharing of commercial intelligence in industry groups and networks. As such relational information sharing has not evolved in the U.S. the services of consulting firms assume special importance, but their analytic strengths tend to be used mainly for the benefit of very large enterprises that can provide the fees necessary for high-volume data processing.[23] For firms in the industrializing East Asian states, it must be reiterated, the requirements of international information processing are very difficult to meet, and technocratic endeavors to assist are significant only in South Korea, Taiwan and Singapore.

The commercial intelligence problems that increase with the continuing internationalization of markets concern not only the difficulties of assessing trends in corporate activity worldwide but also the tasks of technological forecasting and identifying shifts in national policies. In these respects Japanese industrial policy, it must be stressed, supplements corporate information sharing rather effectively. In the United States however market forces do not appear to be substantially broadening the range of enterprises served by consulting firms with international expertise: smaller transnational enterprises and domestic firms remain disadvantaged on this account and because of the absence of industry groups and networks.[24] Meanwhile, over time, the information problems of firms in the industrializing East Asian states are becoming more serious, while improvements in the technocratic assistance by their administrations are occurring slowly. Many of these firms are attracted toward joint ventures and strategic alliances with Japanese enterprises but do not share in the intensive information exchanges between those enterprises. Opportunities for collaboration with U.S. firms tend to be restricted, as their managements are generally reluctant to enter joint ventures.

Transaction costs are lowered as communication, financial, legal, insurance, and trading services operate with greater efficiencies in internationalized markets, but transaction risks are increased for small -and medium-sized firms as they venture into those markets in competition against larger enterprises with more extensive resources. Volatility in financial markets is a serious problem for the small -and medium-sized firms, but the larger enterprises can cope with that volatility through greater flexibility in asset management, the use of transfer pricing, and currency switching for intrafirm and external contracts. Political action costs that may have to be borne to secure and complete international contracts moreover can be borne with less difficulty by the larger transnational enterprises. Their resources for political action can also be used abroad and sometimes at home to assist the building of entry barriers which smaller firms can overcome only at heavy cost.[25]

Transaction cost factors reinforce the utility of relational contracting in the Japanese corporate system as it becomes more extensively involved in the global economy. The nation's industrial policy objectives are served, moreover, by the transaction efficiencies enjoyed by its manufacturing, trading, and financial enterprises on the basis of their mutual relations. These advantages become more significant as regional clusters of Japanese firms become larger, notably in East Asia, North America and Europe. Price competition as well as quality competition in regional and world markets is facilitated. Firms in the industrializing East Asian states can thus be increasingly disadvantaged. While collaboration with Japanese enterprises tends to be sought, especially for entries into Pacific markets, the opportunities offered have to be accepted on a subordinate basis, because of the efforts Japanese managements to preserve the exclusive quality of their managerial and industry group cultures.[26] For American corporations the transaction-costs aspects of rivalry with integrated Japanese corporate clusters are becoming more adverse in the industrializing East Asian states. Because of the attraction of their firms toward collaboration with Japanese enterprises substantial competing incentives must be offered in contractual negotiations, and these have to offset the prospective longer-term advantages which the East Asian firms can anticipate in dealings with Japanese corporations.

Corporate Strategies

Difficulties in competition against the Japanese corporate presence in the industrializing East Asian states have been reflected in a decline of American direct investment in their area, while large flows of that investment into the European Community have continued, as its internal market has become more fully integrated. An industrial policy issue for the U.S. is the competitiveness of American firms that have reduced their involvement in East Asia, and this is complicated by questions about the volume of production and sourcing in that area by U.S. firms, as it affects growth and employment at home, and the U.S. trade balance.[27] For American managements problems of regional and global strategy have to be engaged with while decisions by their home government in the industrial, trade, and foreign direct investment areas remain difficult because of the strong pluralism in their national policy processes. Japanese managements continue to be advantaged by their home government's administrative support, and its assistance in their penetration of foreign markets sustains cooperation that facilitates their adaptation to competitive pressures in those markets. For the present these pressures are potent because of the appreciation of the yen, which obliges Japanese manufacturing firms to shift assembly-type operations to the low-wage ASEAN countries. National firms in the industrializing East Asian states depend very much on support from their governments, but in the larger ASEAN members this is given more significant expression through protectionist trade policies than through industrial cooperation.

American corporate strategies tend to emphasize greater self-reliance in their responses to Japanese competitive challenges, indecision at home on problems of foreign economic policy, and the prospects of higher tax burdens and stresses in the national economy. The increasing challenges of Japanese competition could be met by greater cooperation between U.S. firms, for technological advancement and collaborative production ventures, but distrust of competitors in the home economy is pervasive, and the common response is more intense use of each corporation's own resources. Continuing imperatives to demonstrate short-term profits reinforce the emphasis on self-reliance. Anticipations of further strains in the U.S. economy, in part because of policy failures, add to the perceived importance of enhancing firm-specific strengths, while increasing incentives to build these through expanding foreign operations. Anticipations of improvement in macromanagement and high growth at home are discouraged by the increases in heavy government debt and the effects of slow growth on the political balance in Congress between its distributional coalitions and the advocates of greater fiscal discipline.[28]

Political action to secure greater protection of their positions in the home market has become a further imperative for American firms as they move into or extend their international operations. Their demands for reduced openness to imports tend to be supported by domestic enterprises with little external trade. The retaliatory capacities of major trading partners are recognized by American international firms, but exercise of Japan's retaliatory capacity is evidently not expected to increase significantly the already strong informal barriers sheltering its market. The importance of Japanese investor confidence for stability in the U.S. economy and for the heavy borrowing needs of the U.S. administration appears to have only secondary significance for the managements of American international corporations. This is understandable in view of the absence of strong peak business associations whose leaderships could absorb policy-level perspectives through wide-ranging exchanges with government officials. In a more fundamental way it is also understandable because of the strong pressures on U.S. managements to achieve short-term profits: the intense task orientation which results has a narrow focus.[29]

The technology-promotion endeavors of their administration appear to arouse only modest interest among managers of U.S. international firms. The increasing involvement of the U.S. high-technology transnational corporations in strategic alliances across national boundaries reflects interest in these as the primary opportunities for advanced technology sharing. Anti-trust enforcement focus on the effects of administrative encouragement of pre-competitive technological cooperation between firms, moreover, evidently tends to limit managerial expectations of the value of such collaboration.[30] Traditional distrust of government and doubts about the competence of administrative agencies influence managerial attitudes. There is general awareness that the history of U.S. government efforts to promote technological advancement for the benefit of national firms has evidenced the dysfunctional effects of bureaucratic conflicts and legislative pluralism, as well as divisions within the business community.[31]

Strong emphasis on the substitution of capital for labor is a dominant feature of American corporate strategies, in line with a concentration on price rather than quality competition in world markets. This reflects tendencies to neglect the human resource management aspects of technological advancement. That can be viewed as an industrial policy matter which could be open to engagement because of its significance for equity in industrial relations and because it has some negative implications for the long-term technological rivalry of American firms with their Japanese counterparts.[32] The common managerial culture is not oriented toward the promotion of normative integration in enterprises, and the pressure for short-term profits limits interest in long-term development of the technological competence of the work force.

The managerial emphasis on self-reliant pursuit of market opportunities is expressed primarily by expanding international production. The converging imperatives behind this are becoming more potent, especially because of the interacting effects of strains in the U.S. economy and gains in world markets by Japanese firms. The financing of new technology and of integration and diversification strategies is facilitated by international production, as this yields higher profits because of economies in the expanding use of location advantages, and reduces tax exposure, while U.S. taxes on reinvested profits are deferred indefinitely. The strains in the U.S. economy affect perspectives on domestic financing as well as on the scope for future domestic operations. Meanwhile establishing an active presence in major foreign markets has become increasingly important in the competition against Japanese enterprises. Location in dynamic foreign centers of innovation, moreover, has become more and more important for access to advanced technology and for the management of strategic alliances.[33]

Centralized global management is tending to become more necessary in the international operations of American firms, because of competitive pressures to maximize the use of location advantages on a world-wide basis, that is with respect to information costs, production costs, transaction costs, technology development, regulatory and tax exposure, and trends in general economic conditions. The Japanese competitive pressures, which are assuming larger global dimensions, are presented by regional networks of firms whose activities tend to be integrated into strategies rationalized on a global basis. The distinctive managerial cultures of the Japanese firms facilitate management of these strategies with considerable efficiencies. In the operations of U.S. international enterprises responsiveness to host-economy conditions remains important, but evidently tends to receive less emphasis, especially in Europe, because of the increasing standardization of consumer demands, influenced by very large-scale applications of new technology in global products. The growing importance of centralized global management entails dependence on extensive middle management layers that can be vulnerable to inertia and organizational manipulation, but the tasks of direction and supervision are aided by advances in information and communications technology.[34]

Highly complex diversified organizational learning in U.S. international firms about the factors influencing the development of their global strategies in effect distances them, increasingly, from the commercial and technological knowledge acquired by economic agencies in their home government. This means that in several important respects its potential for efficient ventures into administrative guidance is tending to decline, together with its capacity for devising and monitoring the use of export subsidies.[35] For the administration's political-exchange concerns, of course, subsidies remain very significant, and they deserve attention in corporate political action strategies, but their provision by that administration tends to become less useful for U.S. international enterprises as their foreign operations expand, and as the range of direct and indirect subsidies by host governments tends to increase, because of their efforts to attract manufacturing investment.

Japanese corporate strategies, operating generally in alignment with responsive national industrial policy, are not significantly motivated by desires to reduce domestic regulatory exposure, or dependence on the home economy. The continuing emphasis on expansion into international operations is a single-minded striving for more competitive involvement in world markets, necessitated in a large measure by actual and anticipated foreign protectionism directed against Japanese exports, and by the high cost of assembly type operations at home. The international expansion is in effect a collective endeavor, with manufacturers, suppliers, banks and trading companies working in industry groups and networks, and as it continues there is a collective enhancement of firm-specific advantages through combinations of mutual support and competition. These are sources of advantage over foreign firms that may be engaged in strategic alliances, as those combinations of cooperation and competition are restricted, episodic, less trustful, and less supported by information sharing.[36]

Large integrated Japanese regional corporate presences are strengthened in East Asia and North America by the collaborative outward direct investment. Sustaining the solidarity of those presences is a basic operational principle, because of common awareness of the strengthening of firm-specific advantages in the context of industry group and network-specific advantages. This solidarity makes possible concerted long-term planning, with extensive risk sharing, and ensures collaborative adaptation to problems and opportunities in foreign environments, as well as rapid and often pre-emptive collaborative applications of advanced technology, with leads in competition to influence consumer tastes.

The tacit concern of industrial policy to ensure continued solidarity in the overseas corporate presences tends to be reassured by the reinforcing of collaborative managerial commitments as firms benefit from their linked increases in market shares. The exclusive qualities of their managerial cultures have very important system-maintenance functions in this context. Recognition of this and of the distinctive solidarity potential of the home environment sustains implicit understandings that inward foreign direct investment must be restricted, and must be informally assimilated. On this there is corporate rapport, and a well-established practice of rotating management personnel between the home office and international subsidiaries limits the penetration of foreign cultural influences into the overseas corporate presences. Upward mobility for foreign personnel is restricted for this purpose.[37]

An important consequence of the technocratic-managerial cooperation is that the acquisition of foreign market shares by Japanese firms has a collective dimension, and involves extensive internalization of market processes at the industry group and network levels, not merely at the corporate level. The pervasive relational contracting amounts to an internalization of vast numbers of transactions, undertaken primarily on a basis of solidarity rather than calculated assessments of cost advantages. This solidarity is a source of X efficiencies which tend to increase firm-specific and industry-group as well as network-specific advantages. The X efficiencies operate through the combinations of cooperation and competition, which are functional because of information sharing, technology sharing, risk sharing, and concerted planning. The rapid diffusion of innovations within the industry groups and networks is a constant source of stimulus for further innovations, and these result primarily from intensive intrafirm task-oriented communications, in which working level autonomy is a potent factor.[38]

The more extensive the industry groups and networks become, and the more their Research and Development activities expand, the less necessary it is for their member firms to seek partnerships and strategic alliances with American or European enterprises. Forms of collaboration with such enterprises moreover can be managed with greater bargaining power and with more discrimination. Such collaboration is usually directed at advanced country markets, in which it has some political as well as economic utility. There is little interest in cooperation of this kind for the development of more active roles in modernizing countries. In that context industrial policy has a more visible and supportive function, through involvement in the provision of official Japanese aid. Infrastructure development related to the direct investment of Japanese firms tends to induce preferential acceptance of their proposals by host governments and corporate communities. Industrializing East Asian states are the main focus of administrative and managerial attention. Over the long term, increasing industrialization in these states, with very active Japanese involvement, linking each of them individually more with Japan than with each other, can complement the expanding Japanese manufacturing, trading, and financial presence in North America, and the smaller matching presence in Europe.[39]

For the purposes of Japanese industrial policy and long-term corporate strategy, stresses related to market penetration in North America, and, to a lesser extent, in Europe, can be managed more and more effectively as operations in the industrializing East Asian states are expanded. Over the long term, of course, Japanese planning has to anticipate slow growth in the U.S. economy, and probably related contraction of the politically acceptable limits on penetration of the domestic market by Japanese firms. With the development of a strong corporate presence in East Asian states moving into higher industrialization, however, Japanese industry groups, networks, and associations can anticipate more potent leverage for themselves and their administration on trade and foreign direct investment issues in dealings with the U.S. and the European Community. Collaboration between the U.S. and the Europeans has been a long-standing problem for Japanese policymakers and managements. Although this collaboration has diminished, mainly because of strains over trade issues, it could increase on the basis of shared concerns about Japanese economic expansion.[40]

Industrializing East Asian corporate strategies are evolving in two major patterns, while responding to the challenges of Japanese and American regional economic involvement. Substantially collaborative and rationally ordered responses are being made by South Korean and Taiwan firms, in cooperation with their administrations, while in the development of their strategies difficult choices are being confronted regarding opportunities for linkages with Japanese and U.S. enterprises. Maintaining high degrees of integration in the South Korean and Taiwan industry-administrative complexes is necessary to cope with the increasing requirements for competitiveness in the regional market. National firms in the larger ASEAN states operate with less cohesion, because of communal and political cleavages, and the divisive effects of dependence on administrative favors. Collectively self-reliant rational strategies are difficult to evolve, and for many of these firms, it must be stressed, concentration on opportunities in their protected domestic markets becomes increasingly necessary because of inadequate competitiveness for international operations.

The internationally active South Korean firms are mostly large high -and mature-technology enterprises that were officially sponsored under military regimes and that became significantly competitive in world markets while accepting administrative guidance and support from those regimes. Transitions to representative government in the 1980s reduced the entitlements of these enterprises to official support, and they have had to contend with increasing protectionism in the U.S., their main export market. They have been challenged to achieve greater competitiveness in high-technology manufacturing for the U.S. market, and this has necessitated rivalry with and collaboration with Japanese enterprises, with considerable dependence on the greater resources of those enterprises. Entries into the Japanese market have been difficult, and have been possible mainly in mature-technology sectors where Japanese firms have been losing advantages. Penetration of the ASEAN and Chinese markets has been easier, but encounters increasingly intense Japanese competition. Administrative guidance appears to ensure considerable coordination between South Korean corporate export endeavors, on the basis of solidarity built up over the past few decades.[41]

Taiwan's internationally active high-technology firms are smaller and quite numerous. To overcome disadvantages resulting from their modest resources their administration is encouraging mergers that will be capable of undertaking technology-intensive production for export, to achieve more competitive penetration of the American market, on which Taiwan is very heavily dependent. In rivalry against South Korean and Japanese enterprises the Taiwan firms are disadvantaged by the limitations of size and by greater vulnerability to U.S. trade and political discrimination, because of U.S. business interest in the Chinese market. They are however advantaged by their own expanding presence in that market, based on fairly large-scale assembly-type production for the Chinese economy and for export. They are also advantaged by involvement in a regional network of links with Chinese enterprises operating in the Association of South East Asian Nations. Their administration's industrial policy has to cope with issues concerning the degree of structural interdependence that is evolving with China, the potential for expanding economic ties with Southeast Asian states, and the imperative to reduce dependence on the U.S. market. The strategies of the Taiwan firms appear to be less concerted than those of the larger South Korean enterprises, in part because of opportunities make possible by more extensive commercial links with Southeast Asia and China.[42]

Of the larger ASEAN members Malaysia ranks closest to South Korea and Taiwan in terms of technocratic capacities and levels of infrastructure development, and its industrial development has been less heavily sheltered by protectionist measures than that in Thailand, Indonesia and the Philippines. Strong pro-Malay communal bias in economic policy however has weakened the entrepreneurial and technological potential of what have been mainly Chinese manufacturing and trading enterprises. Predominantly Malay firms, benefiting from the favor of the Malay-dominated ruling elite, have tended to become dependent on official support, and this has not been conducive to efficiency. The attraction of foreign direct investment into assembly-type production for export has been a major feature of the national administration's policy, but incoming firms, most of which have been Japanese, have tended to seek links mainly with local Chinese enterprises.[43]

The scope for independent entrepreneurial initiative is greater in Thailand, that is for Chinese and Thai firms, as the large Chinese business community operates without the official discrimination experienced in Malaysia, and few ventures into industrial policy have been attempted by the presently representative government. Bureaucratic inefficiencies and excessive regulation, however, together with serious infrastructure deficiencies, and high levels of protection, affect the calculations of Thai and Chinese managements. These calculations are also affected by the rapid growth of a large Japanese corporate presence in manufacturing and trading. The sheltered domestic industrial structure does not provide adequate support for Thai and Chinese firms venturing into mature -and higher-technology manufacturing for export. Thailand lacks materials and capital goods industries, and imports of advanced capital goods are necessary for national firms seeking international competitiveness in manufacturing above the low technology level. Links with foreign enterprises tend to be sought for technological support, but Japanese enterprises undertaking direct investment in joint ventures have been quite discriminating on questions of technology sharing and have been reluctant to assist the development of Thai capacities for export. Collective representation of Thai business interests and concerted planning by national firms are prevented by sectoral fragmentation attributable to pervasive clientelism in the Thai political economy. This has reflected the negative effects of long periods of military rule on the development of political institutions.[44]

An industrial policy with neopatrimonial features imposes arbitrary leadership preferences on enterprises operating under Indonesia's military regime, which has sponsored heavily protected import-substituting industrialization. A large Chinese business community enjoys relatively more freedom than its counterpart in Malaysia but must defer to the preferences of a military elite maintaining a highly authoritarian system of personal rule. Serious deficiencies in the administrative services moreover make it essential to secure official favor for routine business activity. Indonesian firms also have to operate with official favor, while contending with the weaknesses of the administrative services, which have been responsible for poor infrastructure development. Both Indonesian and Chinese firms that have been sheltered by high levels of protection have failed to undertake significantly competitive mature -and higher-technology manufacturing for foreign markets. Technocratic efforts are being made to promote such manufacturing, but the fundamental problems of administrative corruption and inefficiency remain serious. While the opportunities for Indonesian and Chinese enterprises continue to be limited by these problems they are also being progressively restricted by the expansion of a large Japanese corporate presence, engaged mainly in assembly-type production and resource extraction. The Chinese enterprises, because of their informal links with their counterparts in other Southeast Asian countries, Taiwan, Hongkong, and China, have more extensive options than the Indonesian enterprises.[45]

Heavy dependence on exports of energy, textiles, and garments is challenging Indonesian industrial policy decision-makers to work for the development of materials and capital-goods industries, to support outward-oriented higher-technology manufacturing. Technocratic efforts in this direction are being influenced mainly by rather high-volume incoming Japanese direct investment, which is likely to continue emphasis on the exploitation of opportunities for assembly-type operations. Movement into research-intensive production will depend on the development of local centers of innovation, which are not yet in prospect. Indonesian and Chinese firms lack capacities for competition against the Japanese assembly-type manufacturing. Meanwhile the expansion of that manufacturing, as it contributes to growth and export development, tends to induce official responsiveness to Japanese proposals for larger-scale direct investment, with related infrastructure improvement.

Administrative and Managerial Planning

The numerous issues for policymakers and managements in the main pattern of relations between the market economy East Asian and North American states raise questions about administrative and corporate capacities for planning. The preferences, options, and decisions that have been identified have to be assessed in the context of trends resulting from interactions between the activities of enterprises and the implementation of policies. These interactions are contributing to rises in structural interdependence with increasing asymmetries due to differences in competitiveness and in the quality of national policies. The advantages of rationally ordered and consensual decision-making at the government and corporate levels are becoming more significant because of disparities in the spread of benefits from higher but imbalanced interdependence. At the same time the costs of disjointedly incremental and conflicted decision making are becoming more serious, for states and enterprises.

Planning capacities in organizations depend very much on information processing and sharing, and tend to be greater if this sharing is broadly inclusive, relational, and integrative: the functional requirements of rational decision-making can then be served more effectively. The scope of the necessary information processing is being widened as markets are internationalized with greater complexities and asymmetries, as leading firms gain global oligopoly power, as technology advances multiply, and as administrations resort to managed trade and strategic trade policies, while often experiencing problems of governance. For firms, then, the commercial intelligence advantages of membership in industry groups are becoming more significant, since the volume of the analytically significant material to be absorbed can strain the cognitive capacities of even large planning units. For firms without industry group affiliations it is becoming increasingly necessary to use consulting services, but these tend to be provided at arm's length outside industry group contexts, with tacit discrimination to maximize exploitation of the needs of the highest paying enterprises.

At the policy level increasing needs for macro information processing can be met to a large extent through upward communications from industry groups, if there is rapport with the corporate level. In the absence of such groups the information processing requirements of policymakers become enormous, and tend to be met in part with biases, through communications associated with lobbying. If there is considerable corporate distrust of government, communications from firms will tend to be related mainly to lobbying, and policymakers will thus have to find ways of supplementing, on a very large scale, that strategically formulated information.

The uses of information are determined by policy styles and managerial styles. The reactive, conflicted, short-term American policy style functions with selective information processing, serving coalition building and bargaining purposes, while its cognitive deficiencies necessitate much experimental incrementalism. Distrust of planning tends to be associated with such a policy style: there is a focus on maximizing the exploitation of current opportunities, and the ordering of these is provisional, within policy designs evolving through trial and error.[46] The consensual, promotional, Japanese policy style tends to operate with broadly functional information flows, in the context of a culture conducive to the formation of industry groups from which communications assist the policy processes. In such a setting aggregated managerial inputs contribute to policy planning.

Managerial styles tend to be similar to policy styles because in each country they are influenced by the same characteristics of the general culture, although the senior personnel of international firms may become multicultural as those firms lose home-country ties. In enterprises with low levels of normative integration managerial decision-making tends to be conflicted because of internal rivalries and attempts at organizational manipulation. Investor pressures for short-term profits, reflecting low levels of integration in the political economy, hinder application to long-term considerations and force concentration on immediate opportunities. These have to be assessed while coping with numerous uncertainties, because of informational problems due to very limited cooperation with similarly constituted firms. Decision-making is therefore experimental and incremental, and it is primarily a top management function. As such it is typically open to only modest planning inputs that do not challenge its subjective preferences.[47]

High levels of normative integration in enterprises, which usually are associated with high levels of normative integration in a national political economy, tend to be expressed in consensual decision-making with much working-level autonomy. Informational problems are managed more effectively on that account and because of relational interactions with other firms. Long-term strategies can be designed with considerable security because of prospects for collaboration with other enterprises in networks and industry groups. These strategies can provide for substantial investments in new technology, based on calculations about expected increases in market shares that are anticipated because of the concerting of strategies with other managements, in operations at home and in foreign economies.

The structural and functional contrasts affecting planning capacities at the governmental and enterprise levels indicate differing potentials for responding to issues of macromanagement and competitiveness in the Asia-Pacific region. The potentials of the U.S. administration and of U.S. firms are weaker than those of the Japanese government and Japanese enterprises. The disparities are especially significant because the problems confronting American decision-makers are extremely difficult. Industrial policy measures to cope with those problems are not likely to be adequate, and accordingly tendencies to seek solutions through managed trade will probably become stronger. Meanwhile the planning of comprehensive long-term solutions may well tend to become politically even less feasible because of the aggravation of problems of governance as asymmetries in the structural interdependence with Japan increase. Japanese planning capabilities will probably remain substantial, in part because of the positive effects of neomercantilist successes on solidarity in the national political economy.

American economic policy will probably continue to be shaped mainly by legislative, sectoral, and community pressures for increased growth and employment, interacting with reactive administrative vote-maximizing moves. Policy planning, especially in critical phases of the political business cycle, must be expected to engage principally with support mobilization tasks in major constituencies rather than with substantive issues. As the main thrust of the conflicted decision processes continues to emphasize managed trade, general confidence in industrial policy as a source of advantages in world markets will probably become weaker. The results of industrial policy measures are likely to be modest, and the conflicting effects of pluralistic pressures will tend to discourage business confidence in the policy process. Strong legislative and societal demands for more domestically based growth, meanwhile, can be expected to influence the orientation of industrial policy decision-making. Such a trend could be made more probable by legislative and business demands for restrictions on Japanese direct investment in the United States.[48]

Policy processes in Japan will no doubt continue to incorporate more rational planning, principally because of the strong role of the economic bureaucracy and the macrostrategic capacities of industry groups, networks, and business associations. The relativizing effects which sectoral bargaining can have on substantive planning concerns will be restrained. Industrial policy, as a major component of the policy mix, will probably give greater attention to guidance of the expanding national corporate involvement in the industrializing East Asian states, while recognizing political limitations on further penetration of the American and European Community markets. Increasing U.S. and European imposition of managed trade arrangements in high-technology sectors, especially automobiles and electronic products, will tend to strengthen the influence of the Ministry of International Trade and Industry on Japanese corporate planning.[49] This will probably also be strengthened by the increasing importance of the administration's economic assistance for infrastructure development in the industrializing East Asian states. Questions about the development of technology research institutes in some of the larger ASEAN members and about the expansion of those in South Korea and Taiwan may well be taken up in industrial policy planning, as the long-term importance of growth in these neighboring states for the Japanese economy becomes more evident. The increasing integration of the Canadian and Mexican economies with that of the U.S. will tend to make that more apparent.

Deficiencies in the planning and decisional capacities of the larger ASEAN members will probably remain serious, preventing the evolution of functional designs for higher technology manufacturing for export, and hindering concerted use of opportunities for market integration within ASEAN. Uncoordinated industrial policy decisions, strongly influenced by leadership idiosyncratic preferences, will no doubt respond increasingly to incentives presented by the entrepreneurship of Japanese corporations. The acceptance of larger-scale Japanese assembly plants and resource extraction projects will narrow the ranges of industrial policy choices, unless there is a willingness to accept reduced entitlements to Japanese official aid and to resort to special incentives for the attraction of high-volume U.S. direct investment. The planning options of national firms in these ASEAN states will tend to be restricted by administrative choices, resulting in greater openness to Japanese direct investment, but Chinese corporations in those states will probably retain considerable scope for independent strategies because of their transnational affiliations, especially with enterprises in Taiwan.

The planning and decisional capacities of the South Korean and Taiwan administrations, which may be impaired to some extent by growing pluralistic pressures, may well be oriented more and more toward cooperation with, and cautious competition against, the growing Japanese regional corporate presence, with acceptance of greater asymmetric structural interdependence in the relationship. This orientation could shift, especially in the Taiwan case, if greater economic liberalization and improved administration in China offered trade and investment opportunities large enough to balance links with the

Japanese economy. The technological dimension of industrial policy is becoming more and more significant for South Korean and Taiwan decision-makers confronting choices relating to Japan and China, especially because the development of strong centers of innovation could open the way for more equal interdependence with Japan, and greater access to scientific research institutes in the U.S. Japanese firms and technology institutions have gained very large leads over all competitors in their efforts to profit from U.S. research, but these leads could be reduced by vigorous South Korean and Taiwan endeavors, especially if those were encouraged by U.S. policy.

Theory

The Pacific configuration of industrial policies and corporate strategies exhibits the efficiency effects--in the context of U.S.-Japan rivalry--of integration logic *above the corporate level*, in industry groups and networks, and their participation in neocorporatist policy-making. The prime example is Japan, but the logic of the Japanese experience has been validated also, to a considerable extent, in South Korea and Taiwan. The motivations in the Japanese case, at the administrative and managerial levels, have derived not so much from the advantages of economizing on transaction costs as from converging normative and efficiency concerns. The normative concerns have derived from commitments to group and community values that have been realized through relational transacting and relational political interaction. The efficiency concerns have been based on understandings of the synergistic consequences of concerting intracorporate and intercorporate as well as supracorporate endeavors, ordering them rationally toward complementary objectives. An optimum national economic structure is emerging, with balanced interdependencies evolving to a considerable extent under administrative guidance. Cumulative achievements in competitive macromanagement have tended to reinforce general acceptance of this large-scale application of integration logic, and of the importance of protecting it against disruptive foreign penetration.

Recognition of long-term oligopolistic trends in markets that are being internationalized evidently contributes also to the acceptance of that integration logic. The formation of integrated corporate presences in North America and East Asia is a major feature of those trends, and has resulted from past awareness of vulnerability to the increasing oligopoly power of American and other foreign firms. Appreciation that the trends have been changed in Japan's favor, and that this has been possible largely because of the pervasive implementation of integration logic, has meanwhile been influenced by nationalist sentiments, roused by discriminatory U.S. and European trade measures.[50]

The multilevel Japanese application of integration logic results in an extensive internalization of markets, not only at the corporate level but, in effect, at the industry group and network level, where relational contracting links numerous patterns of intrafirm commerce. A further degree of virtual market internalization results from the collaboration between industry groups, and between industry groups and networks, under administrative influence. Managements and policy-makers in other major industrialized democracies are challenged by the breadth of Japanese market internalization. Matching applications of integration logic have not evolved in the other industrialized democracies. In several of these states, moreover, problems of governance intensified by declines in international competitiveness have initiated vicious circles, in which macromanagement deficiencies have contributed to further losses in world markets, and to a hollowing out of industrial structures through the outward movement of productive capacity.

The most serious problems of macromanagement and competitiveness to which integrated Japanese neomercantilism has contributed have been those in the U.S. Integration logic has been given little scope in the structuring of the American political economy, as its ethos has been intensely individualistic. Vigorously competitive entrepreneurship was responsible for rapid growth in the domestic economy, but was then expressed in ambitious overseas production ventures which increasingly exceeded manufacturing at home for export. Losses of country identities and loyalties followed. Meanwhile growth and distributional problems in the home economy increased because of the outward movement of industrial capacity but also because of the rising costs of government, which were being pushed higher by vote-maximizing political activities and by related extensions of the administration's role in the economy.

Complex reciprocal causality in the American experience of decreasingly competitive and more difficult macromanagement has evidenced the challenges posed for governments and firms as markets are internationalized. In the exploitation of opportunities in those markets advantages have been gained by Japanese firms whose applications of integration logic have facilitated the implementation of industrial policies. Firms implementing highly self-reliant strategies have been disadvantaged in internationalizing markets because their resources have mostly been smaller and less diversified than those of enterprises affiliated with industry groups and networks. The efficiency effects of the collective enhancement of firm-specific advantages in industry groups and networks have been cumulative. Relative losses of international competitiveness by U.S. firms on that account, together with shifts by those firms into high-volume overseas production, have tended to depress growth in the U.S. economy. Societal demands for improved performance have thus tended to assume prominence in contests for political office.[51] These in turn have been largely responsible for heavy fiscal deficits, yet the increasing costs of government have diverted investment funds from productive use, while raising the costs of capital. In this setting ventures into industrial policy, restricted because of a liberal-political tradition and because of corporate emphasis on self-reliance, have promised less substantial growth results than resorts to aggressively unilateral trade measures. Leverage for these, however, has been diminishing with rises in complex asymmetric structural interdependence between the U.S. and Japan.

The American experience has thus illustrated that the costs of macromanagement deficiencies increase as structural interdependencies rise, through the linking of the home market with foreign economies, as that allows wider scope for expansion by more competitive firms. Supportive strategies by national firms can assist an administration coping with its own deficiencies, but those deficiencies tend to alienate managements and increase their interests in reducing regulatory exposure at home while maximizing the use of foreign location advantages. Such advantages, which include an active presence in overseas markets that are being penetrated, are of course more significant in high-growth countries less burdened with macromanagement failures, for example Germany.

In the larger international context of the American experience the advantages gained by Japanese firms through more comprehensive applications of integration logic have been prominent elements of the oligopolistic global market trend. While national markets have become more open to each other through transnational production and trade, despite import restraints, larger and more efficient firms widening the ranges of their operations have been driving less competitive enterprises into declines.[52] Bargaining strength based on market size has enabled the U.S. to impose restraints on market access, but, it must be stressed, within the limits set by the vulnerabilities of imbalanced structural interdependence, which are increasing. The international firms of U.S. origin which are in many cases leaders of the oligopolistic trend are becoming stateless, but advantages they derive from rationalizing their operations on a global basis are tending to diminish as the concerted strategies of Japanese corporations become more potent, and as relations between the originally American managements remain almost entirely competitive.

Domestic and international contextual factors influencing industrial policy measures and corporate strategies in the U.S. and Japan have thus been evolving mainly in opposite directions. Internal and external challenges have been tending to have disruptive effects in the U.S., while such challenges have contributed to the reinforcement of dynamic integration in the Japanese political economy, through gains in foreign markets. Japanese administrative and corporate capacities to cope with and influence the development of those challenges have been gradually increasing, while there have been no American shifts toward adoption of the Japanese policies and strategies, except for modest initiatives in the technology area. The continued divergence between American and Japanese orientations at the policy and corporate strategy levels has to be explained in terms of cultural, normative, and structural fundamentals, especially in so far as these determine the scope for relational or arm's-length contracting. In explorations of these fundamentals the functional significance of those in Japan for diversified large-scale organizational performance has been especially prominent.

Developmental issues for the industrializing East Asian states have assumed new dimensions with the shift in the balance of regional economic power toward Japan. The competitiveness and bargaining strength of the Japanese presence are increasing, for those industrializing states, in ways that cannot be sufficiently offset by expanding economic ties with the U.S.[53] The potentials of these modernizing states for outward-oriented manufacturing at rising technological levels are being progressively restricted, mainly by Japanese but also by American regional and global market gains, and by continued Japanese and increasing U.S. limitations on market access. No strong political ties between industrializing East Asian states are making possible collective engagement with the increasingly difficult problems of asymmetrically interdependent development. In the larger ASEAN members, meanwhile, political evolution that could lead to technocratic capacities like those in South Korea and Taiwan continues to be hindered by serious leadership failings and institutional weaknesses. In some respects these deficiencies tend to be perpetuated by direct and indirect benefits which political leaderships derive from the expanding Japanese corporate involvement in their economies.

Altogether, then, trends in the linking of Asia-Pacific markets do not encourage expectations of a regional equilibrium. American firms largely unguided and unsupported by industrial policy have competitive advantages over smaller enterprises in modernizing East Asian states, although some of those enterprises, notably those in South Korea and Taiwan, are aided by industrial policies. Japanese corporations, assisted by a solidarity building industrial policy, are gaining competitive advantages over the American firms, and more substantial advantages over enterprises in the industrializing East Asian states. This pattern of change can be expected to continue if there is regional trade liberalization sponsored by the Asia Pacific Economic Cooperation forum. The disparities in the spread of gains from liberalized commerce to be anticipated in any regional trade-liberalization scheme could indeed be very large because of the sharp contrasts in the competitiveness of firms and the qualities of macromanagement.

Notes

1. W. Carl Kester, "Industrial Groups as Systems of Contractual Governance," *Oxford Review of Economic Policy*, 8 (Autumn 1992) 3: 24-44.
2. Roger G. Noll, "Structural Policies in the United States," in Samuel Kernell (ed.) *Parallel Politics: Economic Policymaking in Japan and the United States* (Washington: Brookings Institution, 1991), 230-280.
3. Shumpei Kumon and Henry Rosovsky (eds.), "The Political Economy of Japan," *Cultural and Social Dynamics*, Vol. 3 (Stanford: Stanford University Press, 1992).
4. I. M. Destler, *American Trade Politics*, Second edition (Washington: Institute for International Economics, 1992); and Laura D'Andrea Tyson, *Who's Bashing Whom? Trade Conflict in High Technology Industries* (Washington: Institute for International Economics, 1992).
5. See details of the scale of Japanese direct investment in these states in *Foreign Direct Investment Relations Between the OECD and the Dynamic Asian Economies* (Paris: OECD, 1993), ch. 1.
6. Gavin Boyd, *Corporate Planning and Policy Planning in the Pacific* (London: Pinter, 1993), chs. 5 and 8.
7. Ibid.
8. D.J. Teece, "Technological Development and the Organization of Industry," in *Technology and Productivity: The Challenge for Economic Policy* (Paris: OECD, 1991): 409-418.
9. Kester, "Industrial Groups as Systems..."
10. Kumon and Rosovsky, The Political Economy of Japan...
11. President William J. Clinton and Vice President Albert Gore, *Technology for America's Economic Growth, a New Direction to Build Economic Strength* (Washington: U.S. Government Printing Office 1993).
12. Taiwan is seriously disadvantaged because of its small size, its heavy dependence on the U.S. market, and its lack of official U.S. recognition.
13. This is especially true in Indonesia. On levels of protection in ASEAN, see Boyd, *Corporate Planning and Policy...*, ch. 6.
14. Tyson, *Who's Bashing Whom? Trade Conflict...*; and Robert Wade, "East Asia's Economic Success," *World Politics*, 44 (January 1992) 2: 70-320.
15. Noll, "Structural Policies in the United States..."
16. On one aspect of such a focus, see Margaret Sharp and Keith Pavitt, "Technology Policy in the 1990s: Old Trends and New Realities," *Journal of Common Market Studies*, 31 (June 1993) 2: 129-152.
17. Masaaki Kotabe, *Global Sourcing Strategy* (New York: Quorum Books, 1992) Part II. On the international production strategies of global firms, see *World Investment Report 1993* (New York: United Nations Centre on Transnational Corporations, 1993).

18. Daniel F. Burton, Jr., "High Tech Competitiveness," *Foreign Policy*, 92 (Fall 1993): 117-132.
19. Donald Hay, "The Assessment: Competition Policy," and Lawrence J. White, "Competition Policy in the United States: An Overview," *Oxford Review of Economic Policy*, 9 (Summer 1993) 2: 1-26, 133-150.
20. The influence of the Japanese system on the strategies of U.S. firms in Japan is discussed in Dennis J. Encarnation, "A Common Evolution? A Comparison of United States and Japanese Transnational Corporations," *Transnational Corporations*, 2 (February 1993) 1: 7-32.
21. See comments on complex integrated global production strategies in *World Investment Report, 1993*.
22. Tyson, *Who's Bashing Whom? Trade Conflict...*, deals exclusively with the U.S.-Japan relationship. A similar focus is evident in C. Fred Bergsten and Marcus Noland, *Reconcilable Differences? United States-Japan Economic Conflict* (Washington: Institute for International Economics, 1993).
23. Dorothy I. Riddle, "Business Services in the Pacific," in Gunnar K. Sletmo and Gavin Boyd (eds.), *Pacific Service Enterprises and Pacific Cooperation* (Boulder: Westview Press, 1993), 217-244.
24. Ibid.; and Kester, "Industrial Groups as Systems of..."
25. See discussion of the advantages of large firms in Pari Patel and Keith Pavitt, "Large Firms in Western Europe's Technological Competitiveness," in Lars-Gunnar Mattsson and Bengt Stymne (eds.) *Corporate and Industry Strategies for Europe* (Amsterdam: Elsevier Science Publishers, 1991), 97-116.
26. See comments on cultural influences in Kumon and Rosovsky, The Political Economy of...
27. Kotabe, *Global Sourcing Strategy...*; and Raymond J. Mataloni, "U.S. Multinational Companies: Operations in 1991," *Survey of Current Business*, 73 (July 1993) 7: 40-58.
28. The risk of an economic crisis is an additional factor. See Martin Feldstein (ed.), *The Risk of Economic Crisis* (Chicago: University of Chicago Press, 1991).
29. Michael T. Jacobs, *Short Term America* (Boston: Harvard Business School Press, 1991).
30. On the scope of anti-trust policy, see White, "Competition Policy in..."
31. Noll, "Structural Policies in the..."
32. Peter Enderwick, "Multinational Corporate Restructuring and International Competitiveness," *California Management Review*, 32 (Fall 1989) 1: 44-57.
33. On the significance of such centres in Europe, see John Cantwell, "The Reorganization of European Industries after Integration: Selected Evidence on the Role of Multinational Enterprise Activities," in John H. Dunning and Peter Robson (eds.), *Multinationals and the European Community* (Oxford: Blackwell, 1988), 25-50.

34. A regional approach to operations however is more appropriate for U.S. firms, according to Allen J. Morrison and Kendall Roth, "The Regional Solution: An Alternative to Globalization," *Transnational Corporations*, 1 (August 1992) 2: 37-56.
35. See comments on administrative capacities in Noll, "Structural Policies in the..."
36. See general observations on balancing competition with cooperation in Thomas M. Jorde and David J. Teece, "Competition and Cooperation: Striking the Right Balance," *California Management Review*, 31 (Spring 1989) 3: 25-37. See also Kester, "Industrial Groups as..."
37. Boyd, *Corporate Planning and Policy...*, ch. 4.
38. Ibid.
39. Dennis J. Encarnation, *Rivals Beyond Trade: America versus Japan in Global Competition* (Ithaca: Cornell University Press, 1992), ch. 4.
40. For a brief review of EC relations with Japan in 1992, see Christopher Brewin, "External Policy Developments," *Journal of Common Market Studies*, Supplement to Vol. 31 (The European Community, 1992) 3: 84-85.
41. Ha-Joon Chang, "The Political Economy of Industrial Policy in Korea," *Cambridge Journal of Economics*, 17 (June 1993) 2: 131-157.
42. The Taiwan firms are more numerous, and smaller, and have evidently been treated more distantly by their administration. See Robert Wade, *Governing the Market: Theory and the Role of Government in East Asian Industrialization* (Princeton: Princeton University Press, 1990), ch. 7.
43. Boyd, *Corporate Planning and Policy...*, ch. 4.
44. Somrudee Nicro, "Thailand's NIC Democracy: Studying from General Elections," *Pacific Affairs*, 66 (Summer 1993) 2: 167-182.
45. On the problems of Indonesian firms, see Donald J. Lecraw, "Outward Direct Investment by Indonesian Firms: Motivation and Effects," *Journal of International Business Studies*, 24 (Third Quarter 1993) 3: 589-600. For comments on Chinese communal ties in Southeast Asia, see Jeffrey D. Kapellas and Hsiliang Fred Liu, "The Growth of ROC Trade and Investment in Southeast Asia," *Journal of Southeast Asian Business*, 6 (Fall 1990) 4: 87-98.
46. Ibid., ch. 8.
47. Ibid., ch. 5.
48. On the trade effects of this investment, see Encarnation, *Rivals Beyond Trade...*, ch. 3.
49. MITI's responsibilities for the administration of export cartels will tend to increase. Tyson, *Who's Bashing Whom? Trade Conflict...*
50. The relative cultural closure of the Japanese political economy is an important factor. Kumon and Rosovsky, The Political Economy...
51. See comments on emotions stirred by economic decline in George E. Barcus and Michael B. Mackuen, "Anxiety, Enthusiasm and the Vote: The Emotional Underpinnings of Learning and Involvement during Presidential

Campaigns," *American Political Science Review*, 87 (September 1993) 3: 672-685.

52. This has been in line with the trend noted in the European Community by Cantwell, "The Reorganization of European Industries...," 25-50. See also John Stopford and Susan Strange, *Rival States, Rival Firms: Competition for World Market Shares* (Cambridge: Cambridge University Press, 1991), chs. 3 and 4.

53. See trend in Japanese and U.S. direct investment flows in *Foreign Direct Investment Relations Between OECD...*, ch. 1.

5

Japanese Industrial Policy

Yoko Sazanami

This chapter considers three basic issues in Japanese industrial policy. Firstly, how did that policy, with a neomercantilist orientation, promote economic growth? Secondly, what lessons can other East Asian countries learn from Japanese experiences? And thirdly, how did government-business cooperation in building industrial capacity overseas contribute to Asian exports and growth?

The chapter begins with a historical overview of Japanese industrial policy. A supportive trade policy in the 1960s ensured foreign-exchange earnings to import raw materials and fuel for the growing heavy and chemical industries. When trade surpluses became the government's concern after the late 1970s, policy goals shifted from growth promotion to alleviating the external shocks of yen appreciation and high crude oil prices on domestic industry. The neomercantilist orientation in trade policy then faded rapidly.

Japanese industrial policy has aroused strong interest in methods of government intervention to promote economic growth. Such interest has been particularly strong in East Asian countries. Vogel (1991) stresses the significance of the Japanese model for industrialization in East Asia. Restrictions on imports and inward foreign direct investment (FDI) protected the domestic market for growing industries such as automobiles and electronics in the 1960s. The rationalization of other protected industries such as food and distribution however was retarded. The political and economic costs of the liberalization that became necessary would have been less in the 1970s and 1980s if the shift in trade policy had been made.

In the 1980s, Japan became a supplier of foreign capital to the world. The appreciation of the yen accelerated outflows to rapidly growing East Asian countries. The Ministry of International Trade and Industry (MITI) played an important role in promoting such FDI. MITI provided a lot of information about markets and assisted the technological training of host country workers and others. Such government-business collaboration helped to build the so-called Asian regional production network which helped export-led growth in East Asian countries.

Postwar Industrial Policy

There is a wide range of different views regarding the efficacy of Japanese industrial policy in promoting the competitiveness of specific sectors.[1] But all agree that Japan's rapid economic growth in the postwar period was not made possible by macroeconomic policy alone. There were interventions by the government to alter domestic resource allocations, to supplement factor endowments and to alleviate external shocks. These policies affected various industries and promoted economic growth.

When a foreign exchange shortage was the primary constraint on growth in the 1950s and 1960s Japanese trade and investment policy had a strong neo-mercantilist orientation. Imports of manufactured goods were discouraged to save foreign exchange. Foreign investment was restricted except for natural resource development, which would eventually ensure lower price imports. Such measures can only be well understood when we look into the reasons why MITI promoted the growth of heavy and chemical industries.

Heavy and chemical industries had two basic characteristics that aided economic growth and lifted the balance-of-payment constraint. First, productivity increased more rapidly in these industries than in others. Second, income elasticities of demand for their products in both domestic and foreign markets were high. Thus high rates of growth in the domestic market could result in expansions of demand which would in turn raise the industrial productivity of the economy as a whole. Also the rise in productivity would increase the competitiveness of these products in the world market. It would help Japanese exports to move away from textiles and other light manufactures whose income elasticities tend to be low. A shift in exports from low to high income elasticity products would enable Japan to have more foreign exchange for imports. In 1963 MITI proposed "building industrial structures centered in heavy and chemical industries" as the policy goal for the 1960s. Similar objectives proposed by MITI were "knowledge-intensive industrialization" in the 1970s and "creative knowledge-intensive industrialization" in the 1980s.[2]

To help heavy and chemical industries, the government provided low-cost capital for investment through loans from the Japan Development Bank and gave tax concessions for depreciation. At the same time the government had to alleviate the distorting effects of building capital-intensive and natural-resource-intensive heavy and chemical industries in a country which is extremely poor in both capital and natural resources. In 1960, agriculture, forestry and fishery employed 30% of the total labor force. The number of family workers in small -and medium-size enterprises accounted for 23.9% of total employment.

Protecting agriculture as well as small- and medium-size enterprises from foreign competition was necessary to provide jobs to these workers. By continuing labor-intensive methods in these sectors, Japan was able to pour domestic savings into capital investment in fast-growing heavy and chemical industries.

Japan depended almost entirely on imports of commodities such as crude oil, nickel, bauxite and raw cotton in 1965. One can well understand why Japan tried to save as much foreign exchange as possible until the current account started to show surpluses instead of deficits in the late 1960s.

Indeed, Japan was busy preparing for the liberalization of trade and investment during the 1960s. In June 1960, the Economic Planning Agency published its "Liberalization Plan for Trade and Foreign Exchange" (Boeki Kawase Jiyuka Taiko) which strongly advocated liberalization. Trade-restrictive measures shifted from quotas to tariffs, at very high rates in the early 1960s. A rapid fall in tariff rates started before the conclusion of the Kennedy Round. The number of items left under import quotas was reduced markedly except for agriculture and food. The neomercantilistic stance of trade and investment policy diminished as Japan's industrial policy goals became more complex in the 1970s and the 1980s.

By the end of the 1960s, Japan had to worry about a rapidly increasing current account surplus, which put pressure on the yen to appreciate. Despite the fears of the business community and the government, the yen rate appreciated by 16.8% in 1971. To avert further appreciation, tariff and non-tariff barriers were reduced to increase imports. The oil crisis of 1973 temporarily halted the move for liberalization. But when a large bilateral trade surplus with the U.S.caused severe trade frictions (based on the claim that Japan's recovery from the recession was at the expense of her trading partner) the liberalization policy was resumed.

The rise in energy prices and the appreciation of the yen forced Japan to use industrial policy more for structural adjustment than for the promotion of growth. A shift was made away from natural-resource-intensive industries to sophisticated electronic products with low resource content. In order to get the policy consensus for such adjustment, MITI's "vision" of the 1970s and 1980s became "knowledge intensive" and "creative knowledge intensive" as mentioned previously. Between 1978 and 1988, the government planned to scrap industries whose high energy costs were severely reducing their competitiveness. The planned rates of capacity reduction were as much as 32% in aluminum, 35% in shipbuilding and 36% in ammonia.[3] The Japanese business communities responded to the adjustment policy by "Sho-ene doryoku," which means energy-saving efforts. They were the key words of the period. The efforts extended from setting air-conditioned office temperatures higher in the summer to designing more fuel-efficient automobiles and shifting energy-using smelting processes to resource-rich countries.

In the area of growth promotion, the importance of industrial policy faded in the 1970s and still further in the 1980s except for R&D in basic research. So long as MITI's "visions" could provide general information and consensus concerning where the Japanese economy was heading, private firms found themselves quite well equipped with managerial and technological skills to compete in the world market. By the early 1990s, manufacturing firms found that regulatory practices left in other areas--distribution, agriculture, and transportation--were affecting their interests. Closed markets in these areas were intensifying trade frictions between Japan and her major trading partner, the U.S.

Japan as a Model

Japanese industrial policy has aroused strong interest in other East Asian countries which had similar economic conditions--ample supplies of labor and poor natural resource endowments. For South Korea and Taiwan the Japanese model provided important guidance. Both countries adopted import-substitution policies in the 1950s and export-promotion policies in the 1960s. They stressed the importance of heavy and chemical industries for their industrialization as was done in Japan.[4]

However, there were substantial differences. Export promotion played a more important role in Korea and Taiwan. Inward FDI brought in technology and capital needed for industrialization in Korea and Taiwan but not in Japan. The contrasts reflected differences in population size, factor endowments and institutional frameworks.

Japan's export promotion policy included low interest rates offered by the Japan Export-Import Bank to finance exports, special accelerated depreciation allowances for export industries, and market information gathered through the foreign offices of JETRO (Japan External Trade Organization). Assisted by such measures, Japan's exports of manufactured goods grew at an annual rate of 13.6% between 1965 and 1973, and its world market share expanded from 8.6% in 1965 to 14.0% in 1973. However, the growth in exports was proportional to the growth of GNP during this period. The share of exports in GNP was 11% in 1960 and 11.3% in 1970. It was after 1973, when growth rates declined, that the share of exports in GNP started to rise. The share became 14.8% in 1980.

Exports increased at a much higher rate than GNP in Korea and in Taiwan between 1970 and 1980. The share of exports in Korean GNP rose from 9.8% in 1970 to 28.7% in 1980, while the share increased from 26.3% to 47.8% between the same years in Taiwan. Exports really led economic growth in both countries. The importance of exports in these two countries, compared with Japan, probably reflected the differences in the size of the domestic market.

Japan with more than 120 million people (in contrast to 43 million in Korea and 20 million in Taiwan) had a domestic market large enough for its protected heavy and chemical industries. Growth in the domestic market stimulated investment in these industries, and as the investment embodied the latest technology, they became more competitive in the international market.

The government's support of heavy and chemical industries increased imports of raw materials, and these industries were severely affected by the sharp rise in energy prices in the 1970s. Industrial policy thus had to be used for adjustment to high oil prices. Subsidies were provided to scrap excess capacity in energy-intensive industries termed "structurally depressed industries" (Kozo-fukyo gyoshu). To assist firms that laid off workers with pay an Employment Insurance Law (Koyo Hoken Ho) was enacted in 1974. Through other supplementary measures, the government tried to smooth out the adjustment by increasing unemployment benefits and by providing training to dismissed workers.[5]

Japan meanwhile had to cope with frictions in trade with the U.S. The issues after the oil crisis included the size of the trade surplus, the small share of manufactures in total imports and sector-specific barriers limiting the export opportunities of trading partners.[6]

To alleviate the trade frictions the Japanese government concluded orderly marketing agreements on TVs in 1977 and introduced voluntary export restraints (VER) on automobiles in 1981. On the import side opinions were divided whether the small share of manufactures reflected Japan's factor endowments or high trade barriers protecting the domestic market. Although Japanese tariff barriers declined rapidly in the early 1970s Japanese reluctance to liberalize had made trading partners concerned about informal trade barriers. Discussions of Japanese trade protection had centered on non-tariff barriers (NTBs) including standards and testing (medical equipment and pharmaceutical), a lack of transparency, and unequal treatment of foreign companies.

Except for agricultural and food industries that continued to benefit from a complex system of protection, Japanese NTBs were substantially reduced by the mid-1980s. The liberalization enabled the Japanese market to become more responsive to the changes in the relative prices of imports and domestic goods. When the yen appreciated after 1985, the share of manufactures in total imports started to rise. The share rose from 31% in 1985 to 52% in 1993.

As Japanese trade policy in the 1970s and 1980s shifted from export promotion to export restraint and from import protection to import liberalization, the importance of industrial policy for structural adjustment increased. Manufacturing industries responded to MITI's vision by changing from energy-intensive to technology-knowledge intensive products. Policies targeted to specific sectors were used only in industries troubled with high-energy costs, or in agriculture and distribution. The government thus made it clear that the market mechanism would become more and more important.

MITI's vision of the 1990s stressed market efficiency as the primary policy goal of industrial policy. The shift in policy accorded with the interests of private firms, particularly in manufacturing, which were fully competitive in domestic as well as in international markets. They were starting to feel "regulation" burdensome. Indeed "deregulation" which in fact meant "liberalization" became a keyword of policy in the early 1990s.

The experiences of the 1980s and the early 1990s illustrated the importance of reducing government intervention in business activities. Such experiences were shared with Korea and Taiwan. Inoue, Kohama and Urata (1993) found that the easing of controls over imports, overseas capital and technology, along with targets for export promotion, were effective as industrial promotive measures in Korea. They also pointed out that though martial law had put all economic activities under government control in Taiwan, outward-oriented sectors such as textiles, consumer goods and electronics were set free.[7]

Although Japan's trade barriers for manufactures had been substantially reduced in the 1980s, agriculture and distribution, backed by political interest groups, enjoyed protection. The tariff rates on agricultural products were higher than those on industrial products.[8] And most of the import quotas were on agricultural products in late 1980s. The United States, as the major supplier of agricultural products, pressed hard for the reduction of trade barriers. Controversial import quotas on oranges and tangerines as well as fresh and frozen meat were abolished in April, 1991. However, imports of rice under a state trading system were banned until 1993 when poor weather reduced autumn crops. The conclusion of the Uruguay Round in the same year forced Japan to accept rice imports.

The economic cost of protecting agriculture was borne by Japanese consumers. According to OECD estimates,[9] total transfers in terms of higher price and taxes, from consumers to producers, during 1992 to support agriculture were $600 US per population in Japan. Such estimated transfers were $450 US in EC and $360 US in the U.S. In addition Japan had to face other problems created by protecting agriculture. High domestic food prices had adverse effects on consumer spending. Moreover a decline in import prices after the yen appreciated in 1985 was not reflected in the domestic prices of regulated food items.

Protection in distribution was based on the Large-Scale Retail Store Law (Daikibo Kouri Tempo ni Okeru Kourigyo Jigyo Katsudo no Chosei ni Kansuru Horitsu) enacted in 1974. Its purpose was to protect small retail stores from the competition of department stores, supermarkets, and large chain stores. Small retail stores were influential in local politics, and the protection reflected their political strength. Their prosperity was important to maintain employment. Long waiting periods for government approval limited competition and helped to maintain an inefficient distribution system. Protection in distribution had similar effects as protection in agriculture: it tended to bid up domestic consumer prices relative to world prices when the yen appreciated. In 1991 a new law was enacted to increase transparency in approval, shorten the period necessary for approval, and benefit consumer interests more than previously.

Lessons from liberalization in agriculture and distribution were that delays in reducing the protection further increased the economic as well as political costs of protection. Costs to the consumer conflicted with growth policy since they distorted resource allocations, making prices higher in protected sectors. Moreover, changes in import prices did not reduce domestic prices for protected items, especially when the yen appreciated in 1985. The liberalization of agriculture and distribution sectors had to wait until the early 1990s, but trade barriers on manufactures were swiftly removed in the 1970s and the 1980s. Since protection of automobiles and electronic products was only a part of industrial promotion policy, MITI was quite ready to remove the barriers when these products were competitive.

The main thrust of Japanese industrial promotion policy was the development of new technology. Domestic firms were aided by low interest rate loans and tax credits for R&D activities in the 1960s.[10] But active participation by foreign firms bringing in new technology was not welcomed. MITI tried to introduce foreign technology through licences and encouraged domestic firms to apply this technology in production. MITI seemed to have preferred to prevent foreign competition which might impede efforts to build industrial structure for growth and adjustment.

Japanese policy toward FDI in the 1950s and the 1960s differed from the inward-FDI promotive policies that most of the East Asian countries implemented in the 1980s. FDI to Japan was discouraged unless projects contributed to the balance of payments, the promotion of important industrial activities, or brought in new technologies.[11] As the balance of payments started to show surpluses, Japanese firms accumulated industrial and managerial skills to invest abroad in the late 1960s. FDI to Japan was liberalized swiftly except in industries that needed time for adjustment. Those industries had a larger share of small -and medium-size enterprises in total production. Even after most of the restrictions on inward-FDI were removed by 1973, the screening of individual investment projects was still required in the agriculture, forestry, fishery, mining, petroleum, leather and retail sectors.

Opinions are divided on the importance of protective policies for growth in Japanese manufacturing industries, in particular automobiles and electronics. Although both industries benefited from protection in the 1960s which assured a domestic market for new products and provided breathing space for the accumulation of technological skills,[12] they were always told that protection would be removed soon. Perhaps the pressure to prepare for the termination of protection was more important than protection itself in promoting the competitiveness of Japanese manufacturing industries.

In the 1980s there was increased concentration on automobiles and electronic products. When these were gaining competitiveness by responding to market demand for new products, superior quality and low price, other industries were left behind. Agriculture and distribution that needed protection were examples. The appreciation of the yen in the late 1980s further increased the barriers needed for such protection to block imports sold at lower prices. According to OECD estimates[13] the implicit tax on Japanese consumers for agricultural support increased from ¥3996 billion in 1979-86 (average) to ¥4751 billion in 1990. If similar costs could be estimated for other protected sectors, the total for the Japanese economy would be enormous. An important lesson is that even when protection is needed to promote growth or to provide adjustment, the termination date should be clearly set. Growth-promotive industrial policies should rely more on assisting R&D efforts or providing information on policy and business trends.

Japanese Industrial Policy and East Asian Growth

Japanese industrial policy has been aided by strong government-business cooperation. This was particularly important in the early 1960s because Japan was trying to build an industrial structure centered on heavy and chemical industries in spite of acute resource deficiencies. A neomercantilist trade policy endeavoring to save foreign exchange for imports of raw materials and fuels was implemented with business collaboration. Japanese firms moreover cooperated with government efforts to develop foreign mineral resources and fuels.

Even when outward FDI was still under strict government control four resource-related ventures started in the late 1950s with strong official support. They were Alaska Pulp Co. (1953-), Usiminas Siderurgicas de Minas Gerais, S.A. (1956-), Arabian Oil Co. (1958-) and North Sumatra Oil Development Co. (1960-). In 1971, tax-incentive schemes were introduced to promote foreign natural-resource development. A Reserve Fund for Resource Development Investment (Shigenkaihatsu Toshi Sonshitsu Junbikin) supported 100% of the costs of searching and 30% of the investment costs of petroleum, non-ferrous metals, uranium, coal and iron ore projects. Financing was also provided by an Overseas Economic Cooperation Fund, a Petroleum Development Corporation and a Japan Export-Import Bank. These endeavors promoted business ties between Japan and resource-rich developing countries. When those countries started to industrialize in the 1980s, Japanese business experience in resource development opened the way for FDI in manufacturing, construction and other services, notably in Indonesia and Malaysia. Japanese direct investment in developing East Asian countries increased in the early 1970s. Rises in domestic wages of unskilled workers in the late 1960s and the appreciation of the yen in the early 1970s pushed Japanese firms to start overseas production. This was aided by government schemes including the Reserve System for Overseas Investment Losses (Kaigaitoshi Sonshitsu Junbikin) which allows half of FDI in developing countries to be treated as loss (for five years), and the creation of a reserve fund started as early as 1968.

Japanese policies to promote direct investment in developing countries now cover tax, finance, investment insurance, subsidized research and information services in host countries. The Japan Finance Corporation for Small Business, the People's Finance Corporation and the Shoko Chukin Bank together with the Japan Overseas Development Corporation play very important roles in supplying capital for outward investment by small -and medium-sized enterprises. The shortage of unskilled labor and the subsequent rise in wages in the late 1960s eroded the competitiveness of labor-intensive products that small -and medium-size enterprises were exporting. Assisting their needs to invest in labor, abundant low-wage countries became a very important industrial adjustment objective in the 1970s.

East Asian countries endowed with ample supplies of labor and located near Japan became the major host economies for Japanese FDI in developing countries. This trend was pronounced in manufacturing investment. Asia hosted 64.1% of Japanese FDI to developing countries in manufacturing from 1951-1988.[14]

Japanese FDI became increasingly important, not only in supplying capital and technology, but also in expanding export opportunities for East Asian regional industrial activities in the 1980s and in networking. The share of Japan in total inward FDI increased in most of the East Asian countries; Hong Kong (22.9% to 36.0%), Singapore (from 18.9% to 32.5%), Taiwan (from 29.4% to 37%), Malaysia (from 30% to 33.9%) and Thailand (from 36.2% to 47.5%) during this period.[15]

Various complex macro- and micro-economic factors contributed to the expansion of Japanese FDI. There were macroeconomic factors such as an easy money policy after 1985 to stimulate domestic demand. It boosted the security market and helped Japanese firms raise funds at low cost and invest abroad. Also the appreciation of the yen pushed Japanese firms to globalize their foreign operations. Meanwhile, cost factors induced Japanese manufacturing firms to locate affiliates in low-wage countries like Taiwan and then Thailand. These affiliates in Asia shipped more of their products to Japan and to third-country markets than affiliates located in other regions. Sazanami (1992) found that Japanese manufacturing affiliates located in Asia exported 32.5% of their total sales (15.8% to Japan and 16.7% to third-country markets) in 1986. The expansion of domestic markets reduced the export/sales ratio to 24.9% in 1989, but it was substantially higher than export/sales ratios of affiliates in Europe (3.9%) and in the U.S. (5.3%) during the same year.

Training schemes carried out by Japan Overseas Development Corporation (75% government funded) to assist human capital formation and loans from the

Overseas Economic Cooperation Fund to build electricity, transport and communication systems prepared basic conditions for Japanese firms to invest in developing countries, particularly in Asia.[16]

In 1987, MITI had launched a "New Aid Plan" (Shin Asia Kogyoka Sogo Kyoryoku Plan) to coordinate economic assistance and industrial promotion programs. "The Plan tries to promote industries which earn foreign exchange, and to assist industrialization though coordinated cooperation in both investment and trade. It provides the master plan for coordinated assistance and programs for developing industries. It covers technical assistance to local firms, loans to establish social infrastructure, and various promotive policies towards FDI".[17] It is interesting to find that the "New Aid Plan" reflects MITI's experience in promoting Japan's industrialization.

The Plan tries to build social overhead and industrial infrastructures by providing loans. In Japan, government investment in roads, harbors, railways, telegraphs and telephones during the 1950s and the early 1960s[18] played a very important role in stimulating business activities. Japanese government loans to developing countries were similarly directed in production-related social overheads. Japanese government loans for electricity and gas, transportation, communications, electricity and irrigation projects accounted for 64.6% and 50.7% of the total for developing countries in 1981-1985 and 1986-1990 respectively. In Asia, 31% of the investment in electricity in Indonesia was funded by Japanese government loans. The proportions were 20% in Thailand and 51% in peninsular Malaysia.[19]

The plan also tries to extend Japan's experience in promoting exports. The Japan External Trade Organization (JETRO) which played an important role in gathering foreign market information is used to increase imports into Japan. The change in JETRO's role reflects the change in the interests of Japanese firms. Faced with the appreciation of the yen, Japanese firms were looking for imports that could be supplied from Asia at low cost. Import promotion by JETRO also helped to reduce current account surpluses which caused trade frictions.

In addition, the plan promotes Japanese direct investment in Asia by coordinating Japanese business interests and host country needs. As noted in the earlier part of the present section the government had helped Japanese firms to invest abroad in various phases of industrial development. It assisted natural resource development in the 1950s and 1960s. Japanese small -and medium-size enterprises received capital when they had to transfer labor-intensive production processes to Asia in the late 1960s. In the New Aid Plan, the government helps host countries to absorb direct investment from Japan.

The plan includes the drafting of a general master plan and then industrial development plans for specific industries. The master plan was intended to link business interests and policy goals. A special purpose was to enable Japanese and other Asian firms know in what fields they could expect more demand in the future.

The basic Japanese industrial policy style is to draft the plan, provide the institutional framework (fiscal, finance and information) and build industrial infrastructure while firms respond to these policies. However, successful outcomes depend not on Japan's policy alone but on each host government's policy, especially its decision to restrict or liberalize trade and investment. Fortunately trade barriers seem to have been lowered in East Asian countries except the Philippines in recent years. Average tariff rates declined from 8.18% to 7.09% in Korea, 14.29% to 7.64% in Taiwan, 9.80% to 5.27% in Malaysia, 7.92% to 6.11% in Indonesia and 12.62% to 11.30% in Thailand between 1979 and 1989.[20] In capital markets there were a number of policy changes to invite more inward FDI. Financial deregulation and liberalization in Hong Kong and Singapore started as early as the 1970s. Branches and affiliates of Japanese banks located in these two countries helped Japanese manufacturing affiliates located in other Asian countries by providing not only finance but also giving advice on local market conditions and introducing local partners for joint ventures. Such services by Japanese banks were particularly important for small -and medium-size enterprises' FDI.[21] Thailand abolished restrictions on 100% ownership for export-related FDI in 1983 and Malaysia exempted similar regulations for foreign firms exporting 50% of their products in 1986. Indonesia relaxed regulations on local participation in FDI in 1987.[22]

Deregulation and liberalization in financial and capital markets are inviting Japanese FDI in diverse industries. Even when Japanese FDI to the world had declined for three consecutive years after a peak in 1989 the flow to Asia in 1992 increased by 8.2% from the previous year. Japanese FDI in manufacturing accounted for 48.3% of the total in the same year. Besides expanding in traditional export-related manufacturing fields, Japanese firms were investing into other areas such as distribution and responding to the growth in local consumer demand. Even when their primary motives for FDI were developing local products for exports, they found it profitable at times to supply similar products to the domestic market. Industrialization in neighboring countries made it possible to shift procurements from Japan to those countries. The introduction of a common preferential tariff system in AFTA (ASEAN Free Trade Area) may accelerate such export substitution.

What seems to be important is the cooperation between Japan and host-country governments in coordinating Japanese business interests for growth promotion. Japanese firms are rationalizing and expanding their activities in East Asia because countries in the region provide attractive location advantages. In doing so they pass on technology and managerial skills that contribute to growth in the host countries. Japanese industrial policy experience extended to East Asia can assist host countries to build efficient economic policy systems for government-business complementarity in promoting industrialization and growth.

Notes

1. Different views on Japan's Industrial Policy are summarized in Takatoshi Ito, "The Japanese Economy" (MIT Press, 1992), 201-202.
2. See *Economic Whitepaper* (1992), 333-337 for the summary of industrial policy "visions" followed in the postwar period. For more details, see James Vestel, *Industrial Policy and Japanese Economic Development* (Oxford University Press, 1993), ch. 4, 81-106.
3. Based on Vestel, *Industrial Policy and...*, Table 8.5, 205.
4. R. Inoue, H. Kohama, and S. Urata, *Industrial Policy in East Asia*, JETRO, 1993.
5. Vestel, *Industrial Policy and...*, 178-179.
6. Yoko Sazanami, "Trade and Investment Patterns and Barriers in the United States, Canada and Japan," in R.M. Stern (ed.), (1989), *Trade and Investment Relations Among the United States, Canada and Japan* (University of Chicago Press, 1989), for the details.
7. Inoue, Kohama, and Urata, *Industrial Policy in...*, 14-16.
8. Average tariff rate on agricultural final products was 18.0% while the similar rate on industrial final products was 4.7% in 1991.
9. OECD, *Agriculture Policies. Markets and Trade*, Paris, 1993.
10. Vestel, *Industrial Policy and Japanese...*, 201-214, on MITI's R and D Projects.
11. Law of Management of Foreign Exchange and Foreign Trade (Gaitameho) enacted 1949 and Law Concerning Foreign Capital (Gaighiho) enacted 1950 were basic laws for the regulation.
12. Tariff rates for small cars were set higher than the others in the 1960s to protect a domestic market that was expanding in this type of car. By 1974 the Japanese computer market was mostly liberalized except for computer software. In both trade and investment, Japan's firms were quite ready to compete in the world market.
13. OECD, *Agricultural Policies, Markets and Trade-Monitoring and Outlook*, 1991, Paris.
14. S. Urata, "The Rapid Increase of Direct Investment Abroad and Structural Change in Japan," in E. Ramstetter (ed.), *Direct Foreign Investment in Asia's Developing Economies and Structural Change in the Asia Pacific Region* (Westview Press, 1991) Table 7.1.
15. Yoko Sazanami, "Japanese Service Enterprises in the Pacific," in G.K. Sletmo and Gavin Boyd (eds.), *Pacific Service Enterprises and Pacific Cooperation* (Westview Press, 1993), Table 7.2.
16. Asia's share in Japanese economic development assistance in 1990 was as follows: ODA, 59.3%; loan, 76.7%; receiving technical trainee, 49.3%;

sending technical assistance personal, 54.6%. Based on Ministry of Foreign Affairs "Japan's Official Development Assistance" (1993).

17. Quoted from MITI, *White Paper on ODA*, (1993), Section 3-2, Relationship between Aid, FDI and Trade.

18. K. Inada, S. Sekiguchi, and Y. Shoda, *The Mechanism of Economic Development-Growth in the Japanese and East Asian Economies* (Clarendon Press Oxford, 1992), Figure 14.3 and Table 14.18.

19. MITI, *Whitepaper on ODA*, (1993), Table 3-1-3-6.

20. Y. Okamoto, "Economic Cooperation Schemes in the Asia-Pacific Region," in K. Ohno (ed.), *Regional Integration and Its Impact on Developing Countries*, Institute of Developing Economies, 1993, Table 5-2.

21. Sazanami, "Japanese Service Enterprises...," for details of financial deregulation in East Asia.

22. Economic Planning Agency, *Whitepaper on World Economy 1992*. Appendix Table 4-1.

References

Inada, K., S. Sekiguchi, and Y. Shoda. 1992. *The Mechanism of Economic Development-Growth in the Japanese and East Asian Economies*. Clarendon Press Oxford.

Inoue, R., H. Kohama, and S. Urata. 1993. *Industrial Policy in East Asia*. JETRO.

Ito, Takatoshi. 1992. "The Japanese Economy." MIT Press.

Komiya, R., M. Okuno, and K. Suzumura. 1988. *Industrial Policy of Japan*. Academic Press.

Komiya, R., and K. Yokobori. 1991. *Japan's Industrial Policies in the 1980s*. Research Institute of International Trade and Industry.

Okamoto, Y. 1993. "Economic Cooperation Schemes in the Asia-Pacific Region," in Ohno, K. (ed.), *Regional Integration and Its Impact on Developing Countries*. Institute of Developing Economies.

Sazanami, Yoko. 1986. "Some Policy Implications of Intra-Industry Trade for Japan," in Greenaway, D. and P.K.M. Tharakan (eds.), *Imperfect Competition and International Trade*. Wheatsheaf Books.

______. 1989. "Trade and Investment Patterns and Barriers in the United States, Canada and Japan," in Stern, R.M. (ed.), *Trade and Investment Relations among the United States, Canada and Japan*. University of Chicago Press.

______. 1993. "Japanese Service Enterprises in the Pacific," in Sletmo, G.K. and Gavin Boyd (eds.), *Pacific Service Enterprises and Pacific Cooperation*. Westview Press.

______. 1992. "Globalization Strategy of Japanese Manufacturing Firms and its Impact on Trade Flows between Europe, Asia and North America." Paper presented at the conference *Europe-Japan Concurrents ou Partenaires*, Université de Paris I, Panthéon-Sorbonne.

Urata, S. 1991. "The Rapid Increase of Direct Investment Abroad and Structural Change in Japan," in Ramstetter, E. (ed.), *Direct Foreign Investment in Asia's Developing Economies and Structural Change in the Asia Pacific Region*. Westview Press.

Vestel, James. 1993. *Industrial Policy and Japanese Economic Development*. Oxford University Press.

Vogel, E. 1991. *The Four Little Dragons. The Spread of Industrialization in East Asia*. Harvard University Press.

6

Industrial Policy Issues in the U.S.

Edward M. Graham

This chapter attempts to assess the industrial policies of the United States. It is written at a time when many Americans have become worried about the ability of U.S. firms to compete in world markets. As recently as the early 1970s U.S. firms were, or at least were perceived to be, unchallenged international leaders in terms of product and process technology and managerial sophistication in many industrial sectors, including almost all of the very high technology ones. But many leading U.S. firms have seen their supremacy (and their worldwide market shares) erode over the past twenty years.[1]

The decline has been most associated, in American minds at least, with the rise of firms in Japan and elsewhere in East Asia. Many Americans associate this rise with successful "industrial policies" pursued by the Japanese and by other governments in the region. To a lesser extent, the U.S. decline is also associated with the rise of European firms. European success, again in the minds of many, is also associated with "industrial policy", the Airbus program coming most to mind in this regard.

This chapter also comes at a time when the collapse of the Soviet Union continues to reshape thinking about the future world political order. The United States is involved in a long process of planning future military capabilities. No matter what final decisions are reached in this regard, the outcome will surely be a reduction in resources committed to defense-related technologies. One task facing the nation will be how to redirect those resources to other uses.

The perceived need to increase the competitiveness of U.S. firms and to redirect resources suggests in the minds of many a need for an activist U.S. industrial policy. "Industrial policy" however is a rather vague term. Also, there is considerable (and probably growing) controversy over whether industrial policies adequately explain the success of dynamic economies, especially that of Japan; other explanations include high savings rates (enabling high rates of cap-

capital formation and current account surpluses to be achieved simultaneously) and plain hard work by Japanese workers and management.[2] Furthermore, severe recession in Japan, combined with a series of political scandals, has altered assessments of that country. Many Japanese industrial firms are currently struggling to remain profitable. Indeed, among the hardest hit are the large electronics firms, the very ones that but a few years earlier were seen decimating the U.S. semiconductor industry, and the automotive producers, whose advantages over their U.S. rivals were only recently seen as all but unsurmountable.[3]

At the same time, the United States has had an export boom for several years, and U.S. firms have during the past two or three years reclaimed lost world market share in many sectors where, as recently as the late 1980s, many forecasters foresaw unarrestable U.S. decline.[4] The U.S. export boom is doubtlessly primarily due to the low dollar. However, there is considerable evidence that U.S. firms have also been increasing their competitiveness in terms of non-price variables such as product quality and technological sophistication. Yet there is still considerable concern that major U.S. industrial firms are in a long-term secular decline, and numerous voices have called for activist U.S. industrial policies.[5]

Definitional Problems

The United States has not implemented "industrial policies", or at least not in the European sense. In Europe, "industrial policy" covers any government program or measure *deliberately* taken to make firms more competitive. A rejoinder to the claim that the United States has not implemented such policies is that it has, *de facto*. A wide range of government policies and programs affect business in the industrial sectors, often with unintended and unforeseen consequences.

The United States government has in recent years sponsored programs that would be elsewhere seen as "industrial policy" measures in the European sense, e.g., support for the SEMATECH consortium, the Advanced Technology Program of the U.S. Department of Commerce, and other such programs. However, one year into the Clinton administration, which was expected by many observers to initiate more activist policies, the number of such programs remains relatively small and their total funding represents a fraction of the U.S. federal budget for new technology development.

Ultimately, the competitiveness of firms is determined largely by how well they accumulate and apply useful knowledge (this includes, but is not limited to, those subsets that are labelled "technology" and "management skills"). Indeed, accumulation and application of useful knowledge is one of the most important determinants of economic growth itself.[6]

The slowdown in industrial growth that has affected all of the major industrial economies of the world during the past twenty years or so appears to be caused largely by a slowdown in productivity growth apparently caused by reduced accumulation and application of useful knowledge. This slowdown, in the United States at least, is almost surely a causal factor in real wage stagnation. Presumably, therefore, one important reason why any government might attempt to pursue industrial policies is to raise the rate of growth over the rate that would prevail in the absence of such policies.[7]

The classical case for intervention to support the development of new technology is anchored in the economics of knowledge generation and diffusion. In a static context, gains from the deployment of useful knowledge are maximized when all potential users have unencumbered access to it. The creation of useful knowledge, however, requires real investment and, if knowledge is disseminated to all potential users free of charge, any return that might accrue to this investment will be bid away. Thus, it is argued that, in order to ensure that knowledge continues to be created, the government must subsidize this creation or provide other means by which firms can generate sufficient returns so as to have an incentive to make the necessary investment.[8] The granting of patents or other intellectual property rights is one such means; the holding of a patent in principle grants to a firm a temporary monopoly over the use of a particular technology, to extract from the market monopoly rents during the life of the patent. But other means can enable firms to appropriate rents from the market and the importance of patents for returns from investment in technology varies considerably across industries.[9]

There can be major conceptual differences, however, between the European notion of industrial policy and government support of new technology. The former is meant to assist specific firms at the expense of others. The latter can be conducted so that no specific firm is targeted to benefit at the expense of others, even if there are winners and losers.

Hence industrial policies, if including all measures that benefit firms (even unintentionally), should also encompass almost all policies affecting the generation and dissemination of knowledge, not just those supporting research and development.

The competitiveness of firms of course is affected by any policies which change relative prices. Allocations of resources are made in response to price signals, and ultimately affect a firm's competitiveness. Many government policies and programs affect relative prices, including government procurement, price controls, income or price support programs, regulatory programs, policies towards imports, and competition policies.

In addition, macroeconomic policies affect relative prices, e.g., a short-term economic-stimulus program can stimulate the demand for certain products more than for others, leading (perhaps) to price changes. And, of course, policies affecting the movements of the exchange rate can have both direct and indirect effects on relative prices.

Observers of the U.S. political economy have often cited military procurement practices and trade policies as being the prime drivers of an implicit industrial policy. Military procurement, combined with research and development performed in the private sector but funded by the U.S. Department of Defense, has played a very active (and usually positive) role in the evolution of a number of important sectors, including semiconductors, computers, aircraft, and other major high-technology sectors.[10]

U.S. trade policies, and policies to limit imports in particular, have also affected the fortunes of major firms. The determinants of exactly which firms get protection are by and large, political, and most observers feel that net costs have been borne by the U.S. economy.[11] In terms of real resource transfers, by far the largest beneficiary has been the textile and apparel complex which, in spite of a flood of self-generated propaganda to the contrary, has prospered over the past thirty or so years behind massive protection against lower-cost imports.[12] Cynics indeed contend that the revealed industrial policy of the United States is to sustain via trade protection aging industries such as textiles and steel at the expense of newer and more dynamic activities. This contention bears an element of truth, although the protection is the outcome of a highly political process (rather than any industrial strategy) and the resources transferred are certainly not so great as to preclude other activities.

A controversial issue is whether trade policies can (or should) be used to enhance the competitiveness of firms in the technologically advanced industries.[13] The most important case for the United States where arguably trade policy has had such an effect is the Semiconductor Agreement of 1985 examined below.

In what follows, the policy domain is restricted to include only those governmental measures and instruments that might promote the technological competitiveness of firms in the United States. The discussion is limited to a subset of this domain, but this subset is chosen so as to include issues that this author believes are most relevant to current debate. First an effort is made to sketch the essential elements of current U.S. technology policy.

Technology Support in the United States

In 1991, the most recent year for which, at the time of this writing, detailed figures were available, total U.S. expenditure on research and development (R&D) was slightly less than $151.6 billion, or about 2.49% of GNP on a current dollar basis.[14] Although the amounts were greatly in excess of expenditures in other major industrial nations, U.S. R&D as a percentage of national product lagged behind a number of other countries. For example, in

1989 (the latest year for which comparative international data are available), this figure was 3.0% for Japan, 2.9% for Germany, and 2.8% for Sweden. (In that year, we might note, the figure was 2.7% for the United States.) Other large nations, however, lagged behind the United States, e.g., the figure was 2.3% for France, 2.0% for the United Kingdom, and 1.3% for Italy.[15]

The United States has also spent a relatively large percentage of its total R&D expenditures on defense and thus is even further behind Japan and German in non-defense R&D spending. Again using 1989 figures, the following countries spent the following percentages of GNP on non-defense R&D: Japan, 3.0%; Germany, 2.8%; Sweden, 2.5%; the United States, 1.9%; France, 1.8%; the United Kingdom, 1.6%; and Italy, 1.2%. Reflecting the higher role of defense in the United States, the U.S. government in 1989 funded a higher percentage of R&D expenditure (45%) than the government of any G-5 country except France (49%); the figures for the remaining G-5 are Japan, 19%; Germany 33%; and the United Kingdom 37%. However, even though the United States government *funded* a higher percentage of R&D than in most other G-5 nations, it did not actually *perform* a particularly high percentage of the R&D; the figures on government performance of R&D as a percentage of all R&D expenditure for the G-5 nations are: United States, 11%; Japan, 8%; Germany, 13%; France, 24%; and the United Kingdom, 15%.

Table 6.1 indicates by institution sources of funding of R&D and performers of R&D in the United States, the figures in parentheses being the percentage of total R&D funding in each cell. As can be gleaned from the table, the U.S. government performs less R&D than it funds, whereas the opposite prevails for the other three classes of institutions, implying a net transfer from the government to these other institutions.

Table 6.2 provides salient details for 1991. As can be seen, in addition to transfers from the Federal Government to other performers of R&D, small percentages of the R&D performed by non-profit institutions (including universities and colleges) are funded by industry, and there is a transfer from "other non-profit" sources (mostly foundations) to universities and colleges. Overall, the largest element in Table 6.2 is industry-funded R&D performed by industry itself; this element accounts for over half of all R&D performed in the United States and is greater than U.S. federal funding of R&D or indeed the *total* spending on R&D in any other nation. It doubtlessly is the largest single factor affecting the technological competitiveness of U.S. firms.

Although the federal component of R&D funding is smaller than the industrial component, it is in absolute terms very large and figures importantly in the overall R&D effort. Some indication of the importance of the federal portion is given in Table 6.3, which indicates R&D funded and performed by institution broken down by category, i.e., basic research, applied research, and development. It is evident that the U.S. Federal Government funds the majority of basic research, the crucible for future technologies. The government funds

Table 6.1 Sources of Funding and Performers of R&D in the United States 1991 billions of dollars (% of column total)

Institution	Source	Performer
U.S. Federal Government	66.0 (43.5)	16.40 (10.8)
Industry	78.05 (51.5)	108.45 (71.5)
Universities and Colleges[16]	4.95 (3.3)	22.05 (14.5)
Other Nonprofit Organizations	2.60 (1.7)	4.70 (3.1)
Total	151.60 (100.0)	151.60 (100.0)

Source: U.S. National Science Foundation, *Science and Engineering Indicators 1991* (Washington: U.S. Government Printing Office, 1991, NSB 91-1).

Table 6.2 Sources of Funding and Performers of R&D in the United States 1991 billions of dollars (% of column total)

Institution	R&D Performed	Funded by Self	Funded by Fed.Gov.	Funded by Industry	Funded by Other Non-profit
U.S. Federal Government	16.40 (100.0)	16.40 (100.0)	x.x	0.0 (100.0)	0.0 (100.0)
Industry	108.45 (100.0)	76.15 (79.2)	32.30 (29.8)	x.x	0.0 (100.0)
Universities & Colleges[17]	17.20 (100.0)	3.45 (20.0)	9.65 (56.1)	1.25 (7.3)	1.35 (7.8)
FFRDC's at Universities & Colleges[18]	4.85 (100.0)	0.0 (100.0)	4.85 (100.0)	0.0 (100.0)	0.0
Other Nonprofit Organizations	4.70 (100.0)	1.25 (26.6)	2.80 (59.6)	0.65 (13.8)	x.x

Note: x.x indicates that the relevant figure is included under "Funded by Self".

Source: U.S. National Science Foundation, *Science and Engineering Indicators 1991* (Washington: U.S. Government Printing Office, 1991, NSB 91-1).

Table 6.3 Funding for Research and Development in the United States, by Institution and by Type of R&D 1991 billions of dollars (% of column total)

Institution	Basic R&D	Applied R&D	Development
U.S. Federal Government	14.45 (61.5)	13.10 (37.0)	38.45 (41.5)
Industry	4.88 (20.7)	19.66 (55.5)	53.52 (57.7)
Universities and Colleges	2.90 (12.3)	1.70 (4.8)	0.35 (0.4)
Other Nonprofit Organizations	1.28 (5.4)	0.94 (2.6)	0.39 (0.4)
Total	23.50 (100.0)	35.39 (100.0)	92.71 (100.0)
Note: Column Total as % of all R&D expenditure	(15.5)	(23.3)	(61.2)

Source: U.S. National Science Foundation, *Science and Engineering Indicators 1991* (Washington: U.S. Government Printing Office, 1991, NSB 91-1).

proportionately less applied research and development than it does total research, but more development than applied research (see also Table 6.4). Some industrial policy advocates in the United States (including some members of Congress) have called for smaller government expenditure on basic research, with the savings to be reallocated to applied research or development. For reasons touched upon in the paragraphs following this author believes that this would be an error.

If the United States spends a relatively high proportion of its R&D expenditures on defense and if the U.S. government is a large funder of R&D, a high percentage of total expenditure is on defense-related R&D. This is borne out in Tables 6.4 and 6.5 which indicate Federal Government R&D expenditure by agency and federally funded and non-federally funded R&D by industry. Of the total R&D funded by the Federal Government, over 75% in 1991 was defense-related, counting all R&D expenditures of the Departments of Defense and Energy and of the National Aeronautics and Space Administration (NASA) as "defense related" (but of no other agencies. This accounting probably, however, overstates somewhat the defense-related component.)

The proportion of federal R&D funding commitments that are defense-related varies by class of R&D. For example, basic research is only slightly more than one third defense-related, and this figure almost surely overstates the true proportion because, e.g., much of the Department of Energy's basic research budget is for high-energy physics, an activity that has been on occasion justified as being needed for the national defense but in fact is really pure scientific enquiry. Likewise, much of NASA's basic research budget is for non-defense related activities, e.g., scientific enquiry such as the deep space probes.[19] The largest single funder of basic research is the Department of Health and Human Services, and the bulk (over 82%) of its basic research budget goes to the National Institutes of Health, the main federal performer of medical research.

At the other end of the scale, government-funded development expenditures are almost 96% defense-related by the accounting of Table 6.4, and there is less scope for these expenditures being misplaced in the defense-related than for basic research expenditures. In the in-between category is applied research, of which the defense-related component is just under 50%. Most analysts believe that government-funded research in this category is most likely to result in commercial technological development.

Figuring somewhere in these data--it is a little hard to tell exactly where--is Defense Department expenditure made through the Defense Advanced Research Projects Agency, or DARPA. DARPA is the conduit through which federal money has been channelled to SEMATECH, and some would say that DARPA's implicit mission is to support development of civilian technologies deemed important to the defense effort. In 1991, DARPA's budget was $1.455 billion, or about 4.1% of all Defense Department R&D.

The data of Tables 6.1-6.4 thus suggest, DARPA notwithstanding, that federal support of R&D has been overwhelmingly oriented towards basic research, defense needs, energy development, and maintenance of public health. All of these are arguably legitimate goals of a government to create "public goods", i.e., knowledge that is of social utility but from whose generation little or no private return can be expected.[20] Most economists, including those who truly believe in the "magic of the marketplace", agree that there is a legitimate role for the government in providing such goods.

Unanswered in this statement, however, is to what extent the U.S. government does nonetheless fund commercial technological development by private firms. The detailed information regarding federal funding of private research and development broken down by sector that would be needed to address this issue is incomplete and dated. (See Table 6.5.) Nonetheless, the figures do show, as might be expected given the defense orientation of much federal funding of industrial R&D, that the funding is skewed towards particular industries. The industries indicated in Table 6.5 account for over 95% of all federal funding of R&D performed by industry in 1989 and one industry (aircraft and missiles) accounts for the lion's share (62.6%) while one other industry (communications equipment) accounts for another 14.9%. Exactly what R&D activities in non-manufacturing industries are Federally funded is not clear

Table 6.4 U.S. Federal Government Obligations for R&D, by Agency 1991
billions of dollars (% of total)

Agency	Total R&D	Basic Research	Applied Research	Development
Dept. of Agriculture	1.224 (1.9)	0.563 (4.5)	0.606 (5.2)	0.055 (0.1)
Dept. of Commerce	0.527 (0.8)	0.031 (0.2)	0.433 (3.7)	0.062 (0.2)
Dept. of Defense	35.188 (54.8)	1.022 (8.3)	2.662 (23.0)	31.504 (78.1)
Dept. of Education	0.204 (0.3)	0.007 (0.1)	0.150 (1.3)	0.047 (0.1)
Dept. of Energy	6.057 (9.4)	1.741 (14.1)	1.220 (10.6)	3.096 (7.7)
Dept. of Health and Human Services	9.336 (14.5)	5.101 (41.2)	3.218 (27.8)	1.018 (2.5)
Dept. of Housing and Urban Development	0.030 (0.0)	0.000 (0.0)	0.011 (0.1)	0.019 (0.0)
Dept. of Interior	0.586 (0.9)	0.231 (1.9)	0.315 (2.7)	0.040 (0.1)
Dept. of Labor	0.029 (0.0)	0.006 (0.0)	0.018 (0.2)	0.005 (0.0)
Dept. of Transportation	0.414 (0.6)	0.000 (0.0)	0.146 (1.3)	0.269 (0.7)
Environmental Protect. Agency	0.425 (0.7)	0.097 (0.8)	0.246 (2.1)	0.083 (0.2)
NASA	7.435 (11.5)	1.730 (14.0)	1.734 (15.0)	3.971 (9.8)
National Science Foundation	1.828 (2.8)	1.719 (13.9)	0.109 (0.9)	0.000 (0.0)
All Others	0.978 (1.5)	0.135 (1.1)	0.695 (6.0)	0.148 (0.4)
Total	64.261 (100.0)	12.382 (100.0)	11.563 (100.0)	40.316 (100.0)
Note: Column total as % of all Federal R&D	(100.0)	(19.3)	(18.0)	(62.7)
Note: Defense-related as % of total in column[21]	(75.8)	(36.2)	(48.5)	(95.7)

Source : U.S. National Science Foundation, *Science and Engineering Indicators 1991* (Washington: U.S. Government Printing Office, 1991, NSB 91-1).

Table 6.5 Major Industrial Sectors Performing R&D and Federal Funding of R&D Within the Sector 1989 billions of dollars (%)

Sector	Total R&D Expenditure	Federally Funded R&D Expenditure	Federally Funded R&D in Sector as % of all Federally Funded R&D Performed by All Industry	Federally Funded R&D as % of Total R&D Performed by Sector
Chemicals & Allied Products (includes pharmaceutical)	11.54	0.09	(0.3)	(0.8)
Communication components	10.51	4.67	(14.9)	(44.4)
Electronic components	4.88	0.52	(1.7)	(10.7)
Motor Vehicles	11.21	2.13	(6.8)	(19.0)
Aircraft & Missiles	25.65	19.63	(62.6)	(76.5)
Professional & Scientific Instruments	5.76	0.13	(0.4)	(2.2)
Nonmanufacturing	8.27	2.71	(8.7)	(32.8)

Source: U.S. National Science Foundation, *Science and Engineering Indicators 1991* (Washington: U.S. Government Printing Office, 1991, NSB 91-1).

from the figures, and so to what extent this funding is defense-related cannot be ascertained. The U.S. National Science Foundation does not publish a figure for federal funding of R&D performed in the non-electrical machinery industry, which includes computers. One suspects that much of the unaccounted for 5% or so lies in this sector.

Table 6.5 is most interesting for what it does *not* show. It does not show significant federal funding for R&D performed by industry in any manufacturing sector not closely related to defense. The overwhelming majority of federally funded R&D in the United States that is (1) not defense-related and (2) not performed by the Federal Government is undertaken by institutions other than manufacturing firms. This conclusion is roughly supported by the data in Table 6.6, showing federally funded R&D performed by industry in 1989 broken down by nature of the R&D. The Federal government supports less basic and applied research by industry than development, whether these are mea-

Table 6.6 Federally Funded R&D Performed by Industry as a % of Total R&D Performed by Industry, by Nature of the R&D 1989 billions of dollars (%)

	Basic Research	Applied Research	Development
1. Total Industry Expenditure	4.00	23.08	74.51
2. Amount of Above Funded by Federal Government	1.10	4.83	25.45
3. Line 2 as % of line 1	(27.3)	(20.9)	(34.1)
4. Line 2 as % of all Federally Funded R&D Performed by Industry	(3.5)	(15.4)	(81.1)

Source: U.S. National Science Foundation, *Science and Engineering Indicators 1991* (Washington: U.S. Government Printing Office, 1991, NSB 91-1).

sured as absolute amounts, percentages of the total such activity performed by industry, or the percentage of total federal funding of R&D performed by industry. This is consistent with the notion that, for the most part, federal support for R&D performed by industry has been defense-related.

The figures contained in all of Tables 6.1-6.6, of course, reflect past years and past priorities. Many of these priorities are being changed by the Clinton administration. For example, one stated goal of the administration is to reduce the defense share of federal R&D to about 50% without reducing the overall share of federal R&D in national income. However, the changes are to be implemented gradually. Thus, the proposed federal budget for FY 1994 reflects few of the proposed changes (see Table 6.7) when compared to the FY 1993 budget, set by the Bush administration.

The FY 1994 budget does reveal rather large percentage increases in a number of civilian technology programs. These are, however, all on rather small bases. The much touted Advanced Technology Program (ATP) within the Department of Commerce's National Institute of Science and Technology (NIST) has received close to a 200% funding increase between FY 1993 and FY 1994, but on a base of only $68 million. The ATP was established in 1988 under the Omnibus Trade Act and marks a departure from most other federal programs to support technology because it is not linked either to defense or to other public purposes such as basic research, energy, or health. Indeed, the mission of the ATP under the 1988 trade act was to help U.S. businesses to "commercialize significant new discoveries and technologies rapidly".[22] This mission was ideologically anathema to the Reagan administration, which accepted the program as part of a series of political compromises taken to assure passage of the 1988 act. The successor Bush administration then proceeded to keep funding for the program very small. In the FY 1994 budget, the ATP will be funded at just under 8% of the level of the (significantly reduced) "star wars" program (also known as the "Strategic Defense Initiative" or SDI but now officially the "Ballistic Missile Defense" or BMD).

Even so, the ATP has become the focus of much controversy. During the summer of 1993, the U.S. Congress worked towards legislation that would define what types of enterprise would be eligible for assistance and/or have access to technology created under the ATP. Legislation passed by the House of Representatives--the National Competitiveness Act of 1993 (HR 820 and amendments thereto)--would require that recipients of assistance under the ATP conduct their activities within the United States and either be U.S. citizens or nationals of countries that offer equivalent benefits to U.S.-based firms.[23] It is important to note that HR 820 is not yet law and, indeed, that the Senate counterpart bill (S 4) does not yet contain the nationalistic language contained in HR 820. Action is expected on S 4 in early 1994.

Likewise, the Manufacturing Extension Program, also within the NIST, has received more than 60% increased funding, but on a base of only $18 million. Indeed, while the NIST itself received funding increases of over 35% between FY 1993 and FY 1994, the base budget of NIST was $384 million, barely 10% of the R&D budget of the Department of Defense.

Whether this represents the modest start of something big or simply a modest start remains to be seen. The stated goal of the Clinton administration is for the annual funding of the ATP to reach $680 million by 1997. This would be part of an overall goal of reorienting all federally supported R&D to be "in line with the contemporary needs of industry". If the goal is implemented, the $680 million would represent much less than 1% of industry-financed R&D, even if this latter did not grow at all in nominal terms from 1991 levels.

On a somewhat bigger scale is funding for DARPA, now renamed the Advanced Research Projects Agency or ARPA. (ARPA is now to be involved in the development of nondefense-related technologies and to cooperate with other agencies of the U.S. Government involved in civilian technology development.) The appropriated funding for ARPA for FY 1994 is over $2.6 billion, an amount 114% greater than DARPA's funding in 1990 and 14% greater than ARPA funding in 1993. Still, the budget of ARPA represents less than 5% of budgeted federal R&D expenditure in 1994. From available figures it is not possible to determine how much of the funding is for primarily civilian projects and how much for primarily defense-related ones, although it is clear that the mission of ARPA is now primarily civilian. Roughly one fifth of ARPA's budget is for the Technology Reinvestment Program, designed to integrate military technology into the civilian sector.

The Clinton administration has created a new cross-agency National Science And Technology Council, and a subarm of this, the Committee on Industrial Technology, will manage a $2 billion cross-agency budget for programs to de-

Table 6.7 FY 1993 Federal Appropriations for R&D, FY 1994 Administration Requests, and FY 1994 Congressional Committee Proposed Appropriations, by Agency of Subagency (Billions of dollars)

Agency	Fy 1993 Approp.	FY 1994 Admin. Regs.	FY 1994 Conference
Dept. of Defense	38.238	38.620	35.192
- SDI (now BMD)	3.725	3.637	2.639
- ARPA	2.279	n/a	2.609
- Defense Conversion	1.767	3.342	2.491
NASA	7.080	7.690	7.509
National Science Foundation	1.859	2.205	1.986
Environmental Protection Agency	0.323	0.354	0.339
National Institute of Science & Tech. (Commerce Dept.)	0.384	0.535	0.520
- Advanced Technology Program	0.680	0.200	0.200
- Manufacturing Extension Program	0.108	0.030	0.030
- Qlty Outreach	0.000	0.003	0.003
NOAA (Comm. Dept.)	1.629	1.863	1.928
NTIA (Comm. Dept.)	0.040	0.095	0.700
Dept. of Energy	3.020	3.156	3.224
- Biological & Environmental Research	0.357	0.416	0.416
Dept. of Trans.	0.003	0.003	0.009
Health-related Research	17.649	18.742	19.005
- National Institute of Health	10.327	10.668	10.956
- National Cancer Institute	1.978	2.041	2.082
- Substance Abuse & Mental Health Services Admin.	2.005	2.154	2.125

Note: Line items for the health-related agencies are for total budgets and not for R&D alone.

Source: Carnegie Commission on Science, Technology, and Governments; compiled from U.S. Government Sources; ARPA figures from U.S. Congress.

velop advanced manufacturing technologies. The Departments of Defense, Energy, and Commerce as well as NASA and the National Science Foundation will be primary performers (or funders) of the research. Also, within the Department of Transportation, programs to develop a clean car (with a proposed funding of $141 million in FY 1994), high speed rail, "intelligent" vehicle highways, and more fuel efficient vehicles are being launched.

However, even if all of the funding of ARPA is for commercial technologies, it still is a safe statement that, as of the time of this writing, the industrial policy goals of the Clinton administration, at least in so far as they are reflected in the federal budget for R&D, are being implemented on a modest scale. Nonetheless, a number of serious policy issues are on the table, and it is to these that we now turn.

Industrial Policy Issues[24]

One interpretation of the closing paragraphs of the preceding section might be that the Clinton administration does not yet have its industrial policy in place but that, in spite of a number of unresolved policy issues, much more is in the works. This might or might not be the case. But whether it is or not, this author cannot suppress the desire to offer some policy advice.

One of the fundamental dilemmas of those who would pursue an activist industrial policy is that, while the goals might be to identify and promote those activities *and the business organizations that will pursue these activities* likely to be future "winners", the political process often leads to protection of the "losers". One of the standard criticisms of industrial policy is that the government is not particularly qualified to determine what and who will be the winners and that this is best left to the market. To this author at least, this possibility is less worrisome than the high probability that the political process will be captured by special interests who seek to have incumbent commercial positions protected from the very winds of change that produce the future winners.

Thus, the most salient criterion by which any industrial policy measure should be evaluated is "can this measure be captured by special interests?" An immediate objection might be that the most relevant criterion should not be the above, but rather "does this measure make sense?" Presumably, of course, no policy measure should be implemented if it fails this second criterion. But even if a proposed measure passes this second criterion, it should be viewed with extreme scepticism if it fails the first, i.e., that the measure can be implemented so as to protect the losers. For it is indeed the case, alas, that many measures having this last effect have been implemented in the United States and elsewhere, usually with a plausible rationale. With this in mind, let us look at a number of substantive issues.

The politics of trade are tilted very heavily in favour of incumbent industries.[25] It is very doubtful whether an activist trade policy can be fashioned to benefit potential winners without being captured by incumbent industries fearful of more efficient foreign producers. Trade protection for incumbent industries against foreign competition is almost surely to have a negative impact on real domestic income--this is the classical case against trade protection--*and* reduce incentives to domestic producers to increase their own efficiencies so as better to compete with foreign producers. Trade protection will (almost always) reduce both the static and dynamic efficiency of the economy. The static losses are emphasized in neoclassical trade theory, but it should also be recognized that trade protection likely will also result in *dynamic* losses--the very opposite of the dynamic gains that industrial policy advocates seek.

A standard riposte is that policies can help determine comparative advantage, and that this invalidates classic arguments for gains from trade by comparative advantage. Those who make this riposte then will argue that there is a special case for protecting incumbent producers of high technology goods from new foreign entry, on the grounds that this protection can preserve U.S. comparative advantage.

This author agrees that governments can help shape comparative advantage, but dismisses the conclusion. Persons who believe in this riposte are confusing two separable propositions: that there are gains to trade based on specialization of production (and on dynamic effects created by the enlargement of competition), and that government policy can help determine in what activities the comparative advantage of a nation might lie. By and large, trade protection *undoes* the potential gains brought about by specialization along lines of comparative advantage *irrespective of how that comparative advantage might have come about.*[26]

What has become almost a classic case of how misguided trade-policy-as-industrial-policy can work perversely is the antidumping finding against foreign producers of flat panel displays. The Commerce Department, by finding against foreign producers of these high technology devices, was hoping to promote the fortunes of a number of domestic producers, none of which was particularly competitive against any of the several large Japanese producers that collectively dominate the market for this product.[27] But the decision raised the costs of an important input for the highly competitive U.S. computer industry.[28] Several of the leading computer firms announced that as a result of the Commerce Department decision, they might relocate production embodying flat panel displays to offshore locations. Similar results appear to have followed other protective measures, e.g., the U.S. automotive industry has almost surely been rendered less competitive internationally by a number of actions taken to protect U.S. steel producers.

Advocacy of import protection as a tool of industrial policy has been aided by academic work over the past decade and a half on strategic trade theory.[29] However, as one of the innovators of the new theory has pointed out, the conditions under which strategic trade theory might further national welfare are extremely restrictive, and advocates of the use of protective policies in the name of this theory usually misunderstand the nature of the arguments.[30]

While protection from imports as a tool of industrial policy should be avoided, restrictions on participation of foreign firms in the U.S. economy should also be avoided. The case against such restrictions is stronger than that against import restrictions, because foreign direct investment implies location of economic activities on U.S. soil and hence greater likelihood of capture of spillover effects from these activities. Unfortunately, a number of measures now before the U.S. Congress would condition foreign-controlled firm participation in certain U.S. high-technology ventures. To this author, these measures would close the gate on guests bearing gifts.[31] Elements of such closure, unfortunately, appear in a number of pieces of legislation before the Congress, including most notably HR 820, discussed briefly at the end of this chapter.

The foregoing is not meant to imply that trade policy has no use as an adjunct of industrial policy. Steps to reduce official or unofficial import barriers would be in most instances welfare enhancing. One should note that such steps can be taken with respect to domestic as well as foreign markets with much the same effect; Mexico's new prospects have resulted from steps taken unilaterally by its government to open sectors of its economy that had long been shielded from international competition.

Perhaps the most controversial steps taken to open markets are the newly coined "voluntary import expansions" (VIEs) first applied in the U.S.-Japan semiconductor agreement. VIEs entail governmental mandated import floor levels in a specified nation. VIEs thus differ from normal market-opening measures, in that the latter simply remove barriers to imports and then allow the market to determine levels of trade.

Whether VIEs in the semiconductor industry have had salutary effects is controversial.[32] Proponents argue that without VIEs, Japan would never have increased its semiconductor imports to current levels, with attendant benefits to Japan and the rest of the world. Opponents argue that if any benefits were achieved from the semiconductor agreement, they likely are restricted to this one industry and unlikely to be replicated in other sectors.

It is even more controversial whether VIEs should be applied in other sectors.[33] It is a safe bet to say that the economics profession is largely (but not unanimously) opposed, on economic grounds, to the use of these measures.[34] Whatever the economic rationale, it must be added that this instrument, like trade protective measures, could be captured by special interests. Hence the view of this author is that the presumption should be against VIEs.

Basic Research

To the above rule regarding import restrictions as an instrument of industrial policy might be added the following positive rule: *the government has a very important role to play in fostering basic research and scientific and technical education*. Basic research, as has been detailed above, is very heavily underwritten by the U.S. Government, and this is a proper for at least two reasons. First, the "wedge" between private and social rates of return for this activity is, by almost universal consensus, higher than for applied research or development, and such instruments as strong intellectual property protection do not function very effectively to increase the private returns captured from basic research.

Second, in addition to adding to the basic scientific understanding of the universe (which is, after all, the major goal of basic research), such research often serves as the "crucible" from which, often with a considerable time lag, new useful technologies emerge.[35] The conclusion is, to this author at least, inescapable: basic research is the component of R&D most likely to be underfunded by the private sector relative to the contribution it makes to overall economic well-being (the evidence in this chapter is generally consistent with this observation). Thus, *inter alia, efforts to redirect resources currently devoted to basic research into lines of inquiry having a more immediate commercial payoff are short-sighted and unwise.*

This last statement might apply especially to efforts to redirect the priorities of the national laboratories. It is noncontroversial that these priorities should be directed away from militarily oriented missions, and it is equally noncontroversial that efforts should be expanded to disseminate the fruits of research in these laboratories where this would not carry significant security risks. However, such changes should not be misused as reasons for gutting the (often very substantial) basic research activities of these laboratories.

The importance of basic research is inextricably tied to the issue of scientific and technical education. Much basic research is performed at universities, whose mission it is also to produce the next generation of qualified scientists and engineers, most of whom will be employed by private industry.[36] As is documented above substantial university research is funded by the U.S. Federal Government.

To amplify some of these themes, let us note that the contribution of strong universities to the ability of a nation's institutions (including, most importantly, private firms) to compete effectively is two-fold. First, the universities create a pool of individuals with the necessary skills required to perform industrial R&D. Surveys of industrial firms operating across technologically advanced sectors indicate that this pool is very important to their R&D undertakings and that it would be very difficult to replicate the skills possessed by members of this pool through on-the-job training.[37] Second, the universities generate, through their own research, specific knowledge that can be a vital input to industrial technological development. The degree to which this happens, however, seems to vary considerably by specific industry.[38] Some industrial activities (e.g., biotechnology-based activities) rely heavily on research emanating from universities. Others (e.g., aerospace) do not.

It is self-evident (to this author, at least) that without effective primary and secondary education, the universities will be hard-pressed to impart foundation skills to the new generation of scientific and technical personnel. This is apparently self-evident to most politicians, because the importance of improving U.S. education is high in their rhetoric. What is striking is the little extent to which this gets translated into policy. The reasons for this are beyond the scope of this article (and beyond the competence of this author), but that more needs doing in this area seems clear enough.

If the government has a mission to support basic research, should it also support applied research and development that leads directly to commercialization of new technologies? The answer is a qualified "yes". The qualifications are crucial, however, and in order to make the case for these, it is important to note the constructive U.S. government role in direct support of the development of new technologies.

From the rather extensive literature on this subject, it would appear that this role has been positive (and perhaps vital) when two criteria have been met: *First, the government itself has been a customer for the technology and, second, the commercial risks associated with the development of the technology have been seen as high.* The latter point can be consistent with a large wedge between expected private and social rates of return from the development of the technology: that successful development will confer no special advantages upon the innovator even though the technology might bring benefits to society at large. Equally, however, commercial risks could be high if the endeavor has a high probability of failure.

The development of microprocessors--the example most often cited as a case where the U.S. Government underwrote the development of new technologies that led to the rise of an important industry--clearly met these criteria.[39] Early on, the U.S. Air Force was the major (indeed, at first, the only) customer for these devices. What the Air Force wanted was a very small device that could fit into an aircraft or missile and that could withstand high temperatures and shocks. There was no assurance that such a device was technically feasible and there was little assurance that investment in their development would yield a commercially acceptable return. But, after the feasibility and reliability of such devices was demonstrated, a civilian market rapidly developed and the government's role in fostering of the market rapidly waned.

Likewise, the U.S. Government's involvement in the early commercial aircraft industry met these criteria. Again, the Air Force created substantial demand for military versions of early transport aircraft, most notably the Douglas DC3 and the Boeing 707. And, as was the case in microprocessors, following successful commercialization, the government played a diminishing role in the development of later generations of aircraft.[40]

In each of these cases the major interest of the government was not to "do something" to enhance the competitiveness of U.S. firms, but rather to develop a technologically sophisticated product that met the government's own requirements. But in each case the government's involvement did have the unintended (and successful) effect of making certain firms highly competitive.

These successes contrast starkly with programs designed primarily to enhance the competitiveness of domestic firms. In the United States, for example, the SEMATECH consortium was organized with the mission to restore

U.S. firms as efficient producers of large-scale memory devices. To date, successful results are not wholly evident (although, to be fair, such a judgement is probably premature). In Europe, the Airbus program can probably be fairly called a technological success but a commercial failure.[41] It is too early to write off Airbus entirely--it has preserved competition in an industry that might otherwise have evolved into a monopoly, and one result has been improvement in Boeing products. It nonetheless has been one of the costliest programs imaginable to the European taxpayer. At the very least, it can be argued that whatever the benefits from the Airbus program, few have been captured by the European governments that sponsored the endeavor.

In an era of diminishing need for high-technology military programs, will there be future examples of the sorts of success in the semiconductor and aircraft industries, that is, cases where the above criteria would suggest a reason for government participation? My feeling is that there will be opportunities for constructive government participation in such areas as infrastructure improvements (a network of mag-lev trains?), health care services (where the government already is a factor in the demand for these services) and perhaps even in a renewed program to explore the universe. In all of these areas, future progress will depend on the continuation of basic research, and this of course reinforces the point already made that the government should support this type of activity. What is very dubious to this author is that the government should be underwriting the development of new manufacturing technologies, or that the government's large national laboratories should be recast as public-sector versions of industrial development centers. The bulk of the evidence would suggest that the government is not very good at these sorts of activity, but that private enterprise, given the right incentives (including the maintenance of a competitive environment) is very well suited to perform them. It would be a shame if the *angst* that continues to grip much of the United States were to lead to the U.S. Government abandoning a role in the creation of new technology that it is uniquely placed to perform in order to pursue a role that is both unwise and unnecessary.

Notes

1. However, this erosion is not nearly as great as some people claim, especially if one includes the overseas production of affiliates of U.S. firms. See Irving B. Kravis, and Robert E. Lipsey, "Sources of Competitiveness of the United States and of its Multinational Firms," *Review of Economics and Statistics*, 74 (1992) 2.

2. Masahiro Okuno-Fujiwara, "Industrial Policy in Japan: A Political Economy View," in Paul R. Krugman (ed.), *Trade with Japan: Has the Door Opened Wider?* (Chicago: University of Chicago Press for the National Bureau of Economic Research, 1991); see also Bela Balassa and Marcus Noland, *Japan in the World Economy* (Washington: Institute for International Economics, 1989). The most cited work extolling the role of industrial policy in Japan is Chalmers Johnson, *MITI and the Japanese Miracle: The Growth of Industrial Policy, 1925-1979* (Stanford: The Stanford University Press, 1982).

3. Thus, in *Wall Street Journal/NBC News* poll, reported on December 17, 1993 in the *Wall Street Journal* (page 1), the U.S. public thought that the U.S. economy is more powerful than that of Japan.

4. These include the U.S. automobile and semiconductor producers, i.e., those firms whose misfortunes during the 1980s triggered much of the talk about U.S. decline.

5. These concerns should not be dismissed as a residual of the near-apocalyptical vision of U.S. industrial decline heard so often in the late 1980s. A number of sober assessments of U.S. technology suggest that in many fields the Japanese really do have a technological lead over their U.S. rivals. George Gamota, "Technology Assessment in the U.S.-Japan Context," in Thomas S. Arrison, C. Fred Bergsten, Edward M. Graham, and Martha C. Harris (eds.), *Japan's Growing Technological Capability: Implications for the U.S. Economy* (Washington: National Academies Press, 1992). In the same volume, David C. Mowery and David J. Teece document the growing techno-logical capabilities of these firms, and John Cantwell argues that in many respects Japanese firms are better suited to take advantage of what he calls the "new technological paradigm" than are U.S. firms. But, also in the same volume, William F. Finan and Carl Williams note that Japanese electronics firms are increasingly constrained by their own technological limitations, especially in software engineering. See Mowery and Teece, "The Changing Place of Japan in the Global Scientific and Technological Enterprise"; Cantwell, "Japan's Industrial Competitiveness and the Technological Capability of Leading Japanese Firms"; and Finan and Williams, "Implications of Japan's Soft Crisis: Forcing New Directions for Japanese Electronics Companies," all in Arrison et al., *Japan's Growing Technological Capability: Implications for the U.S. Economy.*

6. Nathan Rosenberg, *Inside the Black Box: Technology and Economics* (Cambridge and London: Cambridge University Press, 1982), ch. 6. That advances in technology are an important determinant of economic growth is by now accepted; the empirical literature is vast, but it is accepted that the pioneering articles are Moses Abramovitz, "Resource and Output Trends in the United States Since 1870", *American Economic Review*, 46, 1956, and Robert M. Solow, "A Contribution to the Theory of Economic Growth," *Quarterly Journal of Economics*, 70, 1956. A recent contribution is Michael J. Boskin and Lawrence J. Lau, "Capital, Technology, and Economic Growth," in Nathan

Rosenberg, Ralph Landau, and David C. Mowery, *Technology and the Wealth of Nations* (Stanford: Stanford University Press, 1993) which both offers new evidence and summarizes a number of the major studies.

7. On this proposition, see Barry P. Bosworth, *Savings and Investment in a Global Economy* (Washington: The Brookings Institution, 1993) and Organisation for Economic Cooperation and Development, "Total Factor Productivity," *OECD Economic Outlook*, 42 (December 1987): 39-49.

8. It has been argued that in a "first best" world the government should always subsidize technology development rather than employ other means to create incentives for this development, on grounds that this would maximize the social rate of return to technological innovation. For the detailed reasoning, Harry G. Johnson, "The Efficiency and Welfare Implications of the International Corporation," in Charles P. Kindleberger (ed.), *The International Corporation* (Cambridge: The MIT Press, 1970). However, this presupposes that the government is able to make optimal choices regarding allocation of R&D subsidies, a matter about which there is considerable doubt.

9. Richard C. Levin, Alvin K. Klevorik, Richard R. Nelson, and Sidney G. Winter, "Appropriating the Returns to Industrial Innovation," *Brookings Papers on Economic Activity*, 3, 1987. For an analysis of individual firms' strategies, see David J. Teece, "Strategies for Capturing the Financial Benefits from Technological Innovation," in Rosenberg, Landau, and Mowery, *Technology and the Wealth of Nations*. Teece emphasizes that in order to appropriate returns to a new technology, a firm often must have "complementary assets," e.g., the ability to provide users of new products with training, maintenance, and other sophisticated "after-market" services.

10. See sectoral studies in David B. Yoffie (ed.), *Beyond Free Trade: Firms, Governments, and Global Competition* (Boston: Harvard Business School Press, 1993).

11. On the political process by which trade protection is generated, see I.M. Destler, *American Trade Politics*, 2nd edition (Washington: Institute for International Economics, 1992). On the costs of protection, see Kimberly Ann Elliott and Gary Clyde Hufbauer, *Measuring the Costs of Protection in the United States* (Washington: Institute for International Economics, 1994).

12. William R. Cline, *The Future of World Trade in Textiles and Apparel*, revised edition (Washington: Institute for International Economics, 1990).

13. I say that this latter is "more controversial" than trade protection for aging industries because such protection is not controversial at all: almost any rationalist would hold that it should not be granted! As noted in the text, only a political dynamic keeps it in place.

14. Unless cited otherwise, all data in this section are derived from U.S. National Science Foundation, *Science and Engineering Indicators 1991* (Washington: U.S. Government Printing Office, NSB 91-1, December 1991).

15. R&D as a percent of national product is on a GNP basis except for the French figures (here and below), which are for R&D expenditures as a percentage of GDP and not GNP. The result is a slightly higher number than would be the case for GNP.

16. Research performed includes $4.85 billion (3.2%) expanded in federally funded research and development centers administered by universities and colleges, including consortia. These are laboratories and other centers established by the Federal Government to fulfil a stated mission or purpose (and, hence, their activities could be viewed as R&D contracted out to university management, e.g., the Lawrence Radiation Laboratory of the University of California).

17. Excluding federally funded research and development centers; in addition to amounts shown on table, U.S. universities and colleges received funding for R&D from nonfederal (primarily) state government sources, totalling $1.5 billion (8.7% of total R&D performed) in 1991.

18. FFRDCs = Federally Funded Research and Development Centers.

19. The National Science Foundation publishes figures for Federal R&D funding by function which show national defense only claiming 59% of the total federal funding for R&D. However, these figures show no defense component in basic research. For this and other reasons it is arguable that some defense expenditures are "hidden" in other functions. Thus, the bottom line is probably that true defense-related expenditures in 1991 were between 60% and 70% of total federal funding of R&D.

20. To be slightly more precise, a public good can be defined as one where there is a significant "wedge" between social and private rates of return accruing to the good. By the arguments given in the previous section, all scientific and technological knowledge can fit into this category, but the wedge is likely to be especially high for knowledge at the scientific end of the spectrum.

21. Includes Departments of Defense and Energy and NASA only.

22. Executive Office of the President, *Technology for America's Economic Growth: A New Direction to Build Economic Strength* (Washington, U.S. Government Printing Office, 1993).

23. An extensive analysis of the HR 820 provisions is contained in Mark A.A. Warner and Alan M. Rugman, "Protecting U.S.: An Emerging Strategy of Discrimination in U.S. Antitrust and R&D Policy?" unpublished manuscript, Centre for International Business, University of Toronto, November 17, 1993. Warner and Rugman also discuss similar provisions in amendments to the National Cooperative Research Act of 1984 that were signed into law in June, 1993.

24. Many of the issues raised in this section are dealt with in Steve Charnovitz, "Designing American Industrial Policy: General versus Sectoral Approaches," *Stanford Law and Policy Review*, 5 (1993) 1: 78-92. The author is also grateful to Steve Charnovitz for insights conveyed during discussions.

The reader should not, of course, assign any blame to Charnovitz, the article or the person, for errors in this section that are mine alone.

25. This proposition is thoroughly explored in Destler, *American Trade Politics*.

26. The present author takes some credit for having made this case early on. Edward M. Graham, "Technological Innovation and the Dynamics of the U.S. Comparative Advantage in International Trade," in Christopher T. Hill and James M. Utterback, *Technological Innovation for a Dynamic Economy* (New York and Oxford: Pergamon Press, 1979).

27. This case is treated in eloquent detail in Laura D. Tyson, *Who's Bashing Whom? Trade Conflict in High-Technology Industries* (Washington: Institute for International Economics, 1992).

28. Further, in the eyes of most analysts, this protection has not significantly raised the prospects for the U.S. producers to compete successfully in this industry.

29. The major ideas of this literature are in Elhanan Helpman and Paul R. Krugman, *Trade Policy and Market Structure* (Cambridge: The MIT Press, 1989).

30. Paul R. Krugman, "Does the New Trade Theory Require a New Trade Policy," *The World Economy*, 15, 1992.

31. This case is made in detail, and the current legislative proposals analyzed, in the revised third edition of Edward M. Graham and Paul R. Krugman, *Foreign Direct Investment in the United States* (Washington: Institute for International Economics, 1994).

32. Laura D. Tyson and David B. Yoffie, "Semiconductors: From Manipulated to Managed Trade," in Yoffie, *Beyond Free Trade: Firms...* Tyson and Yoffie on balance believe that the agreement has had positive effects; however, they cite a number of studies that arrive at different conclusions. Kenneth Flamm, a semiconductor specialist at Brookings, in particular has indicated in oral remarks that market shifts may have had as much impact on the increase in demand for foreign-made semiconductors in Japan as the semiconductor agreement.

33. C. Fred Bergsten and Marcus Noland, *Reconcilable Differences? United States-Japan Economic Conflict* (Washington: Institute for International Economics, 1993), who offer a limited rationale for VIEs but acknowledge the case against them.

34. Thus, a group of leading economists has recently sent a letter to Prime Minister Hosokawa of Japan and President Clinton of the United States urging that VIEs be rejected as a tool of trade policy.

35. This is not meant to imply, however, that all technological innovation springs from basic research or even that the flow of understanding is always from basic to applied research. On the latter point, history is rife with examples where applied research led to development of processes that worked in the

absence of basic understanding. In such cases, the applied research in many cases triggered basic research which in turn led to advances in the applications. See Richard Nelson and Sidney Winter, *An Evolutionary Theory of Economic Change* (Cambridge: Harvard University Press, 1982).

36. The absolutely key link between the technological performance of a nation and the quality of its institutions of higher learning is explored in Richard Nelson, "What is Commercial and What is Public About Technology and What Should Be," in Rosenberg, Landau, and Mowery, *Technology and the Wealth of Nations*. See also Landau and Rosenberg, "Successful Commercialization in the Chemical Process Industries" (in the same volume), who note that the early prowess of Germany in the chemicals industry--this was probably the first of the truly "high-tech" industries--can largely be explained by links between German firms in this industry and major universities in Germany. Basic research in universities has led to discoveries absolutely vital to a number of other "high-tech" industries, including semiconductors, computers and pharmaceuticals.

37. Levin, Klevorick, Nelson, and Winter, "Appropriating the Returns..." The not-easily replaceable skills are those associated with basic scientific and engineering education, including quantitative skills, that are prerequisite for mastering the specific missions of industrial research and development. Companies almost universally reported to Levin et al. that persons hired who had mastered the foundation materials were easily taught the specifics of industrial R&D, whereas persons without the foundations were likely to flounder.

38. Levin, Klevorick, Nelson, and Winter, "Appropriating the Returns..."

39. Michael Borrus, James Millstein, and John Zysman, "U.S.-Japan Competition in the Semiconductor Industry," *Policy Papers in International Affairs*, 17 (Berkeley: University of California Institute for International Studies, 1983) and Kenneth Flamm, *Creating the Computer: Government, Industry and High Technology* (Washington: Brookings Institution, 1988).

40. Burton H. Klein, *Dynamic Economics* (Cambridge: Harvard University Press, 1977).

41. See chapter on aircraft in Tyson, *Who's Bashing Whom? Trade...*

7

Industrial Policies in South Korea and Taiwan

Tun-jen Cheng

While the long arm of the industrial policy in two stellar East Asian economies, South Korea and Taiwan, is well established (Amsden 1989; Wade 1991), the efficiency of government intervention remains a moot question (World Bank 1993). However, the debate between the statists and neoclassical economists has become quite stale, with the former acknowledging the possibility and risk of policy failure, while the latter giving some credit to policies. A more fruitful approach to the state-market debate is to ask more nuanced and specific questions about state intervention, such as, are some policies better (or worse) than others? or at what stage of development can state policy become counter-productive? The comparison of South Korea and Taiwan, two newly industrializing countries (NICs) so strikingly similar in economic preconditions, historical backgrounds and postwar geopolitical contexts, provides an excellent opportunity to examine the effects of diverse policy instruments on economic growth.

South Korea and Taiwan have followed the same strategy for, and same trajectory of, industrial development. Following a brief period of import-substituting industrialization (ISI) in the '50s, these two NICs adopted export-oriented industrialization (EOI) strategies in the '60s, even though ISI policies for some sectors continued. Ever since that shift, these two economies have remained outward-oriented and have been regarded as paradigms of development. However, there have been significant variations in terms of specific policies and ways of interacting with firms as agents for industrial development.

Until recently, with the intensive use of (highly subsidized) credit allocation as the principal instrument, South Korea's industrial policies were designed to assist a few select, usually big, enterprises and to promote a few specific sectors (Cheng 1990). In contrast, Taiwan's industrial policies were by and large targeted at many medium -and small-sized enterprises in broadly designated sectors. The major policy instruments for industrial promotion in Taiwan were fiscal (tax) incentives, which are arguably less discretionary than credit allocation (Bradford and Branson 1987: 21-22; Westphal 1978). Thus, industrial policies in South Korea and Taiwan differed significantly regarding the selectivity of agents, the specificity of industrial sectors to be promoted, and the intensity of incentives.

Industrial policies in the two states indeed differed more in kind than in degree, and accordingly cannot be lumped together under the rubric of the "East Asian model". The contrasts are reflected in the second-tier NICs. Malaysia has adopted various components of the South Korean approach, using subsidized credit to create *bumiputra* conglomerates, while Thailand's more liberal policy toward domestic and foreign firms resembles Taiwan's economic management. In a sense, the contrast between the Brazilian government's economic nationalism and President Salina's bold attempt to liberalize the Mexican economy also reflects the South Korea-Taiwan differences.

Exclusive and Inclusive Strategies

The South Korean government had, until recently, chosen a small number of big firms, *chaebol*, for industrial projects, while the number of "chosen" agents for industrial promotion has always been quite large in Taiwan. The sectors designated for promotion in South Korea were clearly specified and only few received policy support during each stage of industrial development. Many sectors were earmarked for policy support and sectors were broadly defined in Taiwan. While South Korea used highly discretionary methods, mainly preferential credits, to induce industrial entrepreneurship, Taiwan employed more diffused incentives, through tax credits. Both protected their industries, but the tariff level was generally higher in South Korea than that in Taiwan. Further, the South Korean policy style was more authoritarian, while the Taiwanese approach was more liberal and rather decentralized.

Big business--a small group of family-controlled conglomerates called *chaebol*--was the backbone of South Korean industry. Some of these leading business firms originated in the Japanese colonial period (Eckert 1991); others came into being in postwar era. But nearly all of them developed on a large scale during the period of rapid economic expansion under the military regime (1961-1987) which relied heavily on the entrepreneurship of existing business leaders.

Most of these business leaders benefited from the privatization of state-owned enterprises and banks, and from foreign exchange and import permits during the 1950s under the ostensibly democratic but corrupt government headed by Sygnman Rhee. These business leaders were proxies for the ruling party's rent-seeking and political fund-raising activities rather than trustees for ISI development. The military coup leaders who seized power in

1961 vowed to persecute these business captains on corruption charges and began to pursue pro-agriculture and small business policies, but within a few years they reversed policy preferences and cemented a sort of *sword-won* alliance with business captains (Cheng 1990).

The managerial elite collaborating with the military regime undertook very active export promotion. They took initiatives in several projects, such as the planning and construction of industrial estates. They were also reportedly instrumental in the political and economic rapprochement with Japan (Chang 1982). During the 1970s their firms became responsible for major heavy and chemical industrialization projects (HCI) launched to transform industrial and export structures, as well as to lay the foundation for self-reliant defense industries. Later on, these business captains also established nine general trading companies which by the early 1980s accounted for nearly half of South Korea's exports, and were venturing into the Middle Eastern construction markets, earning foreign exchange to offset growing oil import expenses.

The South Korean government under the military regime was a true believer in industrial sectoral planning. Beginning with textiles, then machinery, steel, shipbuilding, petrochemical, automobile and beyond, a small number of well-specified sectors were selected for promotion in each economic plan. Sectoral policy was not just announced; it was armed with incentives, most importantly soft credits (see below). The leadership of the regime focused on the development of these select sectors like a laser beam. And, as mentioned above, round after round, nearly the same select few were called upon to assume the tasks specified in sectoral planning. The government in short picked both winning sectors and winning groups of firms, and the winners were all small in number.

A wide range of incentives including protected (hence profitable) domestic markets, the symbolic payoff (such as the prestigious export award), tax breaks and import tariff rebates were available in South Korea to encourage investment in designated industrial sectors. However, privileged access to bank loans at preferential rates was the premier policy instrument with which the South Korean government influenced its chosen economic agents. The government nationalized the banks in the early 1960s, negotiated with Japan for the conclusion of a peace treaty in 1965, thereby receiving a credit line, and continued to borrow heavily from abroad thereafter. Occupying the commanding heights, the South Korean government then used subsidized credit to induce as well as dictate to the *chaebol*.

Soft credit was a strong incentive because it was perennially tempting to firms and it allowed the government to exercise "discretionary control" over them. The more lending a *chaebol* received, the more subsidized it was, the more financial capacity it had for expansion. But the more debt it incurred, the more leveraged it became, and hence the more susceptible it was to government direction, as bank loans could be called back any time.

Using subsidized credit as the primary mechanism to elicit private sector support for industrial policy was in congruence with the exclusive principle in South Korean industrial policy. The pool of beneficiaries of credit allocation was generally smaller than that of fiscal incentives. Credit allocation also allowed the South Korean government to target any specific recipients it wanted. Subsidized credit was also conducive to large-scale and capital-intensive production and the formation of big business. Soft credit thus could be said to be the staple for *chaebols* groomed as South Korea's "national champions."

Here it should be pointed out that other policies also helped create the privileged small group of national champions in South Korea. The policy toward foreign capital favored foreign borrowing over the entry of multinationals, thereby insulating *chaebol* from the competition of foreign firms in South Korean markets. A policy of industrial zoning for the establishment of a few large industrial estates facilitated expansion by the existing big corporations while discouraging entries by new firms. The chosen few were unstintingly nurtured.

Taiwan's industrial policy was managed to create and preserve a large number of agents and sectors, or at least avoid privileging the few. During the 1950s, the ISI period, the government flexed its financial muscles to promote mainly state-owned enterprises and a few leading private firms in few key sectors (some of them under mainlander industrialists who fled to Taiwan with the Kuomintang regime in 1949, some of them landlord -or merchant-turned native industrialists). Small and medium enterprises (SMEs), mostly owned by indigenous Taiwanese capitalists, were not the main recipients of the government's credit support. However, with the onset of export-oriented industrialisation at the turn of the 1960s, SMEs flourished in Taiwan and became the mainstay of its economy. Their share in the output of the manufacturing sector increased from 26.7% in 1971 to 48.2% in 1984. Throughout the 1970s more than 60% of the non-farming work force was employed by SMEs and in the 1980s they accounted around 60% of export earnings (Wu and Chou 1987).

Taiwan's industrial policy quite consistently adhered to an inclusive principle. When export promotion began in the early 1960s, the expansion of state enterprises was halted, and banks were instructed to manage export financing rather than support specific industries. Moreover, tax credits were given to broadly defined labor-intensive (employment creating) industries while import duties for export firms were rebated. During the 1970s state enterprises took the lead in petrochemical and heavy industrial projects, blocking the entry of large private firms into upstream industries; but compared to South Korea (Watanabe 1978), heavy and chemical industrialisation was on a smaller scale, aimed at deepening the industrial bases to safeguard the supply of intermediate goods for SMEs in downstream industries rather than attempting to turn heavy and petrochemical firms into the backbone export industries. During the 1980s, when information and machinery industries were designated as two strategic sectors, two new crops of entrepreneurs were groomed. These were "black-handed" apprentice-turned machine-tool shop owners and highly educated, foreign-experienced electrical and electronic engineers, rather than the old stock of capitalists in established industries. New firms in the two strategic sectors are basically SMEs. If developmental agents were also chosen in Taiwan, the choices were broadly inclusive and the chosen agents differed from sector to sector, unlike the case of South Korea where *chaebols* remained the same cast of agents across sectors.

The government in Taiwan did practice industrial targeting (or pick winning sectors) as in the case of South Korea, but in a very diluted way. Unlike the case of South Korea, many sectors in Taiwan were favored, very few were left out in the cold, as if there were some sort of fair share arrangement. When information and electronics were enshrined as strategic sectors at the turn of the 1980s, many existing industries were also designated as key sectors, which also received policy support. The promotion of two strategic industries was also quickly by matched, if not overwhelmed, by the promotion of several broadly defined investment activities, including anti-pollution efforts, production automation, and the upgrading of manufacturing capacity. Industrial policy in Taiwan was thus aimed at broad functional categories across many sectors.

To foster industrial entrepreneurship, the government in Taiwan relied primarily on fiscal incentives which were periodically revamped to favor new sectors or activities. Unlike credit allocation which is a highly discretionary policy instrument, usually favoring big firms with good credit rating, fiscal incentives are extended to any firm that qualifies, facilitating the birth of SMEs. Through its controlled banking sector and postal savings institutions, the government mobilized savings and diverted the flow of capital away from consumption and commerce to support industrial exports. Targeted lending for designated industrial sectors was avoided until recently (Cheng 1994). Compared to South Korea, Taiwan had very modest targeted lending or policy loans. Moreover, these loans were underutilized as they were often disbursed by commercial banks. And even after a bank was commissioned as a development bank, it continued to handle policy loans like regular lending and its performance was assessed by the same set of criteria used to assess other banks, including profit (Cheng 1994).

Other aspects of Taiwan's industrial policy were conducive to the rise and expansion of small and medium enterprises. The influx of FDI resulted in a proliferation of small indigenous component manufacturers (as opposed to the big domestic assemblers in South Korea). Widely located industrial estates also contributed to the spread of small rural enterprises which could tap the abundant labor force in the countryside.[1]

Why did the leadership in South Korea embrace the exclusive principle while its counterpart in Taiwan followed the inclusive principle in the pursuit of industrial development? Both cases are equally puzzling, as the military regime in South Korea initially had attempted to purge big business, while the Kuomintang regime in Taiwan initially did follow the South Korean approach to promoting industries, using subsidized credit to leading firms and treating them as the chosen agents of development. Both cases could have gone the other way.

In the case of South Korea, one possible explanation is that it was simply convenient and even imperative for the regime to use rather than purge big business. The military regime came to power via a coup, and thus was in particular need of economic performance to justify its exercise of political power. Entrepreneurship was hard to come by and it was natural for the regime to build on what already existed. Besides, big business was so small a group that it was quite easy for the government to allocate tasks to, stimulate oligopolistic competition among, and monitor the performance of the members of this group.

The *sword-won* alliance was also a result of big business political action to defend property rights threatened by coup leaders. Big business as a group had sought to work with the military regime, in the capacity of a junior partner of the alliance for industrial development. Big business certainly had the motivation to act together as they shared the same high stake: their property and indeed personal freedom were being threatened. Their small number facilitated collective action, as it was easier for everyone to see the linkage between one's contributions and collective output, as well as to identify and exert group pressure on free riders.

The economic expediency argument however is not convincing enough. The political legitimacy of the newly created military regime in South Korea could have been secured by other means, such as redistribution and the re-opening of political space for competition, while maintaining law and order and national security. Moreover, what big business proposed, the regime did not have to accept; the regime could have continuously fostered SMEs rather than reinstate big business. As of 1961, the South Korean military regime was not beholden to any social group, least of all to big business which the coup leaders had vowed to purge.

The policy preferences of the South Korean military regime were probably based more on its leaders' historical learning of economic nationalism than on economic exigency. The prominent coup leader, President Park Chung Hee, had served in the Japanese Kwangtung Army during the 1930s. Young Turks in the Japanese military were extolling nationalism and later fostered patriotic new *zaibatsu*. Park's writings revealed his early vision of a rich and strong (in that sequence) Korea à la successful industrializers (such as Japan and Germany), a vision quite prevalent among colonized peoples, especially the Koreans who had been victimized by periodic great power rivalry. It was only natural for Park to be impressed by Japanese economic nationalism which legitimated *zaibatsu*-dominant prewar capitalism by elevating the profit motive to the patriotic level.

Economic nationalism inspired and rationalized the Korean military regime's adoption of the exclusive principle in its drive for industrialization. Nurturing a handful of national champs and harnessing them for the ambitious task of industrial development was a laudable national project. Such a policy also meant using Japanese methods to counter the Japanese challenge, to which South Koreans for historical and geographical reasons were most sensitive. When the South Korean government signed a peace treaty with Japan in mid-1960s in exchange for economic concessions, primarily loans, (a move bitterly denounced by students and the political opposition) the Korean national-champ policy became easier to sell to the public.

Once the military regime decided to nurture national champs, the choice of credit allocation as the primary mechanism became a logical move. To allocate bank credits is an effective way of controlling the *chaebol*; what the king gives, the king can take away and give to others. While the regime is dependent on business captains for economic performance, the regime is not dependent on any one of them. The regime can be a maker and killer of any *chaebol*, albeit not the *chaebol* as a collectivity.

It seems that the case of Taiwan is more puzzling. As shown above, the prototype of big business already existed when the government launched export-oriented industrialization at the turn of the '60s, and until the late 1980s the government had absolute control over the financial sector. Why then did Taiwan's KMT regime, in promoting private firms, prefer an inclusive policy? Why did the government resist the temptation to use credit allocation as a major instrument of industrial policy?

One possible explanation is that the government heeded neoclassical economists who inculcated the virtue of minimizing government intervention and avoiding distortion in the economy. Five noted neoclassical economists--based in Taiwan's Academia Sinica and/or leading American economics departments--were indeed often summoned for advice. However, while their words on macroeconomic management were taken seriously (Tsiang 1980), their primarily negative views on industrial policies (especially on the targeting part) probably were not.

Statist ideology and political calculus offer a better explanation for the choice of the inclusive principle in implementing industrial policy. Postwar Taiwan, unlike South Korea, had a party regime (the Kuomintang or KMT regime) espousing min sheng chu i (the principle of people's livelihood), enunciated by Sun Yat Sen in the 1920s to promote state capital and restrict private capital. The confrontation with Communist China after the onset of the Cold War and the alliance with the U.S. led this party regime to stress private capital. However, the concern about the concentration of private capital persisted. On the mainland, the KMT leadership was always leery of big private financiers who, despite their social ties to the political elite, had not been submissive to the state's economic policy. Colonial inheritance and relocation to Taiwan made the KMT regime resource rich, reversing its prewar dependence on the private sector. Having dismantled the indigenous landlord class through a land reform in the first half of the 1950s, the KMT regime had every incentive to avoid the formation of big indigenous capital, and hence to foster SMEs.

The sociopolitical structure within which the postwar KMT regime was embedded also contributed to the leadership's preference. The postwar KMT regime was a minority-mainlander-controlled regime in a society where 85% of inhabitants were Taiwanese. Shut off and deterred from the political arena, Taiwanese found it possible and safer to pursue economic activities. From the perspective of the regime's leadership, however, pre-empting the translation of wealth into political power became a major concern. Conceivably, the regime could have created and then controlled, in a rather cost-effective way, a handful of Taiwanese business captains. Yet the South Korean approach as such required some mutual trust between the powerful and the wealthy, a trust that did not exist in the early postwar period, especially after the February 28, 1947 uprising and massacre. Moreover, the South Korean way symbolized the alliance between the regime and the privileged few, an alliance that would have further alienated the bulk of the population. Fostering numerous SMEs and treating most, if not all, industries fairly thus became politically sensible.

Once the KMT regime decided to embrace the inclusive principle, going along with many rather than the few, fiscal incentives became a better policy choice than credit allocation. Generally speaking, while fiscal incentives can be sector-specific as in the case of credit allocation, they are less discretionary than credit allocation, reaching out quite broadly to any firm meeting the criteria. Firms receiving fiscal incentives are not subject to thorough screening and competitive selection processes as in the case of credit allocation. Fiscal incentives as used in Taiwan were not very sector-specific, as discussed above, creating a perception of fairness and non-discrimination. Relatedly, the policy of dispersing many small-sized industrial estates around Taiwan also supported government efforts to even out rather than concentrate business opportunities.

The Larger, The Better?

South Korea's heavy-handed industrial policy seemed to be very effective in channelling capital to designated sectors and in shaping investment behavior of business captains. It allowed state leadership to achieve policy goals in a short period, upgrading industrial structure, strengthening national defense capability, and establishing Korea's position in world markets for high-value export items (Westphal 1990). By the light-heavy industry ratio (the Hoffmann ratio), South Korea transformed its industrial structure faster than Taiwan. As Table 7.1

indicates, the ratio of South Korea's heavy industry in total industrial output was about 10% lower than that of Taiwan's before 1971, but the gap was closed in 1977. In the early 1970s, Taiwan and South Korea exported very similar items. By the early 1980s, many producer goods were already among the ten leading items in South Korea's exports, thanks to the emphasis on heavy and chemical industries. The bulk of Taiwan's exports however were still nondurable consumer goods (see Table 7.2). The South Korean industrialization might well have been very costly, yet without it, the nation's consumer durable industries, such as automobiles, would not have made great inroads in the world market during the late 1980s.[2]

South Korean big business appears to be better prepared than Taiwan's SMEs for industrial upgrading, which is a process of shifting from price to quality as the basis for competition. Economies of scale are needed for capital-intensive and technology-intensive industries, such as machine tools (Fransman 1986). Moreover, big corporations have the advantage of building up reputations for product quality as well as fostering consumer loyalty. An National Bureau of Economic Research (NBER) study surveying 47 leading product groups (using the four-digit schedule of U.S. import classification) that South Korea and Taiwan exported to the U.S. in 1986 suggests that highly concentrated South Korea industries outperformed SME-dominated Taiwanese industries. The unit value of South Korean exports exceeded that of Taiwan's in 30 product categories (out of 49 categories that were surveyed) by an unweighted average of 27% or an weighted average of around 20% (Rodrik 1988: 15). Higher-quality products from large-size Korean enterprises suggest that in the long run South Korea's exports may have a wider profit margin and may generate more skills as they move up the quality spectrum (Rodrik 1988: 18). As *chaebol* have successfully positioned themselves in many capital-

Table 7.1 The Hoffmann Ratio (Heavy-Light Industry Ratio) of South Korea and Taiwan

	1953	1961	1971	1977
South Korea				
A. light	85.6	76.5	57.0	47.8
B. heavy	14.4	23.5	43.0	52.2
C. a/b	5.93	3.26	1.32	0.92
Taiwan				
A. light	73.4	65.7	46.4	47.2
B. heavy	25.6	34.3	53.6	52.8
C. a/b	2.77	1.91	0.87	0.89

Source: Adapted from Wang (1981: 125).

Table 7.2 Top Ten Export Items of South Korea and Taiwan (as of 1981; unit: % of total exports ad valorem)

South Korea		Taiwan	
Item	%	Item	%
Garment	17.5	Garment	13.0
Ship	13.5	Toys	11.9
Textiles	10.4	TV	8.9
Steel	8.8	Textiles	8.0
Plastics	5.3	Plastics	6.6
Electrical	5.3	Electrical	6.1
Metalwares	5.1	Metalware	4.1
TV	5.1	Travel items	3.2
Toys	4.0	Woodenware	3.0
Sea produce	3.5	Fruit	2.9

Source: Adapted from the Korea's Traders Association (1983: 10-11).

intensive industrial world markets, including the automobile, shipbuilding, and semiconductor sectors, South Korea is touted as the next economic giant in Asia, chasing Japan (Amsden 1989).

However, the merits of the South Korean-style industrial policies are probably overstated. First, for an export-oriented economy, the main thing is probably not the Hoffman ratio, but export performance which can be measured not just in terms of trade composition but (perhaps more importantly) profit margins and market shares as well. While big South Korean firms in the shipbuilding, semiconductor and automobile industries have rarely published their profit ratio, suggesting narrow margins of export profit, Taiwan's SMEs have contributed substantially to the buildup of huge foreign-exchange surpluses, now ranked second in the world in absolute terms. Without a South Korean-style big push for heavy and chemical industrial expansion, the composition (measured by factor intensity) of Taiwan's exports did not differ that much from South Korea's, and Taiwan's exports of manufactured goods to OECD countries continue to mount (Yoo 1990). In fact, while the Korean shares in OECD heavy and chemical industry markets were only marginally below Taiwan's in 1974, the gap in Taiwan's favor widened during the subsequent period (see Table 7.3). Within the heavy and chemical sectors, South Korea's market share was higher than Taiwan's in chemical and basic metals; but in electric and other machinery exports Taiwan outperformed South Korea. South Korean economists concluded that the heavy and chemical industrialization policy either had no effect or was actually counterproductive (Yoo 1990: 99). The policy incurred high opportunity costs, including the weakening of export competitiveness in the light-industry group (Yoo 1990: 99).

By the 1980s, many Korean economists had already concluded that Korea's heavy-handed industrial policy was a mistake (Kim 1984).

If the South Korean approach was not necessarily more efficient, it certainly was more conducive to rent-seeking and corruption, as it involved a higher degree of state intervention and discretionary power than that in Taiwan. Consider, again, the distinction between fiscal incentives and credit allocation. In theory, tax holidays and import-duty rebates are extended to firms that have already performed, while credit is allocated to firms that promise to assume new tasks. The former is an incentive *ex post facto*, while the latter is an incentive *ex ante* the effort. Business activities will have to precede tax benefits, while a project on the drafting board plus good political connections may be sufficient for getting a soft loan. The import duty is rebated only after a manufacturing firm exports its products using imported materials. Corporation income-tax holidays do not mean anything to a corporation until it passes the market test and registers profits.

In contrast, the very moment a firm is granted a soft loan, it can reap instant gains. By diverting part or all of soft loan to informal financial markets and/or by other speculative activities, this firm can receive handsome rents without really producing. In practice, Korean *chaebol* did speculate in real-estate markets and did engage in rent-seeking: recent democratic changes have made this sort of information available.

South Korea's national-champion policy created problems. The government used finance to foster *chaebol* and guide their behavior, but ultimately the government was trapped in its own policy. Easy access to soft loans often led chaebol to overexpand and become highly leveraged, therefore even more dependent on the government's credit line. *Chaebol* being the mainstay of the economy, the government thus depended on *chaebol* for economic performance, and hence was obliged to keep loans flowing. Moral hazard problems arose. Soft loans were intended to underwrite the risks of new industrial undertakings, but they only made *chaebol* reckless. Not infrequently, production capacity expanded far beyond any reasonable projection of exports, leading *chaebol* to inflate export figures ("export goods" idled in *chaebol* warehouses overseas instead of being purchased by foreign buyers). The government certainly could and did penalize any careless or non-performing business group by withholding or withdrawing financial support; at least two *chaebol* were allowed to go bankrupt.[3] But the government could not afford to dump or replace the *chaebol* as a collectivity. Bailouts were therefore more frequent than kickouts. Every round of "economic restructuring" (in 1969/70, 1972, 1979/81 and 1986/88) was a government rescue of financially depressed *chaebol* (Choi 1994).

South Korea's national-champion policy also resulted in drastic increases in the degree of industrial concentration. By any indicator (the distribution of firm size, the share of production capacity, the domestic and export market of leading firms in major industries) South Korean business, as of the mid-1980s, was far more concentrated than Japan's (World Bank 1987). Since the South Korean economy hinged so much on the performance of financially fragile *chaebol*, it was thus more vulnerable to world recessions than its competitor, Taiwan.

The socio-political costs of Korean industrial policy were quite significant. The military-big business alliance isolated the regime from the rest of society, which contributed to a legitimacy problem. The rapid rate of expansion not only made South Korean big business highly leveraged, it also seemed to have preempted the growth of SMEs, which in some cases fell prey to *chaebol*. To the extent that the subcontracting links from *chaebol* (which, like Japanese pre-

Table 7.3 South Korea's and Taiwan's Market Shares in OECD Imports (unit: % of total imports in select sectors)

	Mfg	Light	Heavy	Chem & Chem	Basic Metal	Electric Machines	Other Machine
I. South Korea							
1974	0.86	1.59	0.45	0.22	0.51	1.73	0.18
1976	1.15	2.23	0.51	0.23	0.48	2.20	0.18
1978	1.41	2.76	0.67	0.21	0.75	2.47	0.28
1980	1.17	2.24	0.69	0.20	1.01	2.24	0.25
1982	1.51	2.83	0.92	0.30	1.54	2.51	0.44
1984	1.85	3.21	1.26	0.52	1.79	3.70	0.59
1986	2.03	3.64	1.80	0.58	1.53	3.87	0.94
1987	2.40	3.64	1.80	0.58	1.69	4.80	1.24
II. Taiwan							
1974	0.96	1.73	0.56	0.11	0.08	3.20	0.23
1976	1.08	1.96	0.59	0.14	0.09	2.94	0.27
1978	1.44	2.56	0.84	0.27	0.23	3.54	0.47
1980	1.43	2.70	0.86	0.18	0.11	3.52	0.56
1982	1.85	3.42	1.19	0.25	0.27	4.09	0.83
1984	2.46	4.30	1.73	0.39	0.46	4.74	1.43
1986	2.57	4.36	1.76	0.43	0.49	4.42	1.50
1987	2.87	4.52	2.11	0.47	0.49	5.09	1.89
III. South Korea's Shares Less Taiwan's							
1974	-0.10	-0.14	-0.12	0.11	0.43	-1.47	-0.06
1976	0.07	0.27	-0.08	0.09	0.39	-0.74	-0.09
1978	-0.03	0.20	-0.17	-0.06	0.53	-1.07	-0.19
1980	-0.26	-0.47	-0.17	0.02	0.90	-1.28	-0.31
1982	-0.34	-0.59	-0.27	0.05	1.27	-1.57	-0.39
1984	-0.60	-1.08	-0.47	0.13	1.34	-1.04	-0.84
1986	-0.54	-1.07	-0.32	0.11	1.04	-0.55	-0.56
1987	-0.47	-0.88	-0.31	0.11	1.20	-0.29	-0.64

Source: Adapted from Yoo (1990: 96-97).

war zaibatsu, remain family enterprises) to smaller firms existed, the ties were perceived as exploitative, a manifestation of predatory capitalism, unlike the benevolent or "goodwill capitalism" in postwar Japan where big firms absorb market risk on behalf of the loyal and technologically improving small firms (Dore 1983; Kawasaki and McMillan 1987). A careful empirical analysis is needed to shed light on the nature of subcontracting links to determine whether South Korea had a system of predatory capitalism.[4] But given the thoroughness of pro-*chaebol* policy, the perception of predatory capitalism was quite entrenched.

Predatory capitalism, perceived or real, imparted a sense of unfairness, permitted the opposition to mobilize any social force other than big business, and aggravated class and distributive politics. SMEs, especially the self-employee type, could have been an avenue for upward social mobility for unskilled labor, an "exit" option that could have made Korean labor less militant, with a better bargaining position vis-à-vis the management. *Chaebol* were blamed for the deterioration of income distribution in the 1970s and early 1980s, given that capital became a major input in industrial production and that the return to labor, in aggregate terms, was eclipsed by the return to capital-asset holders. Though being instrumental for South Korean industrial transformation, *chaebol* and their sponsor, the military regime, were blamed for any undesirable externalities associated with rapid industrialization.

Here we see the merits of the Taiwanese approach to industrial promotion. Promoting many sectors, allowing many firms to compete and avoiding highly discretionary policy not only instilled a sense of fairness, but also minimized the blame on the government for economic problems. SMEs not only have given Taiwan's economy a number of important characteristics, including flexible production and diversified competitiveness, they have also blurred the borderline between social classes (farmers, workers and the self-employed). The performance and self-reliance of SMEs has allowed the government in Taiwan to escape from being captured by big business, a fate experienced by the Korean government.

Surely, Taiwan's SMEs were not without drawbacks. They also had weak financial structures, though not as leveraged as *chaebol*. Lacking economies of scale, they could not engage in research and development. Lacking economies of scope, they had difficulty in building up their brand name in international markets. Many of them remained subcontractors for foreign firms. The semiconductor industry best illustrates the constraints on the SME-dominated Taiwanese economy (Schieve 1990). In the absence of industrial conglomerates, integrated circuits (IC) designed by the abundant Taiwanese engineers in small firms during the early 1980s were all licensed to South Korean and Japanese firms. The proceeds of technology sales were far short of the costs of research and development, and domestic IC users such as home-consumer electronics firms remained at the mercy of foreign IC producers.

These SME problems are not beyond remedy, however. The government has been assisting in the transformation of small and medium enterprises into modern, market-oriented business units via three interrelated policies. It uses tax incentives and technological support to encourage mergers and help forge the nexus between component producers and assembly firms. It also sponsors all sorts of technology institutions to diffuse engineering know-how and skills. The government itself even undertakes basic research and development activities, and coordinates joint research projects among firms.

It is important to note that in trying to induce the expansion and merger of existing SMEs, the government in Taiwan continues to avoid promoting South Korean-style industrial conglomerates (Cheng 1993). Instead it is encouraging sufficiently large firms in medium- and high-technology sectors that have the potential to create their own brand names and marketing channels. A model to emulate is the type of ever-growing, specialized, reputable American corporation, with its remarkable product recognition, such as the Apple Computer. These dynamic and profitable firms are in no way comparable to industrial behemoths with high-flying (sometimes tarnished) images, such as IBM. Another model that Taiwanese industrial policy advocates have in mind is the sort of national-image-making company in small European countries, such as Philips Electronics in the Netherlands. Still another model is homemade: a few successful medium-size, yet renowned Taiwanese companies such as Kennex (in sporting goods) and Acer (in computers), that have impressive world market shares in their well-delimited product ranges.

Because of the continued predominance of SMEs in the industrial export sector, Taiwan appears to have lagged behind its keen competitor, South Korea, in truly capital-intensive industries such as shipbuilding, steel and automobiles. Taiwan's macroeconomic performance, however, has been as good as South Korea's, if not more so; generally speaking, Taiwan's economic growth rates were only slightly lower than South Korea's, but prices were more stable and foreign exchange earnings were higher in Taiwan. To neoclassical economists, macroeconomic performance and national welfare, not industrial structure, are the litmus test of economic success. Moreover, Taiwan's industry is by no means shrinking, despite the surge of Taiwan's direct investment into Southeast Asia since the Taiwan dollar appreciation in 1986. The Taiwanese industrialists are carving out international niches in small-scale, skill-intensive production, such as automobile components, speciality steel, customer-designed electronics, and numerically controlled (computer-programmed) machine tools.

Convergence

While academicians may continue to debate the comparative advantages of the two approaches to industrial promotion in Taiwan and South Korea, policymakers of these two NICs are emulating each other and their industrial policies seem to be converging rather than diverging. South Korea is replacing its sectoral policy with "functional incentives" (Leipziger 1988) and phasing out credit allocations for industrial promotion, while Taiwan is experimenting with subsidized lending to strategic industries. Taiwan is assisting its SMEs to grow bigger, while South Korea attempts to revive SMEs.

However, while industrial policies can be redesigned in these two NICs, their industrial organizations remain very sticky. Industrial organization, once created, has a life of its own and cannot be easily remolded. Taiwan continues to be a land of SMEs. Incentives encouraging merger are rarely exploited. SMEs are slow in upgrading their production; more visible is their exodus from Taiwan to low-wage countries to extend the life of their products in world markets.

To redress its lopsided and highly skewed industrial organization, the South Korean government has several times introduced affirmative-action policies, such as increasing total lending to SMEs, and setting a ceiling on total loans to *chaebol*, as well as ordering *chaebol* to vacate some business lines which are supposed to be SMEs' reserve domains. Under new economic policies, which include an effort to dismantle the heavy-handed industrial policy, corporate management can become rational and technically oriented, rather than rent-seeking (Rhee 1987). But South Korea's economy continues to be a function of *chaebol*, and the government seems to be learning to live with them rather than reshaping them.

Notes

1. Since this paper contends that policy for the promotion of industrialization is a crucial factor shaping industrial organization, a few words on the cultural hypothesis are in order. Many have suggested that the proliferation of small enterprises in Taiwan, as versus the formation of big business in South Korea, is a function of Chinese cultural attributes. The Chinese mentality of "would rather be a chicken head than an ox tail" as well as the inheritance system--one that distributes wealth equally among all offspring, rather than one that designates one heir (or the primogeniture)--supposedly prevent the emergence of big enterprises (Greenhalph 1984; Wong 1985). But South Korea in the '50s and overseas South Korean communities also witnessed small entrepreneurship. Many studies have shown that South Korean conglomerates or national chaebols had been primarily family-oriented; only during the turn of the '80s did they begin to implant multi-divisional control systems found in modern corporations. Small entrepreneurship is not limited to the Chinese community, it also thrives in India, indeed in any industrial society in the

earliest stage of capitalist development. And only Japan has a primogeniture system and the praxis of adopting "capable managers" to head the family business. Cultural factors may be important, but one cannot demonstrate their relevance unless one controls for economic, institutional, and policy factors.

2. Other factors were equally, if not more, important, such as the appreciation of the Japanese yen as a result of the Plaza Accord, which forced Japan out of the world low-end automobile market.

3. These two were Kuje and Myunsung; note that political reasons were as significant as economic reasons for their collapse; they were reportedly either flirting with the opposition or refusing to subscribe their share in political contribution.

4. Preliminary findings from my own survey on the textile industry show that there are limits to which big enterprises can squeeze SMEs, and some risk-sharing arrangement has been at least tried between two sides of subcontracting links.

References

Amsden, Alice H. 1989. Asia's Next Giant. Cambridge: Cambridge University Press.

Bradford, Colin, Jr., and W. H. Branson. 1987. "Patterns of Trade and Structural Change." In their (eds.) *Trade, and Structural Change in Pacific Asia*. Chicago: University of Chicago Press.

Chang, Daljoong. 1982. *Political Economy of Japanese Foreign Investment in Korea*. Ph.D. dissertation. Berkeley: University of California.

Cheng, Tun-jen. 1990. "Political Regimes and Development Strategies: South Korea, and Taiwan." In Gary Gereffi and Donald Wyman (eds.) *Manufacturing Miracles: Paths of Industrialization in Latin America, and East Asia*. Princeton: Princeton University Press.

______. 1993. "Distinctions Between the Taiwanese and South Korean Approaches to Economic Development." *Journal of East Asian Affairs*. (Winter/Spring), Vol.7, 1: 116-136.

______. 1994. "Guarding the Commanding Heights: the State as Banker in Taiwan." In Stephan Haggard, Chung Lee, and Sylvia Maxfield (eds.) *Politics of Finance*. Ithaca: Cornell University Press.

Choi, Byung Sun. 1994. "Government, Financial Systems, and Economic Development: The Case of South Korea." In Haggard, Lee, and Maxfield, *Politics of Finance...*

Dore, Ronald. 1983. "Goodwill and the Spirit of Market Capitalism." *British Journal of Sociology*. 34:4: 459-482.

Eckert, Carter. 1991. *Offspring of Empire: the Koch'ang Kims and the Colonial Origins of South Korean Capitalism, 1876-1945*. Seattle: University of Washington Press.

Fransman, M. 1986. "International Competitiveness, Technical Change and the State: The Machine Tool Industry in Taiwan and Japan." *World Development*. 14:12: 1375-1396.

Greenhalgh, Susan. 1984. "Networks and Their Nodes: Urban Society on Taiwan." *China Quarterly*. September, 99: 529-552.

Kawasaki, Seichi, and John McMillan. 1987. "The Design of Contracts: Evidence from Japanese Subcontracting." *Journal of the Japanese and International Economies*. 1: 327-349.

Kim, Kihwan. 1984. *The South Korean Economy*. Seoul: South Korea Development Institute.

Korea's Traders Association (The). 1983. *Export Competition of the Four East Asian NICs* [text in Korean].

Leipziger, Danny M. 1988. "Industrial Restructuring in South Korea." *World Development*. 16:1: 121-135.

Rhee, Sungsupp. 1987. "Policy Reforms of the Eighties and Industrial Adjustments in South Korean Economy." South Korea Development Institute. Working Paper No. 8708.

Rodrik, Dani. 1988. "Industrial Organization and Product Quality: Evidence from South Korean and Taiwanese Export." National Bureau of Economic Research. Working paper No. 2722.

Shieve, Chi. 1990. "The Next Stage of Industrialization in Taiwan and South Korea." In Gereffi and Wyman, *Manufacturing Miracles...*

Tsiang, S.C. 1980. "Exchange Rate, Interest Rate, and Economic Development." In L.R. Klein et al. (eds.) *Quantitative Economics and Development*. New York: Academic Press.

Wang, Jin-li. 1981. "A Comparative Analysis of the Structural Transformation in the Taiwanese and South Korean Manufacturing Sectors." *Economic Research*. December [text in Chinese].

Watanabe, Toshio. 1978. "Heavy and Chemical Industrialization and Economic Development in the Republic of South Korea." *The Developing Economies*. (December) 15:4: 385-407.

Westphal, Larry E. 1978. "Industrial Incentives in the Republic of China. Taiwan." Mimeo.

______. 1990. Industrial Policy in an Export-propelled Economy: Lessons from South Korea's Experience." *The Journal of Economic Perspectives*. (Summer) 4:3.

Wong, Siu-lun. 1985. "The Chinese Family Firm: A Model." *The British Journal of Sociology*. (March) 36:1: 58-72.

World Bank (The). 1987. *South Korea: Managing the Industrial Transition*. Vol. II. Selected Topics and Case Studies. Washington.

_______. 1993. *The East Asian Miracle: Economic Growth and Public Policy.* Oxford University Press.

Wu, Hui-lin, and Tein-chen Chou. 1987. "Small and Medium Enterprises and Economic Development in Taiwan." *The Proceedings of Conference on Economic Development in the Republic of China on Taiwan.* Chung-hua Institute for Economic Research. July, 153-181.

Yoo, Jung-ho. 1990. "The Industrial Policy of the 1970s and the Evolution of the Manufacturing Sector in South Korea." South Korea Development Institute. Working paper No. 9017.

8

ASEAN Industrial Policies

Donald Crone

Coherent government-sponsored programs to stimulate private domestic manufacturing activities have not been common in South East Asia. It is undeniable that Singapore, Malaysia, Thailand, Indonesia and the Philippines have industrialized rapidly, if not consistently. There is good reason for the widespread attention to their industrial growth and potential. Their development features some industrial policy objectives, in that they aim to enhance manufacturing and associated employment, in some cases they increase national competitiveness, and they intend positive domestic spillovers. But the results are very different from those that would normally be attributed to industrial policies, for example in South Korea or Japan.

Rather, what has characterized South East Asia are personalistic industrialization programs. Several of the basic components of industrial policy have been absent: sector selection has not been coherent, as personalistic political connections to the state often determine economic policy support. Paternalistic governments have more often been the key actors, rather than the private sector. Manufacturing activities are predominantly those of foreign investors, perhaps with domestic partners. Inefficient industries have often been supported because of strategic alliances between government leaders and entrepreneurs, public and private. The industrial structures created are largely denationalized, dependent on foreign multinational firms, and their outward-oriented sectors frequently have an enclave character.

This has been the case because none of the ASEAN states in their early development met the socio-political requisites of an industrial policy. The rapidly developing literature on industrialization and economic transformation suggests that there are three core socio-political conditions that must be substantially present if coherent economic transformation is to take place (Evans 1992; Grindle and Thomas 1991; Haggard 1990; Ng et al. 1992; Wade 1988). First, an autonomous state agency must have the technocratic capacity to formulate policy goals and guide private actors toward a common end. This requires a high degree of corporate coherence among agency personnel, reinforced by meritocratic selection and high social regard, and mission-oriented tasking within the government. Japan's MITI provides an example. Second, there must be capital and capitalists available to mobilize. This requires the development of rather large corporate structures, and attitudes that lean toward entrepreneurial, rather than rentier, activities. South Korea's chaebol can be taken as a model. And third, the pattern of state-society linkages in the business sector must produce an embedded state capacity, an ability to direct development cooperatively. This presumes that civil associations exist, that barriers to functional state-society linkages, such as kinship or ethnic stratifications, are not determinative, that an ethos of cooperation exists between government and private actors, and that the political coalition is shaped in a manner that will support economic transition. The pattern of relationships in Japan--between MITI and the myriad of industrial associations--is instructive here. Overall, the demands of industrial transformation are high, including accurate intelligence, inventiveness, active agency, and sophisticated responses to changing reality (Evans 1990: 148).

This chapter focuses on the interaction between socio-political structures and industrial policy in ASEAN. It argues that certain features of their socio-political development blocked their abilities to pursue industrial policies. This resulted in a second-best personalistic state-directed industrialization. However, many of these structural obstacles are rapidly being overcome. The chapter is not just a tale of the "dog that didn't bark": some ASEAN states are on the threshold of industrial policy, and some have crossed it.

ASEAN Industrialization

One of the notable features of the ASEAN economies is their rapid industrial growth over the past several decades. A central thrust of their development strategies has been to transform themselves from primarily agricultural economies into industrial ones. Table 8.1 shows the degree to which that policy goal has been met, as well as the heavy reliance on international markets for manufacturing growth, a necessity given the initial inadequacy of ASEAN domestic markets.

In the 1950s and 1960s highly protected import-substituting investment (ISI) was prominent throughout the region. From 1950 to the early 1970s the Philippines stressed import substitution, which led to rapid early expansion of production. Singapore's first elected government literally campaigned on a platform of ISI manufacturing. Up through the late 1960s, Malaysia focused primarily on expanding locally made consumer goods. Into the early 1970s Thailand emphasized food processing, consumer goods, and construction materials within an ISI framework. Indonesia in effect insured stagnation of manufacturing through its strict ISI regime of the 1950s and 1960s. Each country rather rapidly encountered the natural limits of this strategy in underdeveloped economies where an inability to spread widely within sectors or deeply into other sectors is inhibited by shallow demand, paucity of entrepreneurial resources, and domestic capital shortages.

In each case, foreign investment was a quite visible component of manufacturing. Each country except Thailand inherited extensive investment from the former colonial powers. As a proportion of total investment in the mid-1970s, foreign investment was almost 70% in Singapore, over 50% in the Philippines, Malaysia, and Indonesia, and 30% in Thailand. At the end of the 1970s, foreign companies were thought to control close to 50% of all manufacturing investment in the region, concentrated in export sectors. Well over 80% of Singapore's exports derived from foreign firms (Crone 1983: 97).

This extensive reliance on foreign firms conflicted with the rising nationalist climate in some states during the 1960s and 1970s. In every ASEAN member there were public expressions of hostility toward foreign investment, ranging from student riots in Indonesia and Thailand to public debates in Malaysia and the Philippines (Crone 1981). Only in Singapore was the climate more moderate, although even there the political opposition cited excessive promotion of foreign firms as one fundamental difference with government policies. In part, one might attribute this to a climate promoted by widespread critiques of some practices of multinational firms. ASEAN was active in global arenas demanding a New International Economic Order premised on the inherent exploitative character of multinational firms. In the anti-foreign climate of the 1970s, the low industrial development of the ASEAN economies made the few foreign firms more prominent, and national elites were unsure of their abilities to control them. The result was considerable ambivalence toward foreign enterprises, with hesitant steps toward inducing their presence followed by the imposition of new controls to discourage them.

Table 8.1 ASEAN Industrialization

	Industry/GDP		Exports (Primary/Mfd)	
	1965	1989	1960	1988
Indonesia	8.4 %	40 %	100/0	71/29
Malaysia	10.4 %	34 %	94/6	55/44
Philippines	17.5 %	35 %	93/7	38/62
Singapore	15.3 %	37 %	74/26	26/74
Thailand	15.5 %	41 %	98/2	48/52

Sources: Asian Development Outlook, 1990; World Development Report, 1990; Economic and Social Survey of the Pacific, 1976.

State firms expanded rapidly into manufacturing. The Indonesian nationalizations of the 1950s established the military in the economy, a role that was to expand. Thailand's developmental push of the late 1950s was led by state firms. In Malaysia, Singapore and the Philippines, industry was overwhelmingly foreign owned in the 1950s, but the state took a leading role in the 1970s, albeit by very different paths. The Singapore government became an investor in areas like shipbuilding, and in partnership with foreign firms across industrial sectors. Malaysian interests bought out selected foreign sectors, particularly tin and rubber, and forced partnerships with state-controlled holding companies. The Marcos government in the Philippines used state control of finance and "crony capitalists" to obtain controlling positions in major industrial conglomerates. Controls acted to close sectors that were increasingly occupied by state firms.

Those areas left open to foreign firms were, in fact, focused. The primary sectors were in resource extraction and light export manufacturing. Oil and gas in Indonesia were a prime example of the first, but were also representative in that the government gradually imposed stricter state control through contract provisions that channelled more rents to the state. Electrical and electronics manufacture in Singapore represent the leading edge of the latter trend, one that later spread to each ASEAN country. The notable point is the export orientation of areas left to foreign firms, the essence of the ASEAN industrialization strategy.

The forces propelling this type of "industrial policy" can easily be identified. First, professional resources within each state were quite thin. "Technocrats" were few in numbers, and frequently concentrated in Ministries of Finance and Trade. Controlling investment through edict and a screening board was the common pattern, but the Boards of Investment had little technical capacity and less prestige. Actual policy outcomes were constrained by far more powerful social forces. For example, Indonesia's economic policy making was severely constrained by the vested political interests within the government. The power of the technocrats to implement policies which conflicted with the interests of military-associated firms remained very limited. Major economic institutions, such as the national oil company, Pertamina, and the rice trading agency, Bulog, were managed by army officers who used them to siphon off funds for patronage. Many important developmental projects had to be allocated to firms with military connections which often failed to meet technical criteria; conditions imposed by the technocrats were often waived. (Crouch 1984: 83).

Second, local capital was relatively scarce. Perhaps as important, those who had it operated within a tradition of trade, property investment, speculation, and land ownership--all rent-seeking activities (Yoshihara 1988). But most important, local capitalists were overwhelmingly Chinese. This led to overt restrictions in Thailand and Indonesia, what were in essence quotas in Malaysia after 1969, and restrictions on citizenship in the Philippines that were aimed at curtailing the Chinese economic role. Relations between the governments and national private entrepreneurs were everywhere tense. Personalistic means of control were common, whether "Ali-Baba" in Malaysia, military board members in Thailand, or military-Chinese "partnerships" in Indonesia. The most common group of domestic entrepreneurs were treated like pariahs.

Third, relationships between state and society were hostile. Coalitions supporting South East Asian governments were overly narrow: Thai military and bureaucrats dominated other social forces; Malaysia's dominant party, the United Malays National Organization, commanded support only from the secular Malays; Indonesia's military coercively excluded other social groups; Singapore's "administrative state" had yet to build a social base; Philippine factionalism was rife (Crone 1988). Collaborative relationships between government units and groups of entrepreneurs were completely absent. The Malaysian Industrial Development Authority in the late 1970s had no contact with local Chinese entrepreneurs, as a government dominated by Malay interests saw itself in opposition to them. Few independent associations of local entrepreneurs existed in South East Asia. The governments and their Boards of Investment dealt overwhelmingly with foreign businesses. Often, these relationships were quite collaborative, as the role of Singapore's International Chamber of Commerce (representing foreign firms) in the National Wages Council (the body that established yearly salary guidelines) illustrated. With their own domestic entrepreneurs, high officials maintained only parasitic relationships.

The combination of state intervention, foreign firms, and weak domestic capital resulted in what one analyst has called "ersatz capitalism", lacking domestic technology, but relying on foreign firms for it. Certain groups of domestic entrepreneurs--the Chinese--were discriminated against, and government policy was of low quality (Yoshihara 1988). State and foreign-led industrialization were the only options.

The environment of the 1960s and 1970s prevented a focused industrial policy due to weak bureaucratic capabilities, inadequate capital resources, and fragmented state-social linkages. State-led industrialization was one possible path, and it was taken. Foreign-led industrialization was another, and it led. The result was a combination of rather inefficient industrial enterprises in some sectors, and foreign dominance in others. By the 1980s, these strategies were under attack from both domestic and foreign pressures. Personalistic industrialization wasn't working in the international economic marketplace or in the domestic political one.

Social and Political Transformations

The "industrial policy" of the 1960s and 1970s had, to some degree, met its objective. In most ASEAN countries, the economy was in the hands of "local" forces, albeit mostly the state and its cronies (Yoshihara 1988). Nationalistic objectives were met with the combination of state industry and extensive crony capitalism. The partial industrial transformation, however, was accompanied by social and political transformations that to a large extent reshaped the environment.

The combination of domestic savings and external investment greatly increased the availability of capital during the 1980s, as Table 8.2 shows. Capital shortages were no longer a characteristic problem in South East Asia as savings rates increased dramatically, and the contribution of foreign investment to domestic capital formation had become correspondingly smaller by the early 1980s, while it increased in absolute terms (Lim and Pang 1991: 35). Some of the ASEAN economies, Singapore and Malaysia in particular, had even become capital exporters. In all of the ASEAN countries, domestic banks, either state or private, had by and large displaced foreign banks. Capital availablilty had changed from a limiting condition of industrial development in the 1960s to a facilitating condition by the 1980s.

At the same time, the number of South East Asian entrepreneurs and the size of their businesses increased vastly. In part, this was a positive reflection of the state enterprise efforts, in that they occasionally served as a training ground for individuals who then moved to the private sector, perhaps more in Malaysia than elsewhere. In other cases, state patronage was instrumental in the development of large private entrepreneurs. This was the case to some degree in Thailand, where merchant bankers built large conglomerates from bases connected with bureaucratic patrons in the 1960s; but agribusiness groups grew

Table 8.2 ASEAN Capital Accumulation

	Gross Domestic Savings Rate		Foreign Investment (US millions)	
	1970	1991	1970	1991
Indonesia	14 %	36 %	83	1 482
Malaysia	27 %	30 %	94	3 455
Philippines	22 %	19 %	-29	544
Singapore	18 %	47 %	93	1 066[a]
Thailand	21 %	32 %	43	2 014

[a] 1988

Source: World Development Report (various years).

without close state connections in the 1970s, and manufacturing groups developed more in alliance with foreign capital (Akira in McVey 1992; Hewison 1989). By the late 1970s, the combination had created a dynamic core of business leadership centered in large corporate holdings.

More decisive in Malaysia and in Indonesia were programs designed to foster the development of "indigenous" (as opposed to local Chinese) business. Malaysia's New Economic Policy (NEP) after 1971 channelled vast resources into the building of a "bumiputra" (Malay) business class through educational and state preferences (Gale 1981). In the 1970s the numbers of Malay professionals and managers more than doubled, substantially increasing their share in these occupations relative to other races (Jesudason, 1989: 112). Still, the major initial beneficiaries of the NEP were those who already had direct access to wealth, individuals connected to the royal families who created "princely" business holdings of increasing size (and controversy). By the late 1980s the ruling party, confident enough in a small group of Malay entrepreneurs, was able to privatize business holdings of the ruling party to select groups, fostering the creation of large (or larger) Malay conglomerates (Milne 1992). A new generation of Chinese entrepreneurs found grounds for cooperation with politically connected Malays and state agencies to construct large conglomerates, and more "traditional" Chinese businesses expanded into conglomerates, perhaps defensively. The balance, however, shifted decisively toward Malaysian business ownership (including parastatal trustee ownership) in a wide variety of industrial sectors serving both domestic and international markets (Heng in McVey 1992: 131). The NEP thus accelerated the formation of a Malay business class, and fostered a dynamic reshaping of the Chinese business class.

Indonesia in the early 1970s also initiated a "pribumi" policy, which included many non-Chinese business operators in pervasive clientelist networks. Although the ethnic basis of distinction was de-emphasized during the 1980s in favor of all "weak" national business interests, requirements for domestic partnerships and preserves of "domestic-only" businesses provided a larger number of opportunities for domestic entrepreneurs. While the outcome favored those with close political connections, especially with the Suharto family, by the 1980s a sizable increase in domestic entrepreneurs had occurred including former military officers and bureaucrats as well as civilians (Robison 1986). Truly large business empires were also created, mostly in the form of ethnic Chinese joint ventures with military units and figures, the so-called "cukong" system; some of these had even become transnational by the early 1980s.

Several of the ASEAN members also attempted, with little success, to imitate South Korea and Japan in fostering large business structures that might address the shortage of entrepreneurship. "Thailand Inc." illustrates: In the late 1970s, Thai technocrats, based on World Bank recommendations, proposed that Thailand attempt to emulate the developmental successes of countries such as

South Korea and Singapore. The concept was introduced by the Social Action Party (SAP) and supported by banking interests behind the SAP, but was opposed by industrial interests represented by the Chart Thai Party; implementation of the policy was thus obstructed (Ho 1980: 40-46). President Marcos' "crony capitalist" structures in the Philippines had more severe problems (Hawes 1987). Centered in agricultural monopolies, they were so shot with corruption that they provoked opposition to the regime in the business circles of Makati toward the end of Marcos' rule. If Philippine industrial restructuring attempts of the 1970s had any effect on the number and size of domestic entrepreneurs, it is likely that it reduced them, as smaller "national entrepreneurs" were forced out of the economic system in favor of those linked to foreign capital (and to Marcos personally) (Broad 1988). State-led attempts to create large private industrial structures were not successful.

Singapore did not try this strategy, relying primarily on foreign firms and the state for entrepreneurship until the mid 1980s. By the late 1970s foreign firms accounted for more than half of employment, two-thirds of value added and over 80% of exports in manufacturing; at the same time some five hundred government -linked or-owned firms penetrated most sectors of the economy, comprising a significant pool of domestic entrepreneurial talent (Lee and Low 1990). The number of private Singaporean entrepreneurs also increased, but they were concentrated in smaller service enterprises while the state and foreign business dominated manufacturing. The overwhelming dominance of foreign firms and government inhibited the development of local entrepreneurs (Krause et al 1987: 95). Reacting largely to recession, in the late 1980s Singapore adopted a more self-reliant policy to assist the development of small domestic entrepreneurs as a buffer to international business cycles (Lee and Low 1990: 184ff). Whether the Singapore state can create private entrepreneurship to match that of the public sector remains to be seen.

The pool of domestic business leaders matured considerably in most ASEAN countries during the 1970s and into the 1980s. What had been a limiting condition on industrial growth (and other economic development) in the 1960s was, in most cases, substantially alleviated by the late 1970s. State sponsorship contributed greatly to this outcome in several countries, but was largely unsuccessful in fostering private domestic conglomerates; one might question the sincerity of state efforts in this direction, as state conglomerates were certainly developed, and in some cases dominated the economy.

The great expansion of state involvement in the economy also directly affected the numbers and positions of technically skilled government personnel, often referred to as "technocrats." In every ASEAN state the role of public spending increased quite dramatically in the 1960s and 1970s: for example, government expenditures as a percentage of gross national product increased from 19% to 38% in Malaysia from 1965 to 1980, from 9% to 27% in Indonesia, and from 11% to 22% in Singapore (Crone 1985: 10). Many of the officials administering expanded programs, particularly in the economy, could be considered technocrats (Milne 1982). Their increased presence was bolstered in its effect by a general cultural predilection to accord respect to authoritative actors (Ng et al. 1992). Given the importance of technical skill in industrial policy, the relative position of technocrats in the different ASEAN states is worth examination.

The most dramatic shift took place in Singapore. As Milne notes (1982: 421), because there had been no real political competition since about 1965 in the Republic a policy of promoting technocrats into government after that time was greatly facilitated. The "Second Generation" of leaders who now occupy the highest political positions, including the elected Presidency, are all technocrats, a feat duplicated in the region only during the brief Anand government of Thailand in 1991. Technocrats have virtually absorbed government in Singapore. This has much significance for industrial policy, especially as shaped by the Economic Development Board. This highly prestigious and effective agency implements government preferences, in guiding the involvement of firms (mostly foreign) in Singapore's manufacturing sector (Encarnation and Wells 1985).

Elsewhere in the region, political figures remain in control, but technocrats play a larger role. Malaysia's relative shortage of technically trained Malays (Chinese and Indians were predominant in this area) caused emphasis on their training and combination of technical and political skills, especially in such new agencies as the Prime Minister's Office. In Thailand, the traditionally strong bureaucracy, primarily the domain of generalists, was infused with a large cohort of mostly foreign-trained technical personnel. In the mid-1970s one-third of the highest grade in the bureaucracy and one-fifth of the next grade had foreign training, much of it sponsored by the United States Agency for International Development (Muscat 1990: 64). In the Philippines the Marcos administration, especially after the declaration of martial law, boosted the number of technocrats in government economic agencies. He also increased the importance of those agencies in policymaking, in liaison with international financial institutions. The National Economic and Development Administration (NEDA) was a notable example (Broad 1988: 72-80). Cesar Virata, a classic technocrat and Prime Minister from 1981 to 1986, served to highlight their more prominent role in government, but policy decisions were made in the Presidential palace, often without regard to their technocratic merit.

In Indonesia, the military government brought a core of technocrats, sometimes referred to as the "Berkeley Mafia," into central financial ministries with the New Order government at the end of the 1960s, to rationalize economic policy and reopen links with international financial institutions and multinational corporations (Milne 1982: 412). But they have also been carefully balanced with other factions in the struggle over policy mediated by President Suharto, rising in influence in times of crisis (such as that of Pertamina in 1976 and of the oil price crash in the mid-1980s), but eclipsed during prosperity by nationalists and the military (Bresnan 1993: 72ff).

The relative status of bureaucratic actors has been important for their effectiveness. Government has traditionally been one of the most prestigious occupations in Thailand, a status reinforced by increasing technical competence. In Singapore rigorous meritocratic selection and the tradition of impartiality firmly cements the high status of upper-level civil servants. The Malaysian case is similar, if somewhat less meritocratic and clean. In the Philippines and Indonesia manifest subservience to politicians reduces the authority and legitimacy of civil servants, in the latter case especially because of the colonial and immediate post-colonial experience. Business leaders, except in Singapore, seem to prefer to deal with political leaders rather than senior civil servants.

Partly as a result of the forgoing changes, political coalitions altered from the 1960s through the 1980s. Each of the ASEAN governments had an initially narrow political base, centered in the military in Thailand and Indonesia, in an extended landed elite in the Philippines, in a nearly rootless political party in Singapore, and in a shaky multiracial coalition in Malaysia. The rise of a business class challenged the base in Thailand and Indonesia, while the military core lost its unity. The Malaysian regime was purposefully broadened after 1971, and business interests supplemented the rural school teacher core of UMNO by the 1980s. Singapore came to rely on a strong multinational-firm base, while broadening the party's popular base in the housing estates and appealing to the new middle class. Only in the Philippines did the regime of the 1990s resemble that of the 1960s, despite considerable rotation among individuals through the Marcos and Aquino years. In Singapore, Malaysia, and Thailand, the state emerged with greater capacity to effect change. This did not happen in Indonesia, where hard authoritarianism has limited state capacity. In the Philippines optimism is the only solace (Crone 1988).

Where all the changes combine--a more capable state staffed by technically competent civil servants, with greater financial resources, and a larger pool of entrepreneurs--there has also been discernable movement toward linking it all together. Networks of civil servants in key agencies and private entrepreneurs are emerging, sometimes facilitated by changes in government attitudes toward the role of the private sector in economic development.

Malaysia has experienced such integrative change. In its early 1980s attempt to create "Malaysia Inc." the Prime Minister stated (Quoted in Nor 1984: 2):

> The Malaysia Incorporated concept, therefore, requires that the private and public sectors see themselves as sharing the same fate and destiny as partners, shareholders and workers within the same "corporation", which in this case is the Nation. The "corporation" will only prosper if this commercial and economic arm, that is, the private sector, does its best to promote such things as production, marketing and sales, while optimizing the returns on investment. The service arm of the "corporation", in other words the Government, will provide all the support needed.

To some degree, this philosophy was the outcome of successful attempts to develop Malay entrepreneurs, and it influenced the direction of subsequent privatization efforts, as they focused heavily on turning government business operations over to "private" firms with solid government connections and "bumiputra" credentials (Gomez 1990; Nor 1984). It marked a shift in economic strategy from reliance on foreign investors as its partners against domestic Chinese business interests (Jesudason 1989). Still, the predominant strategy for the 1980s was state-led industrialization (Bowie 1991: 111ff).

In Indonesia, as noted above, technocrats and managements connected to the state dominate economic policymaking. At least in the major economic sectors, clientele systems determine outcomes, not independent and cooperative relations between economic bureaucrats and private sector groups. However, in part due to the economic pressures of the mid-1980s, which increased the importance of production outside the state-associated sectors, and in part due to the development of a larger private sector organized in business associations, recent analyses reveal slowly-developing influence of business groups on economic policy in some sectors (Macintyre 1990), but not in others (Doner 1991: 233). At least around the margins of the Indonesian political economy, there is a modest trend toward combining the strengths of the public and private sectors for economic development.

The Singapore model also combines the public and private sector, but until quite recently it was the foreign private sector. From the inception of multinational-led growth a close network of international executives and public sector employees, primarily in the EDB and Ministry of Finance but also in the National Wages Council, has cooperatively developed the island's economy. More recently, with the emphasis on indigenous small business, the network has extended to domestic entrepreneurs. With both foreign and domestic private actors, though, the state retains the leading role, creating niches for private actors to fill.

In contrast, Thailand's lively and influential business sector has developed more autonomously. Anek (1992) argues that the image of a bureaucratic polity dominated by military and government figures is no longer applicable. He attributes this change to the rapid growth of firms and business associations since the mid-1970s. During the 1980s administrations started developing cooperative relations with private sector organizations, a process that continues. This has been undertaken in the traditional Thai top-down manner, as these quotes from the Sixth National Economic and Social Development Plan reveal (Thailand 1987: 189):

> The government will promote more participation by private sector organizations in the process of economic administration. For instance, certain duties and responsibilities will be assigned to private sector organizations... The government will promote and strengthen organizations in the private sector... The government will encourage cooperation between the public and private sectors to spread systematically into various fields of development.

The administrative mentality has not changed entirely, but social forces are weakening it.

In the Philippines, the Marcos years eroded previous collaborative government-business relationships. Deinstitutionalization of those relationships resulted from the growth of "crony" firms' ties to the Presidential palace and a concentration of decisions there, while the role of economic bureaucrats was undercut (Doner 1991: 245). Chaotic policymaking based on special relationships continued in subsequent administrations.

Social change and political transformations have thus affected the environment of industrial policymaking in each ASEAN country. In some, notably Malaysia, Singapore, and Thailand, the combined changes have been significant, but in Indonesia they have been limited, while in the Philippines there has been very little change.

Directions in Industrial Policy

Socio-political environments have changed in some cases, altering the structure in which industrial policy is made. Policy outcomes, however, involve not just structures, but also active agents. Have South East Asian agents capitalized on new opportunities? Current policy mixes do suggest that change is underway where blockages have been eroded.

Singapore's industrial policy has been the most dynamic in ASEAN over the past decade. It shifted from promoting multinational manufacturing in the 1960s and 1970s to a "high wage" policy in 1979 which was directed toward raising levels of technology (Krause et al. 1987). By the late 1980s increasing attention was devoted to assisting domestic entrepreneurs, and supporting their international investment with policies such as the "Growth Triangles" with Indonesia and Malaysia. Throughout, careful government planning and analysis combined with effective implementation through the Economic Development Board have been maintained, and linkages between the government and foreign investors have been supplemented by rapidly developing ones with domestic entrepreneurs. At the same time, the government has devoted great effort to providing the infrastructure for manufacturing in the broadest sense, including not only plant sites but also financial services, communications, and technical education. Singapore has evolved a dynamic and effective industrial policy, yet under a patrimonial government.

Malaysia forged ahead in the 1980s with its industrial policy. Manufacturing development was targeted from 1981 as a sector for emphasis. The major effort was the 1986 Industrial Master Plan supplemented in 1990 with the Action Plan for Industrial Technology Development. These were to promote leapfrogging development in manufacturing toward an industrial nation combining resource-based industries with export-oriented ones. A market-based approach was to be replaced by a target-oriented one like Japan and Korea within a free-enterprise economy (Ali Anuar 1992). Twelve major sectors were to combine foreign investment with domestic, stimulate collateral domestic industry, draw on existing state investments like those of the Heavy Industry Company of Malaysia (HICOM), and link with the agricultural sector. While it would be premature to evaluate the effort, the ambition of its goals and the apparent commitment of the government is striking. Malaysia has, finally, an industrial policy framework.

Indonesian industrial policy is changing only in some regards. A struggle between technocrats and nationalists has been eclipsed to some degree by a group advocating large, government-sponsored, technology-intensive projects, currently led by Dr. Bachruddin Habibie (Hill 1992: 225). Technocrats were prominent in liberalizing reforms of the late 1980s that stimulated wider private-sector industrial growth and set up Bantam as a joint manufacturing zone with Singapore. Habibie's Agency for Strategic Industries, however, has poured several billion dollars into import-substituting firms in the aircraft, telecommunications, electronics, and shipbuilding sectors (*Far Eastern Economic Review*, 13 May 1993, 20 May 1993). Planned for leapfrog development, these firms generate little or no economic return (Hill 1992: 237). They represent a shift from reliance on foreign investment, but evidence continuity in the personalistic basis of policy, as Habibie's position depends on the continuation of his close relations with President Suharto.

Neither Thailand nor the Philippines has evolved a substantial industrial policy. In the Philippines political chaos and economic instability have kept attention focused on reconstruction rather than new directions; an ambitious plan of the early 1980s that identified a series of sectors for industrial projects was dropped without implementation. The Thai case is more interesting, as many of the blockages to policy change there have eroded. But, aside from an ambitious Eastern Seaboard development scheme to move manufacturing out of the immediate Bangkok area, the government has adopted few industrial policy initiatives. The planning board, NESDB, has had an unstable history. Gradually brought into the central arena of policy formation (participating in Cabinet) during the 1980s, it was displaced with the rise of business-oriented civilian government in the 1990s. Despite that, at least in the auto sector, Doner (1991) found Thailand to have the greatest degree of concertation between public -and private-sector actors in ASEAN. Thailand is poised to formulate industrial policy, with few adjustments in the role of government.

Conclusion

Socio-political obstacles hindered the development of industrial policies in South East Asia. In the Philippines, serious obstacles have prevented the emergence of industrial policies, despite the highest initial level of industrial development in the region. In Indonesia, and in some cases in Thailand and Malaysia, decisions continue to be personalistic. Throughout ASEAN, the role of the state contends with the private sector, perhaps dampening opportunities. Still, those countries whose social and political structures have evolved the most--Singapore and Malaysia--have come to frame industrial policy effectively. Aspects of the Thai sociopolitical structure, although lacking integration, now support greater industrial transformation. Indonesia lags behind, and is mired in a state-led mode of industrial development, under personalistic rule.

In each ASEAN country foreign investment plays a distinctive role. In their early development the ASEAN members were largely passive recipients; now more active, they are still subject to the forces that determine global flows of investment. However, some of the ASEAN experience suggests that drawing on foreign investment may not reduce industrial policy's effectiveness, if planning and execution are effective. Still, the large presence of foreign investment makes domestic ownership of strategic industries a distant prospect in South East Asia. There industrial policy measures will remain conditioned by the system of international production of which they are an integral part.

References

Ali, Anuwar. 1992. *Malaysia's Industrialization: The Quest for Technology.* Singapore: Oxford University Press.

Anek, Laothamatas. 1991. *Business Associations and the New Political Economy of Thailand.* Boulder: Westview.

Asian Development Bank. 1990. *Asian Development Outlook.* Manila, ADB.

Bowie, Alasdair. 1991. *Crossing the Industrial Divide: State, Society and the Politics of Economic Transformation in Malaysia.* New York: Columbia University Press.

Bresnan, John. 1993. *Managing Indonesia: The Modern Political Economy.* New York: Columbia University Press.

Broad, Robin. 1988. *Unequal Alliance: The World Bank, the International Monetary Fund, and the Philippines.* Berkeley: University of California Press.

Crone, Donald. 1988. "State, Social Elites and Government Capacity in South East Asia." *World Politics.* Vol. 40, No. 2, January: 252-268.

______. 1985. "The Growth and Equity Experience of South East Asia." *Occasional Paper No. 8.* East Lansing, Center for the Advanced Study of International Development.

______. 1983. *The ASEAN States: Coping With Dependence.* New York: Praeger.

______. 1981. "Emerging Trends in the Control of Foreign Investment in ASEAN." *Asian Survey*. Vol. XXI, No. 4, April: 417-436.

Crouch, Harold. 1984. *Domestic Political Structures and Regional Economic Co-operation*. Singapore: Institute of South East Asian Studies.

Deyo, Frederic. 1987. (ed.) *The Political Economy of the New Asian Industrialism*. Ithaca: Cornell University Press.

Doner, Richard. 1991. *Driving a Bargain: Automobile Industrialization and Japanese Firms in South East Asia*. Berkeley: University of California Press.

Economic and Social Commission for Asia and the Pacific (1976). *Economic and Social Survey of the Pacific*. Bangkok: ESCAP.

Encarnation, Dennis, and Louis Wells, Jr. 1985. "Sovereignty en Garde: Negotiating with Foreign Investors." *International Organization 39*. Winter: 373-386.

Evans, Peter. 1992. "The State as Problem and Solution: Predation, Embedded Autonomy, and Structural Change." In Stephan Haggard and Robert Kaufman (eds.), *The Politics of Economic Adjustment*. Princeton: Princeton University Press.

Gale, Bruce. 1981. *Politics and Public Enterprise in Malaysia*. Singapore: Eastern Universities Press.

Grindle, Merilee, and John Thomas. 1991. *Public Choices and Policy Change*. Baltimore: Johns Hopkins University Press.

Haggard, Stephan. 1990. *Pathways From The Periphery*. Ithaca: Cornell University Press.

Hawes, Gary. 1987. *The Philippine State and the Marcos Regime: The Politics of Export*. Ithaca: Cornell University Press.

Hewison, Kevin. 1989. *Bankers and Bureaucrats: Capital and the Role of the State in Thailand*. New Haven: Yale University Press.

Hill, Hall. 1992. "Manufacturing Industry." In Ann Booth (ed.), *The Oil Boom and After: Indonesian Economic Policy and Performance in the Soeharto Era*. Singapore: Oxford University Press.

Ho Kwon Ping. 1980. "Thailand Inc." *Far Eastern Economic Review*. May 23: 40-46.

Jesudason, James. 1989. *Ethnicity and the Economy: The State, Chinese Business, and Multinationals in Malaysia*. Singapore: Oxford University Press.

Krause, Lawrence, Koh Ai Tee, and Lee Yuan. 1987. *The Singapore Economy Reconsidered*. Singapore: Institute of South East Asian Studies.

Lee, Tsao Yuan, and Linda Low. 1990. *Local Entrepreneurship in Singapore: Private and State*. Singapore: Times Academic Press.

Lim, Linda J.C., and Pang Eng Fong. 1991. *Foreign Direct Investment and Industrialization in Malaysia, Singapore, Taiwan and Thailand*. Paris: OECD.

MacIntyre, Andrew. 1991. *Business and Politics in Indonesia.* London: Allen and Unwin.

Mackie, J.A.C. 1988. "Economic Growth in the ASEAN Region: The Political Underpinnings." In Helen Hughes (ed.), *Achieving Industrialization in East Asia.* Cambridge: Cambridge University Press.

McVey, Ruth. 1992. (ed.) *South East Asian Capitalists.* Ithaca: Cornell South East Asia Program.

Milne, R. Stephen. 1992. "Privatization in the ASEAN States: Who Gets What, Why, and with What Effect?" *Pacific Affairs.* Vol. 65, No. 1, Spring: 7-29.

______. 1982. "Technocrats and Politics in the ASEAN Countries." *Pacific Affairs.* Vol. 55, Fall: 403-429.

Muscat, Robert. 1990. *Thailand and the United States.* New York: Columbia University Press.

Ng Chee Yuen, and Norbert Wagner. 1989. "Privatization and Deregulation in ASEAN: An Overview." *ASEAN Economic Bulletin.* Vol. 5, March 3.

Ng Chee Yuen, and Sueo Sudo. 1991. *Development Trends in the Asia-Pacific.* Singapore: Institute of South East Asian Studies.

Ng Chee Yuen, Sueo Sudo, and Donald Crone. 1992. "The Strategic Dimension of the 'East Asian Developmental States'." *ASEAN Economic Bulletin.* Vol. 9, No. 2, November: 219-233.

Nor, Abdul Ghani et al. 1984. (eds.) *Malaysia Incorporated and Privatization.* Selangor: Pelanduk Publications.

Robison, Richard. 1986. *Indonesia: The Rise of Capital.* London: Allen and Unwin.

Rodan, Garry. 1989. *The Political Economy of Singapore's Industrialization: National State and International Capital.* London: Macmillan Press.

Thailand. 1987. *The Sixth National Economic and Social Development Plan.* (1987-1991) Bangkok: Office of the Prime Minister.

Wade, Robert. 1988. "The Role of Government in Overcoming Market Failure." In Helen Hughes (ed.), *Achieving Industrialization in East Asia.* Cambridge: Cambridge University Press.

World Bank. 1990. *World Development Report.* 1993. New York: Oxford University Press.

Yoshihara, Kunio. 1988. *The Rise of Ersatz Capitalism in South-East Asia.* Singapore: Oxford University Press.

9

China's Industrial Reforms

Gunnar K. Sletmo and Alain Van Peeterssen

After 15 years of reform, China is still experimenting with ad hoc measures in industry, agriculture and distribution. As the country goes from reform to reform, it is premature to talk in terms of industrial *policy*, and it seems more appropriate to use the term *reforms* in the title of this chapter.

China's industrial reforms reflect conflicting pressures, towards modernization and fundamental restructuring on the one hand, and fear of too rapid change and loss of central control on the other. Efforts to maintain central control have been combined with local "regulation" by market forces. State planning and state enterprises have co-existed with private entrepreneurship. A major concern has been to maintain a balance between these different and frequently conflicting objectives.

It has been suggested that a common view of China's industrial policies is that they constitute primarily a form of industrial targeting,[1] resulting in conflicting approaches by different interest groups, administrative levels and regions, as priorities vary significantly with the local context. As a result, much of China's industrial policy framework has taken the form of experimentation, sometimes limited to a region or even to a small number of specifically chosen firms. This experimentation may not always have had the approval of the central government and may not even have been known to it.

China's economic management system in the early 1950s was built on the Soviet model with its unified distribution of the means of production and state purchase and marketing of all consumer goods. Mao Zedong's egalitarianism played a key role in shaping the allocation process and gave rise to "the iron rice bowl", a concept described as follows by a well-known Chinese economist:

> The practice of "everybody eating the rice cooked in one big pot", a practice that seriously fettered the initiative and enthusiasm of enterprises and of workers and staff members and thus hampered the growth of the productive forces.[2]

It is against this background that one must observe the industrial achievements of today's China. Clearly, the changes which have taken place over the last 45 years involve major adjustments in the thinking of the central government, planning, management practices, and consumer behavior.

This chapter analyzes some of these changes, starting with a review of the pre-reform system. This is followed by a discussion of the nature of China's industrial reform and its industrial enterprises. A third section summarizes the financial reforms in industrial state enterprises and is followed by a review of labor and wage reforms. The contractual responsibility system is discussed, and a concluding section provides an analysis of the price reform.

Pre-reform: The Inherited System

Despite China's long history and early technological achievements in many fields (metallurgy, pottery, navigation, etc.), industrialization and large-scale manufacturing were largely seen as foreign and a tool of domination for the 19th century industrialists. Foreign technology was frequently rejected as when in 1876 the governor-general of Shanghai purchased the first 12-mile railway from Shanghai to Wusung in order to promptly dismantle it. Although the official was a leader in trying to modernize China, he explained to the Emperor that:

> He could not let the British have a joint railway ownership with China or even a joint management; China must control her own modernizing, and moreover the local feeling was violently against railways.[3]

Such attitudes clearly influenced the thinking of socialist China's first planners and economic managers who intertwined socialist ideals with isolationist, nationalistic fervor. It is against this background that one must attempt to understand China's at times rather circuitous route towards industrial and market reform. Two prominent Chinese economic planners have summarized the economy of "Old China" (pre-1949) as semi-feudal and semi-colonial. China's first steps towards industrialization after 1949 relied heavily on industries already in place. In 1932, the Kuomintang created an organization which subsequently became the National Resources Commission (NRC) directly under Chiang Kai-shek and the military in order to create state-run basic industries for steel, electricity, machinery, and military arsenals.[4] By 1949, the NRC controlled two-thirds of China's industrial investment and its existence greatly facilitated Mao Zedong's subsequent monopolization of the industrial sector.

Factory Towns

State factories are giant enterprises which constitute complete societies. It has been observed that each time a state factory was established, a small town was created. An example is the Baoji Nonferrous Metal Works built on an isolated spot along the old Silk Route. It became China's leading producer of titanium sheet and tubing for the country's nuclear industry, and developed into a town of 10,000. It is a self-contained island, complete with dwellings for employees, schools, infirmaries, bakeries, transport pool, etc.[5]

The extensive support system built around the traditional state factories requires substantial resources and the manager of a factory may find his responsibilities are akin to those of a small town mayor. The Capital Iron and Steel Corporation in western Beijing reportedly at one time employed a staff of 135,000 to grow vegetables and rice, teach the children of employees, take care of parks, bakeries and theaters. The number of workers directly involved in the corporation's steel production was less than 15,000.[6]

The state factory became a mini-municipality providing a range of services not provided by central or local governments. It provided life-time employment and the iron rice bowl, health services, education and entertainment. Children of employees were expected to get jobs at the factory, or at least inherit their parents' positions when they retired. And of course retirees would be expected to live out their lives within the factory compound.

For the management of such factories, the welfare of their employees--their dependents--weighed as heavily as any consideration of profitability and efficiency. The strong involvement of the Communist Party in all aspects of the factory management made it difficult, if not impossible, in many instances to develop a professional and economically rational management strategy. Leadership of the party committee existed in each factory, down to each workshop.[7] Party committees intervened at all levels within the enterprise, and the professional managers were bound by their decisions. Consequently, decision-making authority was separated from the management staff who would be afraid or reluctant to act decisively.

The dilution of executive responsibility understandably frequently resulted in slack discipline, absenteeism and sloppy work. It became difficult to introduce changes and productivity improvements, and a technological rigidity developed as there was a strong resistance to adopt new methods or to change work rules. The long-term effect on productivity and product quality was disastrous in many cases. The difficulties which existed on the firm level were aggravated by the nature of the economic planning system.

The Economic Planning System

The first attempts by China to set up a central planning system relied heavily on the Soviet model. In the 1950s, tens of thousands of Soviet experts came to China to help it establish an administrative system for the economy and to help in the running of major enterprises. The first step in developing an industrial policy was the socialization of virtually all industry and large-scale commerce. This was achieved by 1956. A Soviet-style central plan was developed covering major investment projects. The first such five-year plan was for the 1953-1957 period, but was not published until 1955.[8]

The central planning system was based on physical measurements for targets (quotas) combined with a state-run allocation system, both for inputs (labor, capital, raw materials, energy, etc.) and outputs (i.e., enterprises did not control their marketing and normally sold their entire production to a state or provincial agency).

The Chinese were never entirely comfortable with the rigid Soviet allocation system and its highly detailed planning model and were doubtful about its effectiveness. When agricultural production for 1957 (the last year of the first plan) turned out to be disappointing, it gave rise to considerable concern in Beijing. In fact, agricultural output had increased by only 1% for the year, while population grew at 2%. For China's heavy industry to continue to grow at a rapid pace, agricultural output had to be dramatically increased. Mao Zedong therefore decided to promote agricultural production through the use of "moral incentives and mass mobilization under the direction of inspirational local party leaders."[9] At first, the approach appeared to work when agricultural production increased significantly in 1958, and expectations were high for the new forms of organization that emerged under the slogan of The Great Leap Forward.

The Great Leap Forward gave rise to a new social organization. The social changes resulting from the Great Leap Forward included the pooling of most key household activities, such as child raising and cooking. Huge work-teams were created to undertake large-scale terracing (for rice), irrigation and other projects. A million small steel mills went up in villages to provide locally produced steel. The decentralization of steel production was a devastating failure, due to the inability to achieve economies of scale and to produce quality products. Other projects led to a transformation of the landscape as mines were developed, dams constructed and new boulevards and atomic shelters were built in major cities.

Mao Zedong was determined to assert the primacy of the commune system, bureaucratic decentralization and mass mobilization. However, the movement went out of control as Mao Zedong insisted on ever greater contributions from the agricultural sector. Grain exports to the Soviet Union were increased in order to pay for imports of heavy machinery. In 1959, investment in industry rose to 43.4% of national income while peasants were starving to death in many regions.[10] The funds for industrial investment were extorted from agriculture and in some areas the rural population was left with as little as one half--in some cases even as little as one-fifth--of their normal subsistence grain supply.[11] Fairbank concludes that:

> ....the Chinese path to socialism had led over a cliff. Several years of saner economic policies in the early 1960s were necessary to get back to the levels of livelihood of 1957.[12]

Chinese economists recognize that the Great Leap Forward gave rise to a number of fundamental distortions in the economy, while at the same time, emphasizing that those three years (1958-1960) did result in a number of key projects, resulting from the mobilization of an unprecedented amount of labor, equipment and financial resources. It is estimated that the Great-Leap-Forward years contributed as much as one-fourth to one-third to the total increase in production capacity added during the 1950-1979 period.[13]

The distortions created by the Great Leap Forward were of course not alleviated by the withdrawal of Soviet experts and the subsequent pressures from the Soviet Union for repayment of debts. Major disagreements developed between the Soviet Union and China in the late 1950s as Krushchev's caution in international and economic matters came to be seen as "reactionary" by the Chinese. The conflict resulted in the withdrawl of 1,390 Soviet experts and advisers in September 1960. The Chinese have claimed that their departure led to the cancellation of 343 major contracts and 257 other technical projects.[14] Specific imbalances identified include:

1. disproportionate capital accumulation at expense of consumption: marginal productivity of capital declined and even became negative in 1960; consumption fell to starvation levels;
2. disproportionate development between industry and agriculture: from 1957 to 1960 industrial output value increased by 130% while agricultural output declined by 23%;
3. disproportionate development within the industrial sector and communications and transport: overemphasis on increased steel production led to the creation of small, inefficient enterprises producing sub-standard pig iron; various sectors, including mining, not able to keep up with targets; 10 million peasants were drafted to operate short-haul transport companies without training and ships and vehicles were severely damaged, reducing transport capacity; and
4. imbalance between revenue and expenditure widened: the investment fervor led to constant increases in financial credit resulting in significant deficits, shortage of goods, depletion of foreign-exchange reserves as exports declined, and depletion of stocks of grain and consumer goods.[15]

These imbalances were due not only to policy mistakes, but also to enormous inefficiencies throughout the bureaucracy, down to the village level.

Readjustment and Experimentation

The years of the Great Leap Forward were followed by a period of readjustment, including cutbacks. A greater realism in economic matters was achieved as China's leadership recognized that determination, propaganda and slogans were not enough to increase production "a dozen times". The earlier success in increasing agricultural production could not be transferred to industry without modifications, and it became clear that industrial development could not be accelerated beyond a certain point. Sheer manpower alone is not sufficient to support industrial growth, and the need for coordination, infrastructure and large markets (regional and national) for inputs and outputs is far greater for manufacturing than for basic farming.

It was recognized that one cannot selectively give priority to a limited number of industrial sectors without regard for their dependence on other sectors. Diverse forms of management were again recognized as necessary, and most importantly, it became clear that industrialization requires a long gestation period and must be based on available resources. However, a number of practical difficulties continued to interfere with the targeting process as varying and incompatible output measures were used. Thus, in one sector value added might be the key target while in others it was gross output or units produced. Such difficulties resulted in problems related to estimates of productivity and required capital investment.

The Chinese experiment with industrialization was, interrupted by the Cultural Revolution. While this "revolution" was most disruptive from late 1965 to April 1969, it severely affected the economy for a much longer period, and the decade 1966-1976 became China's "Ten Lost Years".[16] In spite of the major upheavals which affected millions of lives, the economy continued to function primarily because the vast rural population was relatively little affected. Urban areas, on the other hand, experienced a disastrous decline in output.

The third five-year plan (1966-1970) went into effect after a period of intense internal debate over the speed of development. This plan envisaged a new China not only catching up with, but even surpassing the industrial world. In order to achieve this, China was to pursue the modernization of agriculture, industry, national defense, and science and technology (which later became the policy of "The Four Modernizations"). At the same time, China would build an integrated industrial system based largely in the interior to protect installations from military attacks. As part of this movement to a new strategic rear, priority was to be given to basic industries, communications and transportation facilities.[17]

In summary, the 10 years of turmoil (1966-1975) had severe effects on the Chinese economy, the most important being:

1. Imbalances in the economy
   - excessive investment, primarily in heavy industry, at the expense of consumption as well as investment in "non-productive" sectors such as housing and urban infrastructure;
   - disproportionate emphasis on steel production, severely distorting the industrial structure;
   - excessive emphasis on grain production at the expense of cash crops, forestry and fishing; and
   - overemphasis on construction of new railways in the interior while severe bottlenecks developed in the national trunklines.

2. Relatively inflexible economic management structure
   - power concentrated in the hands of the state while enterprises had no autonomy;
   - direct control through central planning of virtually all aspects with little room for management or worker input;
   - financial revenues and expenditures handled in a unified manner (i.e., through the central state) with no profit retention for the firms; and
   - while the perceived need for greater national defense led to a decentralization of many economic powers to local administrative organs, this transfer generally did not give more power to enterprises.

3. Overall decline of productivity and economic return
   - marginal productivity of capital dropped; and
   - profits and tax income fell.

4. Living standards declined
   - wages declined by 4.9% from 1966 to 1976;
   - net income of peasants stagnated; and
   - many farmers starved and left their villages, begging for a living.[18]

There were of course also some achievements during these years, the most important being a steady growth of grain production, construction of a number of giant, technically advanced industrial firms (although some if not most of these later have become a major economic and environmental problem), construction of inland trunk railways and bridges, and progress in science and technology, including the development of nuclear power and weapons.

Table 9.1 shows annual growth rates of industrial output value for various years and illustrates that except for the disastrous Great-Leap-Forward period, industrial growth was maintained at respectable rates, even allowing for some doubt about the overall quality of the statistics. The rates are of course aggregate rates, giving averages for a wide range of different sectors and firms. Behind these averages there were clearly great discrepancies between the best achievers and the worst non-performers. There are also serious questions relating to the quality and reliability of the statistics, many of which appear to have been estimated retroactively. The figures given for growth should therefore be viewed with caution.

A major goal in the subsequent modernization and reforms was to eliminate the waste that came from poor planning, lack of incentives for managers and the absence of relevant performance criteria in most instances. The rigidity of the system, reinforced by dogmatic fallacies and deep-seated fear and distrust of foreign powers, all contributed to keep down the overall performance of pre-reform China. The following sections will look at the nature and effects of the economic reforms that followed 30 years of experimentation.

Table 9.1 Industrial Output Index, China 1949-1980

Year	Period	Annual Growth Rate (%)
1949-1952	Pre-plan	34.8
1953-1957	First Five-Year Plan	15.1
1958-1962	Second Five-Year Plan and Great Leap Forward	-6.0
1963-1965	Readjustment Period	23.0
1966-1970	Third Five-Year Plan, Cultural Revolution, emphasis on interior	9.5
1971-1975	Fourth Five-Year Plan, continued emphasis on interior, Gang of Four	7.7
1976-1980	Fifth Five-Year Plan, shift from class struggle to socialist modernization	11.2

Source: Suinian Liu and Qungan Wu. *China's Socialist Economy - An Outline History (1949-1984).* Beijing: Beijing Review. 1986. Growth rates calculated from data on p. 477.

The Need for Reform

Under Mao Zedong's rule, total factor productivity remained low. Perkins estimates that while productivity increases contributed 4.1% per year to China's growth during the period 1953-1957, this figure dropped to -1.4% for 1957-1965. It then improved slightly for the period 1965-1976 when productivity increases reached 0.6% per year.[19] Thus, the "achievements" during the first 25 years of the People's Republic of China were primarily due to a massive increase in the resources used, in the form of mass mobilization of labor and capital.

The poor performance had several fundamental reasons. Official prices had remained largely frozen since the 1950s with no periodic reviews. Hence, even if the price structure reflected relative scarcity at the time of their determination (something which is far from certain), they became increasingly removed from actual relative scarcity as time went on.

Capital was generally provided by budgetary grants and allocations, and appeared costless to the firm. As a result, there were many cases of wasteful investment and excess inventories. As the price mechanism was not allowed to play its role in allocation of resources and goods, administrative mechanisms determined allocation in principle. In reality, due to the lack of rational economic performance criteria waste existed at all levels in the economy. Managerial responsibility was eroded as subsidies were easily obtained to compensate for losses. The quality of products declined to disastrous levels as production quotas rewarded quantity without regard to quality.

Consumption suffered, both because it was preempted by investment and because of the low quality of consumer goods when they were available. Distribution systems were inefficient and agricultural products were delivered in insufficient quantities and often badly damaged, while elsewhere excess stocks of produce were left to rot in warehouses. Seeds were eaten by vermin and harvests were damaged, exposed to the weather in outdoor storage areas. As a result, there was increasing discontent among consumers, a fact that for a long time may have been concealed from Mao Zedong. It became increasingly important to find ways of improving the quality and quantity of goods and food products available to consumers.

It became urgent to contain the ideologically driven pursuit of investment, particularly in heavy industries, while at the same time maintaining aggregate growth. In order to do this, it would be necessary to introduce new technologies to improve productivity and to develop new methods for managing the economy. Increased exports were required to generate foreign exchange to acquire the needed technology. Only in this manner would it be possible to reduce the share of investment in GNP without sacrificing growth.

In the first decades following Mao Zedong's ascent to power, China had been content, even determined, to exclude foreign influences and technology.

The determination to exclude foreign trade was motivated mainly by the Marxist view that international trade was primarily for the benefit of imperialist nations; it was further believed that socialist nations "properly" organized with internal division of labor had nothing to gain from trade. Mao Zedong was stongly concerned with social and political structures and believed such questions to be far more important than the practical aspects of economic management. As was evident during the Cultural Revolution he was afraid that the Communist Party would develop into a new bourgeoisie and he was more at ease with the revolutionary spirit of adolescents than with developing a strong administrative apparatus built on professionals and continuity. Given the discrepancy between political ideology and Mao Zedong's personal convictions on the one hand and the economic realities on the other, it was not possible to introduce large-scale sweeping reforms. Instead, reform started in a piecemeal fashion and frequently took the form of local experiments that could easily be contained or aborted if the political leadership found it expedient to do so. As a result, there was--and still is in many instances--a considerable discrepancy between official pronouncements and local realities.

The early reform policies introduced by Deng Xiaoping following the death of Mao Zedong and the overthrow of the Gang of Four in 1976 have been described in the following terms:

> These new economic policies and reforms do not represent a well-defined economic program introduced at a particular point in time. Rather, the post-Mao Zedong leadership's economic program is the result of a continuous process of experimentation in their search for the path of sustained growth; a process which has encountered problems and undergone several twists and turns, but which is likely to continue throughout the 1980s.[20]

This prediction turned out to be true. Thus, one writer describes the reforms during the 1980s as a confusing plethora of measures:

> No overall blueprint or plan for reform has guided the process. Instead, reforms have been headlong and unpremeditated, sometimes haphazard, often seemingly chaotic, with highly ad hoc implementation, with considerable regional variation. Typically, reforms began with "experiments"; where these were deemed successful, usually after only a short period of implementation and a superficial evaluation, they were often rapidly instituted nationwide.[21]

This does not mean that the reform process was haphazard or totally arbitrary. It can better be seen as a trial-and-error approach, which can be assessed on a case-by-case basis.[22] The general theme which can be observed in these cases is an effort to "marketize" the industrial sector,[23] by allowing firms (or *some* firms) to become largely autonomous, profit-oriented economic agents. Thus, flexible prices (not always entirely competitive) began to replace central planning and administrative directives as an allocative mechanism. The Chinese authorities saught to limit this marketization process by applying it selectively to certain sectors and to certain markets. For instance, factor markets such as those for labor, land and capital, until recently, remained largely under government control. In the following sections, we shall review specific aspects of the reforms, but first it is useful to briefly examine the different kinds of enterprises which operate in China.

Chinese Enterprises

Based on different forms of ownership and administrative control, Byrd identifies five main categories of Chinese firms. Reform measures vary with the type of firm and organization, and the relative role of different firms has changed over time as a result of this selective approach to reform. The categories of firms are:

1. large State Enterprises. Small in total number but contributing a major (now declining) share of industrial output; tightly controlled by the government planning and administrative apparatus;
2. smaller State Enterprises. Controlled by county or municipal governments; declining share of industrial output;
3. urban Collective Firms. Nominally owned by urban community entities but actually controlled by various government agencies;
4. small Rural Firms. Owned by township and village governments; increased in numbers during recent years; and
5. private Enterprises. Found mostly in rural areas; rapidly increasing in numbers after 1984, accounting for a significant share of total industrial output.[24]

In addition to these domestic firms, joint ventures, normally based on foreign direct investment, have come to play a major role in China's foreign trade. Many of these ventures involve large multinational corporations seeking to take advantage of China's vast pool of cheap labor in order to stay competitive in global markets, as well as to gain access to the rapidly growing Chinese domestic consumption and industrial markets.

As each type of firm has different institutional characteristics, reform strategies and measures have been adapted to the fit the circumstances of each category. However, all enterprises, except small private firms, remain under the jurisdiction of government supervisory agencies. Such agencies can be ministries of the central government or provincial, municipal or county industrial bureaus. For rural enterprises, urban neighborhood committees and rural townships and village governments play a key role.[25]

Key Features of the Industrial Reforms

For China, the question of reform goes beyond the technical, economic level. Chinese thinkers are concerned with the relationship between economic growth, institutional structures and social attitudes. There has always been a debate over "the relationship between Chinese essence and 'foreign know-how', between *ti* and *yong*."[26] Some believed the key to economic change was to be found in ideology and in social change rather than in the field of economics, and in fact, the economic policies of the 1950s to 1978 were greatly influenced by Mao Zedong's preoccupation with institutional change and social forces.[27] In 1975, Deng Xiaoping suggested that the introduction of modern technology may place new demands on social institutions.[28] Specifically, the Chinese have been and are still concerned that economic pluralism may lead to social and political pluralism as well. The Central Government is therefore faced with the problem of "two systems", having to develop a limited market economy in some areas (sectorial or geographic) while maintaining a controlled distribution system for other areas. Both are considered key elements in the progress towards an ideal communist society. This duality, this tension between conflicting goals explains the tentative, even erratic, experimentation with reform.

Against this background, one finds a gradual move towards greater use of the market in the allocation of industrial goods with a concomitant reduction in the reliance on administrative planning. A key step in the direction towards marketization was the establishment of financial incentives for enterprises and to a lesser extent for individuals: State Enterprises were allowed to retain a share of their profits. State Enterprises historically returned all their profits to the governing authority which in return supplied them with funds for investment and operations in accordance with the central plan; with reform, this system was replaced by profit retention (after taxes) and bank loans as major sources of new investment, thereby hardening the previously soft budget constraints. At the same time, wages and bonuses were to be used as incentives towards greater productivity, rather than as rewards for loyalty and connections.

The Contract Responsibility System

In order to encourage personal initiative and commitment, the Contract Responsibility System (CRS) was introduced. It combined greater decision-making autonomy for individuals and enterprises in return for greater yields. In its original form, it was known as the "agricultural production responsibility system" and was an integral part of the 1979 reform in the agricultural sector.[29]

By 1983, the responsibility system existed in different variations, but the key element was to create a new social relationship between the individual or group of individuals and the governing authority. Municipalities were given greater power at the expense of the old system of communes and were to exercise economic leadership. "Document Number 1", the first document of the year issued by the Central Committee in 1984, summarized the new economic policies:

> Extending the period for which land is contracted will encourage peasants to increase investment, conserve the natural fertility of their land and practice intensive farming. In general, the period for which land is contracted should be more than 15 years. Where production is of a developmental nature or takes longer to be realized--for example fruit growing, forestry or the reclamation of barren hillsides and wasteland--the period should be even longer.[30]

By requiring contracts to be for at least 15 years, the system effectively transfers a considerable amount of land control to private hands. This was accompanied by safe-guards placing severe constraints of the ability to transfer contracts or to use land or buildings for purposes other than those specified in the contract. However, Document Number 1 went further, allowing peasants to freely use their capital:

> Capital belonging to peasants and the collective should be allowed to flow freely, or in an organized manner, without any geographical restriction. Peasants should be encouraged to invest and become shareholders in all manner of enterprises... The legal rights and interests of investors must be protected by the state.[31]

The success of the agricultural responsibility system led the government to apply a similar approach to the industrial sector. Essentially, the CRS took the form of a lease between the state and the enterprise, under which managers accepted responsibility for profits and losses, normally for an initial period of three years, subject to renewal or termination. The contract system led to a certain degree of competition among groups that were interested in assuming managerial responsibilities. Thus, a government supervisory agency would announce that an enterprise was available for contracting, and invite interested parties to submit bids for the contract. The agency would then accept what it considered to be the most desirable offer. An important aspect of such contracts was that they clearly allocate responsibility:

> Although the manager signed the contract on behalf of all the workers, he is personally responsible for the outcome. Autonomy or discretionary powers are given regarding internal organization, personnel administration (including hiring and dismissal of workers), setting wage rates, production planning,...[32]

Contracts were typically very specific about the manager's obligations in matters such as the amount of taxes on annual profits, their rate of annual increases in tax payments, form of supervision and submission of reports.

Evaluation criteria included the upgrading of the enterprise, improvements in technology, product development and safety record. Rewards and penalties to be applied were also detailed in the contract.

The CRS gave a new autonomy to managers as they were no longer appointed by the state, but rather elected or chosen by public selection. In theory this should have opened the field to new entrepreneurs and increased the available pool of managerial talent. In reality, it remained difficult for outsiders to enter established enterprises. It is reported that 90% of all managers who take part in the bidding for management contracts are from within the enterprise they bid for. Although the Contract Responsibility System is credited for some achievements, it also has drawbacks.[33]

In the following, we shall consider four specific aspects of China's attempts to modernize and restructure its economy: financial reform, wages and labor reform, price reform and the creation of Special Economic Zones (SEZ). Although these different kinds of reforms are interrelated and frequently overlap, they can also be seen as identifiable pillars of China's industrial policy.

Financial Reforms

With reforms came greater financial responsibility for the enterprise. It was mentioned earlier that under the original central planning system, the state allocated funds to enterprises according to the plan and the industrial enterprise was not much more than a plant operation, a sort of remote-control subsidiary of the state.

The responsibility system implied that the enterprise became responsible for its profits and losses.[34] This meant it should now pay taxes on profits and interest on loans. It would also be responsible for depreciation and replacement of equipment and buildings. In return it was free to use its profits for a number of purposes. These included setting up funds for the expansion of production, collective welfare and bonuses, and a reserve fund in accordance with government regulations. Losses due to mismanagement became the personal responsibility of the manager, and enterprises with sustained continued losses could be closed down.

Thus, financial incentives and managerial autonomy were directly linked. The financial reform was introduced in stages, based on the usual trial-and-error approach. In late 1978 a limited experiment with greater enterprise autonomy started in Sichuan Province. Originally intended to be confined to Sichuan, it quickly spread to the national level. In July 1979, the State Council issued documents relating to financial reform, including rules for the retention of profits and charges for the use of fixed capital and interest on circulating capital.

As part of these regulations, enterprises were made responsible for eight criteria set by the state:

1. output levels;
2. product quality;
3. variety and product assortment;
4. use (waste) of materials, fuel and power;
5. labor productivity;
6. cost levels;
7. use of working capital; and
8. profits.[35]

Successful fulfillment of these norms allowed the enterprise to keep up to 5% of planned profits. Profits over and above the target could be retained up to 25%. Up to 60% of the depreciation could also be retained, and for two years, any additional profit attributable to self-financed technological innovations.

This phase of reform ended in late 1980, when it was recognized that the rules failed to produce the desired stimulus towards greater market responsiveness and innovation. Despite the apparent increase in managerial authority and responsibility, profits were more attributable to the price structure imposed by the state and other regulatory agencies than to managerial initiatives. The profit-retention system turned into a negotiating framework, preventing the hardening of the soft budget constraints and threatened to retard the necessary price reforms as "each price adjustment would affect retained earnings and thus be a ripe source of conflict."[36]

Rigid input and output prices clearly hindered early success of the enterprise reforms, but were not the only contributing factor and may not have been the most important. The multiple criteria for success (listed as eight points above) were not always mutually consistent. In addition, the two-tiered pricing system helped to alleviate the allocative inefficiencies associated with the rigidity of the official procurement prices, but was capable of being abused by enterprise managers. Finally, most of the "rule changes" which formed the basis of the early Contract Responsibility System were directed towards short-term gains. Partly as a result of the political struggle between the reformers and conservatives, the changes appeared to have a "foot in each camp."

In early 1981 a brief period of austerity was imposed. The government had been losing control of investment priorities and saw the risk of its revenues rapidly diminishing. Investment expenditures were cut and the spread of profit retention was halted. However, in subsequent years (1983-1985) a gradual move towards a generalized profit tax system was introduced, and by 1985, 81% of all state-owned enterprises were operating under some form of profit tax system.

The tax rate on profits was a uniform 55%, but severe distortions in profits resulted from the artificial and rigid price structure. To compensate for this, "adjustment taxes" were used in order to link the tax burden more closely to performance. In certain circumstances this could reduce the effective tax rate to zero.

The lack of effective sanctions against poor performance allowed many of the large state enterprises to accumulate deficits, thus draining the resources of the central government. The bankruptcy law promulgated in 1986 was seldom used and financially unsound practices continued to flourish.

The financial sector has undergone a series of changes as part of the reform movement.[37] During the 1978-1983 period China had essentially one major bank, the People's Bank of China. In addition there were specialized banks operating in sharply delineated areas. Then, in 1984, the People's Bank of China became the country's central bank, no longer engaged in commercial activities which were transferred to a newly created bank, and specialized banks acquired the right to engage in commercial banking, including, from 1986, foreign transactions. Also in 1986, provincial banks were established.

Following the economic and political difficulties of 1988-1989, reform in the financial sector slowed while attempts were made to bring investment and inflation under control. Beijing took back some of the control over the financial system and competition was reduced. Banking remained subject to considerable political control and pressures, both centrally and locally. Specialized banks were often faced with requirements to provide loans not based on economic criteria.

In late 1992, the government presented plans to transform the specialized banks into competitive, autonomous, and self-accountable commercial entities. Key elements in these reform measures include:

1. separating commercial from policy-based lending;
2. separating quasi-fiscal from commercial operations, with all loans to be provided at market interest rates;
3. any interest subsidy to be provided through government budgets outside the banking system;
4. long-term loans for investment projects to come from long-term funds; and
5. banks to be encouraged to improve their loan evaluation and portfolio management.[38]

Labor and Wage Reforms

Mao Zedong built a society based on egalitarianism symbolized by the iron rice bowl. There would forever be rice for everyone in the collective socialist system which was to be the road to an ideal communist society beyond a distant horizon. The price to pay for the right to dip one's rice bowl in "the big pot" was to conform to the rules established by the party. In the effort to marshall the resources of China's vast population, discipline became more important than performance, and conformity more valued than initiative. Jobs and careers were too important to leave to personal choice and preferences, and job allocation became the norm. The difficulty with job allocation, however, is that it is ill suited to respond to the rapidly changing needs of fast growing industrialization. Economic growth is closely linked to improving labor productivity, and this generally requires labor mobility.

Traditionally, the Chinese labor force is a local labor force. Most people work in or near the village where they were born. With the institution of reforms, excess labor pools developed in many areas as improved productivity in agriculture and industry gave rise to hidden unemployment. For instance, out of fear of urban unemployment, during the first half of the 1980s, the government crammed many young people into urban enterprises that were already grossly overmanned, thereby further reducing an already low labor productivity.[39] At the same time severe shortages developed for skilled labor and managers in the expanding industrial sectors. Job allocation of university graduates was intended to alleviate the problem of shortages of specialists and to distribute scarce graduates in a politically acceptable manner.[40] A fundamental weakness of an assignment system is of course that individual job performance is directly related to the employee's personal interest and motivation.

China's wage system under Mao Zedong was basically just as rigid as the job-allocation system.[41] Bonuses, piecework and other systems of remuneration linking pay directly to productivity were prohibited for many years. A large share of a worker's income was given in kind, such as housing, schools for his children, social services, etc. This part of the worker's compensation varied little from worker to worker and was more tied to status or rank than to work performance.

The rigidities of the job-allocation system and wage structure became increasingly serious as economic reform began to take effect both in the industrial and agricultural sectors and specific reforms affecting the labor market became necessary. Some Chinese economists have argued that the inefficiency of the pre-reform Chinese economy was due to two problems:

1. the low allocative efficiency arising from the deviation of industrial structure from the pattern dictated by the comparative advantages of the economy, (i.e., the policy of prioritizing heavy industry and large state-owned enterprises); and
2. low technical efficiency due to managers' and workers' low incentive to work, due to inadequate wage and labor policies.

Labor Markets

Labor markets in China, to the extent they existed in the past, were always heavily influenced by geography. To this day, rural labor markets are heavily fragmented and not functioning smoothly in most areas.[42] While in some areas there is much less administrative control or interference, various elements continue to impede the development of truly efficient labor markets. A survey of workers in four counties (Wuxi, Hainan, Jieshou, and Shangrao), demonstrate that great differences exist between them. For instance, in the case of Nanhai, the share of the work force in township and village private enterprises (TVP) made up of permanent workers declined from 91.8% in 1980 to 40.2% in 1985. In the same county only 47.7% of workers came from the village. For the other townships or villages in the sample, this figure was 80% to 95%.[43] Thus, labor markets evolved differently and at different rates not only in various regions, but even within provinces. Also state enterprises began to experiment with nonpermanent labor:

> State enterprises gained additional flexibility through hiring various kinds of non-regular employees, often on a temporary basis. Parcelling out activities to rural concerns was another way of achieving the same objective.[44]

A major step toward labor reform was the introduction of the labor contract system in 1986 for all newly recruited employees in state-owned enterprises. Until then the general rule had been that of the three irons, i.e., *the iron rice bowl*--the obligation to feed and house the worker; *the iron chair*--job security; and finally, *the iron wages*--fixed, guaranteed wages unrelated to performance. The labor contract system aimed at breaking these three irons, leaving employer and employee free to end or renew the contract at its expiration.[45] Progress in introducing the contract system has been slow, and it is estimated that by 1992 only 16 million workers, or about 21% of the total number of employees in state-owned enterprises were operating under labor contracts.

Making labor a hard budget constraint means that unproductive, excess labor will no longer be absorbed by external government budgets, thus rising the specter of dismissal and unemployment. China therefore set up an unemployment insurance scheme in 1986 which provides unemployment benefits under the following circumstances:

1. bankruptcy of enterprises;
2. restructuring of the enterprise;
3. termination of labor contract; and
4. firing because of violation of rules.[46]

The unemployment scheme covers some 70 million employees in the state-owned enterprises. In certain regions unemployment coverage has also been extended to employees in collectives, joint ventures and private enterprises.[47]

Another important aspect of labor reform relates to housing. The practice of supplying heavily subsidized housing to all employees severely restrains labor mobility. In recent years several cities have experimented with housing reform. Rents have increased substantially, and since 1991 most municipalities have started to increase rents in order to cover the maintenance and administrative costs, as well as depreciation and interest charges and in order to provide a normal return on capital. This is expected to raise rent levels from about 1% of average household expenses to about 6%. In some cases, it is also becoming possible for people to buy apartments or houses. In a number of cities financial institutions are being set up to provide mortgage financing for housing, using funds from newly established retirement funds.[48] Although the number of households involved is small, housing reforms represent an important step towards greater labor mobility.

The labor contract system is also being modified. Starting in 1992, enterprises were encouraged to adopt a modified version of labor contracts, under which all employees, including managers, technicians and operators, are tied to the enterprise hiring them. Contracts can be for a fixed period or open-ended and must spell out the rights, duties and benefits of the employee.[49] The system of job allocation is being replaced by employment agencies, facilitating job searches for individual employees.

Price Reform

We have left the discussion of price reforms towards the end of the chapter although logically one can argue that such reforms must precede other measures. However, one can also argue that a review of price reforms is well suited as a basis for a synthesis and conclusions. It has been suggested that China's reforms can be grouped into four main phases. In each phase, the concepts of flexible prices and marketization played a progressively important role. Table 9.2 summarizes the four phases.

The first phase of reform started in 1978 and was aiming at selectively introducing material incentives, first of all in agriculture, but also to some extent in industry. The government raised the prices paid to farmers for their products. Rural markets were given greater freedom to sell a diversity of agricultural produce as farmers were allowed to diversify their production. Farming households were given greater control over their work and were encouraged to specialize their production in response to market demand.

In industry, the system of paying performance-related bonuses to employees was reintroduced. Such systems had been used earlier, following the Great Leap Forward, in an attempt to rebuild the economy after the economic chaos

Table 9.2 Phases of China's Price Reforms

Phase	Period	
1	1978-1984	Agricultural product procurement prices increased; restrictions on rural markets relaxed; farming decentralized from collective to household level (contract responsibility system); bonus system reintroduced in industry; experimentation with profit retention; creation of Special Economic Zones as laboratories for market reform.
2	1984-1988	Establishment of two-track pricing system; introduction of entreprise taxation; reform of wage system; introduction of bank lending (hard budget constraint); introduction of industrial contract system; opening of 14 coastal cities for foreign investment.
3	1988-1991	A period of retrenchment; because of inflation, further price reforms postponed; stabilization program for prices successful, but at expense of growth; following stabilization, substantial realignment in relative prices and liberalization of some prices.
4	1992-Oct.1992	Communist Party formally embraced Deng Xiaoping's view that market system is compatible with ideals of socialism; a new paradigm: the socialist market economy; March 1992: references to planned economy deleted from constitution.

Source: Adapted from Michael W. Bell, Hoe Ee Khor and Kalpana Kochhar. *China at the Threshold of a Market Economy*. Washington, D.C.: International Monetary Fund, September 1993, pp. 2-4.

caused by that policy. During the Cultural Revolution, however, bonuses were simply added to wages and thus lost their incentive role. During the first phase of reform certain incentive schemes were introduced also on the enterprise level. Thus, some state-owned enterprises were allowed to retain a share of their profits in order to reinvest in technology and improved production equipment.

The second phase of reform started in 1984 and applied to the urban industrial sectors. It built on the success of the reforms which had been instituted in the rural areas during the previous four years. The two-track pricing system, originally set up in farming, was extended to a wide range of commodities. Under the two-track price system a producer, agricultural or manufacturing, would still have to produce according to a quota established by the authorities. The quota output would be sold at the centrally established price, but any surplus production could be sold on the open market or to the state at specially negotiated prices.

This two-track pricing system proved to be tremendously popular, and by 1988, the share of the value of the retail market transacted at market prices had reached 53%.[50] The second largest share, transactions at fixed (government set) prices, represented 28% of total retail value. The remaining 19% was sold at prices under "state guidance".

The third phase of reform, a period of consolidation or "rectification", began in 1988 and lasted only until 1991. The various reforms introduced prior to 1988 had proven to be very successful in stimulating not only production but also demand which threatened to outrun supply. The rapid growth of the previous years led to strong inflationary pressures with annual price increases reaching double-digit levels. While many developing countries would be unconcerned by such price increases, they were troublesome to the Chinese who had achieved a remarkable price stability over time. Measures were taken to slow down the economy. Some planned reforms were delayed while others were reversed with a return to central control of many prices.

The fourth phase of reform started in 1992 and is still continuing (1994). The rectification program of the previous period came officially to an end early in 1992 and the government announced its intention to accelerate the reform process. Deng Xiaoping declared the market system compatible with socialist ideals and promoted the concept of a socialist market economy. This represents a major break with the past and, in March 1992, China's Constitution was amended "to delete references to a planned economy and to enshrine the new goal of establishing a market system".[51]

Some Lessons from the Price Reforms

One of the key problems faced by China in its efforts to reform its economy and to modernize its industrial sector has been the danger of seriously overheating the economy. This remains an ever-present threat requiring a difficult balancing act between growth and restraint. In the early years of reform, the introduction of the two-tiered price system resulted in reduced distortions in resource allocation both in agriculture and in industry. The reforms started in the agricultural sector and gradually spread throughout the economy. New entries in the light-industry sector increased supply of scarce consumer goods. This, combined with "free markets"--street markets which bypassed state stores--brought better quality, greater choice, more products and, over time, reduced prices in real terms as efficiency was greatly improved.[52]

The measures which were introduced starting in 1978 improved productivity and market efficiency; as a direct result, the economy measured in real gross national product (GNP) expanded at a rapid rate, reaching a staggering 14.6% in 1984. In 1988 inflation reached levels which were deemed socially unacceptable and in the fall of that year, the government started applying brakes to the economy. Planned price reforms were postponed and the emphasis was on consolidation. As a result, the economy slowed to a 4.3% growth rate in 1989.

Many observers in the West incorrectly concluded that the Tianmen Square uprising in the spring of that year led to the slowdown of the economy. In fact, the inflationary pressures and the subsequent deflationary measures preceded Tianmen to which they in fact may have contributed. However, the imposed slowdown was soon reduced in severity and the economy returned to its trendline of about 10% or more of real annual growth. By 1992, the growth had reached 12%.

China has gained considerable experience with price reform and several lessons have been identified, following the 1988 surge in prices. Some of these lessons are:

1. if price adjustments are announced too far in advance (as in 1988), demand will accelerate as consumers attempt to beat the deadline, while producers will hold back in order to benefit from the new (presumably higher) prices; as a result prices surge and black markets develop;
2. demand shocks are stronger when expansive credit policies have been in place prior to price adjustments; if additionally interest rate controls prevent yields on state bonds and deposits to respond to inflation, consumers have a strong incentive to move their savings into real assets, notably consumer goods;
3. full price liberalization can best be achieved when a clear majority of prices are close to market clearing levels;
4. supply conditions in the industrial and agricultural sectors affected by the price adjustments must be such that producers can respond rapidly to the new prices; and
5. price reforms and adjustments must be accompanied by appropriate measures, both on the macroeconomic and the sector levels to ensure adequate factor mobility in response to the price signals.[53]

China's industrial policies depend on a smoothly functioning price and market system in order to assure the most efficient use of the country's resources. The creation of well-functioning markets has been remarkably successful. While in 1978 government mandatory prices applied to 97% of retail sales, only 10% of such prices were subject to mandatory control in 1992. In the case of retail sales of agricultural products, the percent of controlled sales declined from 94.4 to 15% over the same period. For production materials the controlled share declined from 99.7% to 20%.[54]

Considerable progress has also been made in the areas of grain and energy price adjustments. Future price reforms will focus on further rationalization of crude oil, power and transport, including the all-important rail services which have already undergone several important increases in order to bring prices closer to real costs.[55]

Price reforms will not suffice to bring about efficient national markets. Major efforts must be made in the areas of distribution and logistics, including the development of a national system of warehousing and industrial and agricultural storage facilities. Continued development of commercial legislation is needed, including competition laws. The authorities appear to be fully aware of these requirements and have set up a new Ministry of Internal Trade under whose mandate many of these areas will fall.

Special Economic Zones

The creation of Special Economic Zones (SEZs) was formally proposed by Deng Xiaoping in 1979 as an integral part of China's reforms, providing a strategic link to the outside world. All those established thus far are located in coastal areas, they represent a total break with the old principles of the "third front" development strategy, favoring interior regions far away from what was considered likely enemy threats. Their primary objective is to attract foreign direct investment and technology and to gain access to foreign markets while remaining separate from the main domestic economy. They were seen as a method for introducing market mechanisms selectively without endangering the government's domestic political and economic agendas.

The SEZs encompass all the complexities and difficulties of the country's modernization and their fate and performance have been closely tied to the "stop-and-go" policies of the government. They have been moderately successful in attracting foreign investment. In 1991 the five SEZs had attracted about one-fifth of all foreign investment, with the majority of these investments coming from Hong Kong and Taiwan.[56] Reduced to the simplest formula, the Chinese started out seeking foreign technology to modernize their industries and increase exports, while keeping foreigners out of their domestic markets. Foreign investors on the other hand hoped to gain access to cheap labor to be used in export-oriented production and to the vast Chinese market, but without giving China free access to their technology or their overseas markets. Out of these opposing objectives a market for technology exchange has emerged, albeit reluctantly, and China's domestic market share indeed has become increasingly more open. Most of all, however, the SEZs have significantly contributed to China's conquest of world markets, notably in areas such as clothing, footwear, toys and increasingly also in consumer electronics.

SEZs As Economic Laboratories

SEZs were instituted in 1979 and were closely linked to the Four Modernizations. Three zones, Shenzhen, Zhuhai and Shantou, were established in Guangdong Province, and a fourth, Xiamen, in Fujian Province. A fifth zone, Hainan Island, was formally added in 1988.

The zones are loosely modeled on Export Processing Zones (EPZs) found in other developing countries.[57] They provide a more attractive environment for foreign investors: preferential tax rates, reduced tariffs, flexible labor and wage policies, modern infrastructure, and less bureaucracy.[58] The "outward-oriented" strategy pursued by many SEZ administrators aims at the creation of export-oriented joint ventures and foreign subsidiaries that will provide employment for Chinese workers, managerial experience for Chinese technicians, and markets for Chinese raw materials and inputs.[59] Foreign technology would be absorbed and diffused to the inland regions. Others would rather advocate an "inward orientation" of import-substituting production by foreign firms. In either case, improved quality and more efficient production are prerequisites for export promotion and import substitution and the SEZs have emerged as leading areas of advanced production techniques, quality control, and eventually, marketing expertise.

In the early years SEZs were regarded as:

> ...a laboratory where Chinese officials can observe and learn from the outside world through direct participation in different types of joint production and business operations... It also provides a testing ground for new reforms in enterprise management, finance and labor matters...[60]

The zones were physically and legally separated from the rest of the country. This was intended to:

> ...[provide] it with a special economic, political and institutional set-up, while allowing what are considered to be beneficial elements, such as technology, management skills and well-tested reforms, to filter through and spread to the rest of the country.[61]

The barrier not only protected the zones from uncontrolled migration and provided an enabling economic environment, it also (and perhaps more importantly for the Chinese authorities) shielded the rest of the country from too rapid change.

Following the early success of the SEZs, 14 coastal cities were opened to foreign investors in 1984. While the SEZs were largely built from scratch, each city already had a significant industrial base supported by adequate infrastructure and technical and managerial expertise. In early 1985, three delta regions were granted similar preferential treatment. The single most ambitious project being developed is the Pudong New Area of Shanghai as a pivot for the entire Yangtze

River valley.[62] The intent is to make Pudong the focal point in China's development from the second half of the 1990s and well into the next century. As a result of the Pudong three-decade project, Shanghai expects to become the dominant economic, trade and financial center not only for China but also for East and Southeast Asia.

The proliferation of zones with greater economic freedom also led to greater autonomy of these areas. The Chinese leadership at times was divided over the desirability of letting the SEZs and coastal cities freely pursue their capitalistic road, and there have been repeated attempts by Chinese leaders to control and restrict this form of liberalization; however, the swift reactions of foreign investors (reduction of investments, delays in expansion), affecting not only the SEZs but the country as a whole, usually made these interferences short-lived.[63]

Shenzhen

It is interesting to look at the example of Shenzhen, which is the most successful and largest of the SEZs. Located just across the border from Hong Kong, it has become an extension of that city. More than three-quarters of the foreign investment in Shenzhen comes from Hong Kong, some of it originating in China or Taiwan.[64] The great majority of companies in Shenzhen are small processing and assembling operations from Hong Kong, but some large-size manufacturing plants are also present. Concern has been raised about environmental conditions in Shenzhen, affected by industrial and automotive air pollution as well as by the impact of a rapidly expanding urban population.

As early as 1982, it was announced that Shenzhen was to develop into a special kind of border city with its own laws and a market-based economy, mostly financed by foreign investors.[65] It was decided that it would develop its own approaches to development and management. The emphasis would be on incentives, entrepreneurship and professionalism. It was to become physically separated from the rest of the country as illustrated in Figure 9.1. In fact, in 1984 the entire zone was surrounded by an electrified barbed wire fence some 200 miles long in order to strictly control the flow of people and goods between Shenzhen and the rest of China. This protective membrane was originally intended to shield the zone from the rest of China, even to protect China from its capitalistic ways.

Shenzhen has served as a laboratory from which the rest of China could learn from and observe different kinds of joint ventures and other foreign busi-

Figure 9.1 The SEZs as a Sub-System Within China

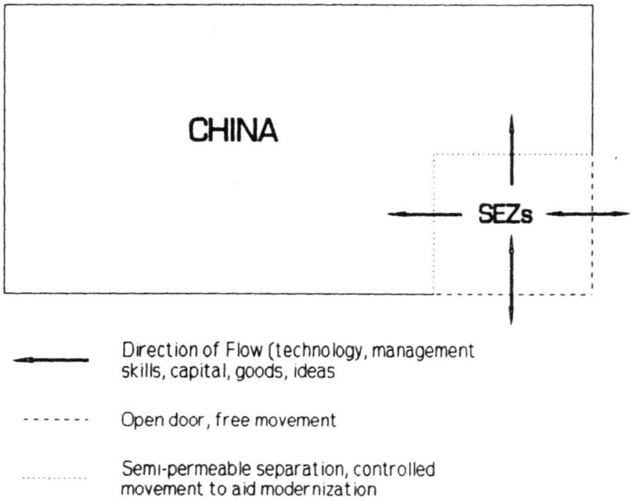

Source: F.S. Sit, "Industries in Shenzhen: An Attempt at Open-Door Industrialization," in Y.C. Jao and C.K. Leung, *China's Special Economic Zones* (Hong Kong: Oxford University Press, 1986), p. 229.

ness operations. Indeed, during the early phases of Shenzhen's development, Chinese officials stated that:

> China will be able to gain an understanding of modern capitalist economies, accumulate experience in the formulation of regulations for economic development programs, cooperate with overseas businesses, and obtain access to advanced technology and management techniques.[66]

Over the years, many Chinese officials have been on organized tours of Shenzhen to observe and marvel at its flamboyant success. Today, Shenzhen, like the other SEZs, has come of age.[67] They continue to be important sources of foreign exchange and will play an even greater role in the future as China's key links with Hong Kong and Taiwan.

The major open development areas, namely the SEZs, the coastal cities and the major river deltas have been supplemented by a virtual free-for-all adoption of the concept of special zones for foreign investment and trade. According to some estimates the number of new development zones opened in 1992 and early 1993 at and above the county level reached 1,800. The number of zones at all levels, including townships and villages, may be as high as 9,000.[68] The open economic zones have played an important role in the introduction of the market economy both on the national and local levels. They have greatly stimulated the development of light industries and entrepreneurship and have contributed towards greater resource mobility. They have been successful in attracting large amounts of foreign investment and foreign technology. They are nodes of development that now influence economic development throughout China.

However, open areas have also given rise to concern. Ferocious competition has developed in some instances between areas and counties as they outbid each other in terms of concessions offered to foreign investors, resulting in lost government revenue. There is also concern that much agricultural land of good quality has been lost in the new land rush that has developed. The government has attempted to slow down the opening of new zones and may consider phasing out transitional incentives offered in the past.

Concluding Remarks

We suggested at the outset of this chapter that China cannot be said to have a consistent set of guiding principles which taken collectively can be said to constitute an industrial *policy*. Rather, China's industrial development has been based on a series of ad hoc measures and experimentation. China's greatest economic success has been achieved in agriculture and in foreign trade. Within manufacturing, by far the most dynamic elements have been in the non-state sector, made up of town and village enterprises, private businesses and foreign joint ventures.

China's greatest failure in the industrial sector remains the giant state-owned enterprises which have found it difficult to break the iron rice bowl and which have failed to respond to new market conditions and new rules. The domestic market remains fragmented both by geography and by policy and within this framework state-owned enterprises remain as isolated regional industrial towns, increasingly irrelevant to the needs of today's China. Until the domestic market becomes more integrated and the state-owned enterprises are exposed to both domestic and international competition, it is not realistic to think of China as having a clearly defined industrial policy. Yet, it must be said that China's gradual and piecemeal reforms appear to have served the country remarkably well as witnessed by its growth record since the introduction of the open-door policy and the largely pragmatic experimentation started in 1978.

Notes

1. Inderjit Singh, *China: Industrial Policies for an Economy in Transition* (Washington: The World Bank, 1992), Discussion Paper 143, ix.
2. Ibid., x.
3. John King Fairbank, *The Great Chinese Revolution 1800-1985* (New York: Harper & Row, 1986), 4.
4. Fairbank, *The Great Chinese Revolution...*, 225.
5. James B. Stepanek, "China's Enduring State Factories: Why Ten Years of Reform Have Left China's Big State Factories Unchanged," in Joint Economic Committee of the Congress of the U.S., *China's Economic Dilemmas in the 1990s: The Problems of Reforms, Modernization, and Interdependence* (Washington: U.S. Printing Office), 2 (1991) S.Prt 102-21: 440-454.
6. Ibid., 447.
7. Antony Y.C. Koo, "Contract Responsibility System: A Bridge of Transition from a Planned Economy to Market Economy," *Economic Development and Cultural Change*, 38 (1990) 4: 797-820.
8. Dwight H. Perkins, "Reforming China's Economic System," *Journal of Economic Literature*, 26 (1988) 2: 606.
9. Jonathan D. Spence, *The Search for Modern China* (New York: W. W. Norton & Company, 1990), 575.
10. Mark Seleden, *The People's Republic of China: A Documentary History of Revolutionary Change* (New York: 1979), 402. Here cited from Spence, *The Search for Modern...*, 583.
11. Fairbank, *The Great Chinese Revolution...*, 304.
12. Ibid., 305.
13. Suinian Liu and Qungan Wu, *China's Socialist Economy: An Outline History (1949-1984)*, First ed. (Beijing: Beijing Review, 1986), 264.
14. Spence, *The Search for Modern China...*, 589.
15. Ibid., 265-271.
16. Fairbank, *The Great Chinese Revolution...*, 316.
17. Lui and Wu, *China's Socialist Economy...*, 338-339.
18. Ibid., Ch. XXVII.
19. Perkins, "Reforming China's Economic...," Table 4, 628.
20. Robert F. Dernberger, "The Chinese Search for the Path of Self-Sustained Growth in the 1980's: An Assessment," in *China Under the Four Modernizations. Selected Papers.* Joint Economic Committee of the Congress of the U.S., Part 1. August 13, 1982 (Washington: U.S. Printing Office, 1991), S.Prt 102-21, 440-454.
21. William A. Byrd (ed.), *Chinese Industrial Firms under Reform* (Washington: The World Bank & Oxford University Press, 1992), 2.

22. The World Bank has taken this approach and has published several cases that analyze the nature of reforms on the firm level. Byrd, ibid., contains seven lengthy cases which taken together give an excellent review of the nature and effects of the reforms.
23. Ibid., 2.
24. Ibid., 1.
25. Lina Song and He Du, "The Role of Township Governments in Rural Industrialization," in Byrd, William A. and Qingsong Lin (eds.), *China's Rural Industry: Structure, Development and Reform* (Washington: The World Bank & Oxford University Press, 1990), 2.
26. Andrew Watson, *Economic Reform and Social Change in China* (New York: Routledge, 1992), 4.
27. Ibid., 5.
28. Deng Xiaoping, "On the General Principles for the Work of the Party and the Country," 7 October 1975, *Zhonggong Nianbao 1977*, Section 5, 62. Here cited from Watson, *Economic Reform and Social...*, 5.
29. Koo, "Contract Responsibility System...," 797-798. It should be notd that if Small Rural Firms were traditionally owned by township and village governments, they are now mostly privately owned.
30. Spence, *The Search for Modern China...*, 700.
31. Ibid., 701.
32. Koo, "Contract Responsibility System...," 799. Carl Riskin, *China's Political Economy: The Quest for Development since 1949* (Oxford: Oxford University Press, 1991), 340-379.
33. Some of these drawbacks were identified in Jinglian Wu, *Large State Enterprise Reform: Establish Modern Enterprise System* (Tianjin: Tianjin People Press, 1993), 162-163.
34. Haibo Wang, "Greater Power for Enterprises," in Wei Lin and Arnold Chao (eds), *China's Economic Reforms* (Philadelphia: Philadelphia University Press, 1982), 81.
35. Riskin, *China's Political Economy...*, 344.
36. Ibid., 345.
37. The following synopsis is based on Michael W. Bell, Hoe Ee Khor, and Kalpana Kochhar, *China at the Threshold of a Market Economy* (Washington: International Monetary Fund, September 1993), Appendix I, 80-81.
38. Ibid., 31.
39. Edwin Lim and Adrian Wood (mission leaders), *China: Long-Term Development Issues and Options* (Baltimore: The Johns Hopkins University Press, 1985), a mission report published for the World Bank, 127.
40. For a discussion of the allocation of university graduates, see Zou Ji, "The Assignment of Jobs to College Graduates," in Timothy King and Zhang Jiping (eds.), *Case Studies of Chinese Economic Reform* (Washington: The World Bank, 1992), 51-79.

41. Lim and Wood, *China: Long-Term Development...*, 133.
42. Byrd and Qingsong (eds.), *China's Rural Industry...*, 275.
43. Meng Xin, *The Rural Labor Market*, in Byrd and Qingsong, *China's Rural Industry...*, 303, Table 14.4.
44. Byrd and Qingsong (eds.), *China's Rural Industry...*, 9.
45. Bell, Khor, and Kochhar, *China at the Threshold of...*, 19-20.
46. Ibid., 20.
47. Lilian Liu, "Social Security for State-Sector Workers in the People's Republic of China: The Reform Decade and Beyond," in Joint Economic Committee of the Congress of the U.S., *China's Economic Dilemmas in the 1990s: The Problems of Reforms, Modernization, and Interdependence* (Washington: U.S. Printing Office), 1 (1991) S.Prt 102-21, 270-289.
48. Bell, Khor, and Kochhar, *China at the Threshold of...*, 30-31.
49. Ibid., 48.
50. Ibid., 18.
51. Ibid., 4.
52. *China: The Achievement and Challenge of Price Reform* (Washington: The World Bank, 1993), 1.
53. Ibid., 1-2.
54. Luo Zhiling, Director of State Price Bureau, "Accelerating the Establishment of a Pricing Mechanism Based on the Market," *Price Theory & Practice*, (1992) 12; here quoted from Peter Harrold and Rajiv Lall, *China: Reform and Development in 1992-1993* (Washington: The World Bank, 1993), Discussion Paper No. 215, 49-50.
55. Harrold and Lall, *China: Reform and Development...*, 50.
56. George T. Crane, "Reform and Retrenchment in China's Special Economic Zones," in Joint Economic Committee of the Congress of the U.S., *China's Economic Dilemmas in the 1990s: The Problems of Reforms, Modernization, and Interdependence* (Washington: U.S. Printing Office, 1991), 2, S.Prt 102-21, 841-857.56.
57. For a review of how export processing zones in developing countries started and developed, see *Export Processing Zones* (Washington: The World Bank, 1992), Policy and Research Series, Paper No. 20, Appendix, 24-28.
58. Crane, "Reform and Retrenchment in China's...," 843.
59. Ibid., 843.
60. Victor F.S. Sit. "Industries in Shenzhen: An Attempt at Open-door Industrialization," in Y.C. Jao and C.K. Leung (eds.), *China's Special Economic Zones: Policies, Problems and Prospects* (Hong Kong: Oxford University Press, 1986), 226-246.
61. Ibid., 228.
62. Bell, Khor, and Kochhar, *China at the Threshold of a Market Economy* (Washington: International Monetary, September 1993), 43.
63. Crane, "Reform and Retrenchment in China's...," 842.

64. Ibid., 845.
65. Sit, "Industries in Shenzhen: An Attempt...," 229.
66. Chi Fu, "China's Newborn SEZs and their Strategic Significance," Economic Reporter (August 1981), 14, here cited from Sit, "Industries in Shenzhen: An Attempt..."
67. Lawrence C. Reardon, "The SEZs Come of Age," *The China Business Review* (November-December 1991): 14-20.
68. Bell, Khor, and Kochhar, *China at the Threshold of...*, 54, No. 80.

10

Industrial Policy Issues and Pacific Regional Cooperation

Gavin Boyd

The interaction of industrial policy measures, and related trade and foreign-direction investment measures, is having very extensive effects in the Asia-Pacific regional political economy. Diverging, competitive and cooperative strategies implemented by firms as they respond to the diverse governmental measures are shaping national economic structures and linking them in complex interdependencies. This is happening with often stressful asymmetries, as there are many disparities in the spread of gains from arm's-length and intrafirm commerce, and from transnational production. Problems of efficiency and equity posed as markets are internationalized demand national and collective attention. The most prominent problem in the functioning of the internationalizing markets is an oligopolistic trend in high-technology industries, which has consequences in mature- and low-technology sectors, as well as in the extractive and services sectors. Associated with this trend is a shift in the balance of regional economic power toward Japan.

Some imperatives to engage collectively with issues posed by rising structural interdependence are activating national policymakers, because of trade imbalances. Their views however differ because of concerns as rivals in competitive macromanagement, and because of diverging beliefs about the economic functions of governments. Regional trade liberalization is recognized to be in the general interest, but on this there is unevenly shared consensus. In the industrializing East Asian states there is concern that the main beneficiaries of reductions of tariffs and non-tariff barriers will be the larger and more competitive firms operating out of the U.S. and Japan. In the U.S. there are expectations that Japan and most of the industrializing East Asian states will continue informally restricting access to their markets after agreeing to regional trade liberalization, and will make further competitive gains in the American market. In Japan there appears to be optimism that deeper penetration of markets in the industrializing East Asian states and of the U.S. market would be possible after a regional trade-liberalization agreement, but that informal barriers protecting the home market would remain rather effective. Confidence in the national capacity for implementing industrial and industrially related policies is an important factor in Japanese elite perspectives. In the U.S. there is little business confidence that a similar technocratic capacity could develop in the American political economy, and accordingly aggressive management of trade policies tends to be viewed as the main imperative in foreign economic relations.

Some regional trade liberalization may result from exchanges within the Asia Pacific Economic Cooperation forum, comprising the market economy states of East Asia and North America, and China. This consultative association, formed mainly because of Japanese and American business initiatives, has given priority to the study of ways of reducing barriers to regional commerce. The participating governments, however, have shown no interest in the possibility of undertaking trade liberalization in a way that would lead to wider economic cooperation.[1] Replication of the European Community's experience in deepening integration has not been envisaged, primarily because of the sharp cultural contrasts that limit the growth of understanding and trust across the Pacific. Industrial cooperation has not been in view. The U.S. administration's efforts to establish forms of managed high-technology trade with Japan however have involved pressures to promote some industrial cooperation, notably through Japanese procurement of automobile parts and semiconductors.

Regional industrial cooperation could help to reduce structural imbalances and enhance growth in Asia and the Pacific. This could be possible through the harmonization of national industrial measures and concerted sponsorship of direct investment planning by corporate management conferences. A consensus for this could emerge from discussions of issues arising out of ventures in trade liberalization, but increasing inequalities in the spread of benefits from that liberalization might well cause resentments that would prevent further cooperation.

Questions about the feasibility of regional industrial cooperation have to be considered with reference to the orientations of corporate strategies in the Asia Pacific region. Compatibilities and conflicts between these strategies and the policies of governments differ greatly from the pattern in Europe, where significant identities have been seen between the interests of firms expanding through integration strategies and the interests of governments working for regional economic integration.[2] The identities of interest between European firms and member governments in their economic community could sustain a common industrial policy, directed mainly against the competitive challenges of American and Japanese enterprises. In the Asia-Pacific setting similar identities are not evolving. The ambivalence in national policies regarding options for regional trade liberalization is being influenced mainly by pressures to achieve greater international competitiveness, without concessions on market entry.

Japanese and U.S. firms are dominating the regional economy by gaining oligopoly power and internalizing segments within national markets that otherwise remain separated by administrative barriers and informal restrictive business practices. These restraints on entry are being breached from the internalized market segments, and this is happening in an imbalanced pattern in which national decision-makers are tending to give more competitive thrusts to industrial policies.

Industrial Policies and Regional Interdependencies

The evolution of structural interdependencies in the Asia-Pacific region is being influenced by industrial policies mainly from the East Asian side, while from the North American side it is being shaped principally by the independent activities of firms. There could be regional convergence if the U.S. became much more active in the industrial policy area and if Japanese industrial policy decreased its informational and administrative guidance functions. U.S. industrial policy initiatives however have only minor significance for the managements of American international firms, while for their Japanese counterparts the utility of cooperative interaction with the Ministry of International Trade and Industry remains quite high.

Japanese industrial policy, influencing the operations of the nation's international firms, tends to have very extensive effects on the regional interdependencies resulting from transnational acquisitions of market power and corporate internalizations of market processes. As these extensive effects are possible because of the wide-ranging cooperation between Japanese firms in industry groups and networks, there is technocratic interest in maintaining rapport with and working with the managements of those enterprises. As their operations become more extensive and their resources become larger they can act with greater autonomy, but the complexities and uncertainties of their operational environments make the informational and guidance functions of the technocrats more valuable, in so far as these supplement synergistic interactions with affiliated enterprises.[3]

At the policy level, it must be stressed, the Japanese corporate presence in the industrializing East Asian states is especially significant, as a means of balancing the superior leverage of the U.S. on regional economic issues, and of increasing leverage against the European Community. Alignment with this perspective appears to be pervasive among Japanese managements, especially because of the importance of production bases in the industrializing East Asian states, and the opportunities of their rapidly developing markets. Questions of Asia-Pacific regional economic cooperation are evidently seen from this standpoint at the administrative and management levels. The regional dimension of industrial policy thus appears to be directed toward strengthening the integrated configuration of national industrial capacity in the immediate Southern environment while linking the countries in that environment more closely with Japan.[4]

The potential benefits of general trade liberalization in the region seem to be secondary concerns, and it may well be considered that, on balance, there could be substantial gains by U.S. firms after such liberalization. Continued advantages secured by Japanese enterprises through their capacities to obtain informal preferential treatment of direct-investment and trade proposals by industrializing East Asian states are probably hoped for while issues of regional trade liberalization remain difficult to negotiate. Participation in trade liberalization negotiations moreover could be an unwelcome prospect because Japan could face coalitions of Asia-Pacific governments pressing for market access and for more balanced trade. While American leadership of such coalitions could be very active, U.S. political and economic links with industrializing East Asian states could be strengthened through exchanges within the coalitions.

American industrial policy initiatives are intended to promote general improvements in the competitiveness of national high-technology firms, and are not devised on the basis of active interests in the industrializing East Asian states, which have been of diminishing importance in the strategies of U.S. manufacturing enterprises.[5] The trade interests to which the industrial policy initiatives are related are primarily global. The possibility of negotiating substantial Asia-Pacific trade liberalization is given secondary attention, primarily because of emphasis on aggressive unilateralism in separate dealings with each of the East Asian trading partners, which can be an effective means of maximizing the use of bargaining power. In regional negotiations on trade liberalization collective representations of East Asian interests could be confronted, and although the U.S. could well cope with these more successfully than Japan, the benefits from leverage in a series of bilateral relations could be greater.

The operations of American firms directed at East Asian markets, while generally uncoordinated by affiliations at the corporate level or by industrially related trade measures, are likely to remain less effective than those of their Japanese rivals in shaping regional interdependencies. The cross-sectoral and intrasectoral transnational linkages resulting from the Japanese operations are becoming much wider, while setting up extensive entry barriers and restricting the scope for U.S. and other host-country industrial measures aimed at more balanced interdependence.[6] Restrictive trade and foreign direct investment measures are important options for the U.S., but weak bargaining strength tends to prevent their use against Japanese interests in the industrializing East Asian states.

Industrial cooperation within ASEAN, after substantial improvements in the technocratic capacities of its larger members, could produce major changes in the regional pattern of structural interdependencies. Japanese and American corporate involvement in shaping the economies of those members could be reduced and made more compatible with requirements for self-reliant growth. Problems of political development in those members however and of community formation in their association continue to prevent the introduction and harmonization of functional industrial policies.[7] The strategies of their national firms, restricted by administrative failings, are not promoting outward-oriented industrial growth on a scale sufficient to reduce the structural effects of Japanese and American corporate involvement and make them more compatible with designs for the building of optimum national economic systems. Trade liberalization, for the formation of an ASEAN Free Trade Area by the end of the century, is proceeding slowly, because of weak political commitments. Support for market integration among national firms in the member states is fragmented by the effects of administrative biases and of the generally high levels of protection sheltering the import-substituting enterprises.[8]

While collectively more self-reliant outward-oriented ASEAN growth remains difficult to achieve, weak community formation limits the bargaining strength that can be used in dealings with Japan and the U.S. on trade and investment issues. Each member government is individually vulnerable to Japanese and American pressures and inducements, and the vulnerabilities are tending to increase, especially because of the collective dimension of Japanese corporate penetration. The investment from Japan and the U.S. in manufacturing, while contributing to growth and employment, in effect limits the scope for industrial policy measures that might be aimed at the development of national productive capacities. The foreign direct investment policies of the larger ASEAN members, which have become relatively liberal over the past decade, could be under pressure to become more liberal if negotiations for freer trade in the region were being sponsored in the Asia Pacific Economic Cooperation forum by the U.S. As the pressures took effect, the scope for industrial policy endeavors to enhance self-reliant growth could be further reduced.[9]

Japanese corporate expansion in ASEAN, facilitated by the technocratic deficiencies of its larger members, is virtually unchallenged by South Korea and Taiwan, as their opportunities for competing involvement have been limited not only by weaker resources but also by insufficiently developed political ties with ASEAN members. With the multiplication of Japanese economic activities in the ASEAN area, it must be stressed, governments in the larger member states tend to be drawn into increasing dependence on Japanese direct investment in manufacturing, services and resource extraction. Although disparities in the spreads of benefits from Japanese involvement are recognized, the costs of alienating Japanese corporate groups through rejections are evidently seen to be substantial because the direct investment that can be attracted from the U.S. tends to be smaller and less permanent.[10]

The structural interdependencies which Japan is shaping in the industrializing East Asian states are linked with those in its relationship with the U.S. Japanese industrial policy evidently tends to have somewhat weaker influence on the activities of national firms in this relationship, as they have incentives to develop ties with U.S. firms for technology sharing and production sharing, and do not have to seek favorable allocations of official aid from their home government like those made available for the larger ASEAN members.[11] Japanese technocratic objectives, while clearly concerned with promoting a favorable balance between research-intensive production in the U.S. and at home, are evidently sensitive to political constraints affecting the acceptability of foreign firms producing in the United States for the host market. As much of the manufacturing in the industrializing East Asian states is for export to the U.S. moreover the technocratic influence on Japanese corporate strategies in those states may well be guided by recognition of the problems caused by large surpluses in their trade with the U.S. Exports from Japanese subsidiaries account for increasing proportions of the manufacturing items in those surpluses. Diversification through increased emphasis on exports to the European Community is possible, but it is unclear whether guidance from the home administration for that purpose is a significant factor in Japanese corporate decision making.

The influence of Japanese industrial policy on the strategies of national firms shaping structural interdependencies with the U.S. is challenged principally by American trade policy in the bilateral relationship. As the main thrust of this policy is toward the development of managed trade in high-technology products a major task for Japanese decision-makers is to promote technological leads in their nation's firms that can be maintained, with increasing market advantages, while U.S. demands are accommodated quantitatively according to product standards that become inferior. The dynamics of pluralistic policymaking in the U.S. cause those demands to be made after some lags during which faster Japanese advances in applied technology continue. Market shares that have to be granted to the U.S. meanwhile tend to be more than offset by the gains of Japanese firms in the American market.[12]

The Japanese gains in the U.S. market tend to activate protectionist demands by American producers, and these are encouraged by successes in triggering administrative restrictions on imports from Japan. The sheltered American firms then profit from their domestic market strength. The resulting benefits, however, do not lead to superior competitiveness. The generally strong emphasis on financial management, entailing less concern with manufacturing efficiency, tends to be increased, mainly because of pressures for short-term profits. Japanese emphasis on quality as well as price competition ensures strong influence on demand patterns among U.S. consumers, while the quality competition is maintained by further rapid advances in applied technology. At the same time the gains in product markets are paralleled by Japanese acquisitions of larger shares in markets for production equipment, against which there is little scope for restrictive U.S. trade policy measures, because of the dependence of U.S. manufacturers on such supplies.[13]

Macromanagement Interdependence

Asia-Pacific industrial policy measures influence corporate strategies in a larger context of macromanagement interdependence, in which the combined effects of interacting policy mixes reflect affinities and dissimilarities between national political economies, together with contrasts in bargaining strengths. In this setting Japanese capacities for competitive macromanagement through neocorporatist processes challenge pluralistic American policymaking within the restricted scope set by a tradition of limited government.

The regional macromanagement interdependence has evolved in conditions of regional disequilibrium. The principal cause has been strong fiscal expansion in the U.S., which, by increasing consumer demand, has substantially raised imports of highly competitive manufactures from Japan, enabling the exporting firms to finance technological improvements for more intense competitiveness and to undertake large-scale manufacturing in the United States. In the initial phases of this sequence severe monetary tightening to restrain the inflationary pressures of fiscal expansion resulted in appreciation of the U.S. dollar, adding to the rise in imports while causing losses of foreign market shares by U.S. firms and giving impetus to outward direct investment from the United States. After depreciation was promoted by the U.S. monetary authorities in 1985, to avert what could have been a heavy fall in the value of the dollar, Japanese investment in manufacturing within the U.S., which had begun to overcome trade barriers, surged to fairly high levels. While the manufacturing in effect substituted for exports from Japan, this effect on the trade balance was offset by procurement of inputs from Japan, and Japanese exporting firms retained and even increased market shares in the U.S. through price competition with very low profit margins. Meanwhile U.S. firms sourced products from Japan on a relatively large scale. The overall U.S. trade balance, while altered on that account, was also changed by continuing rises in overseas production by American international firms, increasing the already large ratio between such production and U.S. exports.[14]

The adverse trade effects of heavy fiscal expansion could have been overcome by shifts to fiscal discipline, but politically these were not feasible because of distributional pressures in the policy process. Increased protection of the internal U.S. market was an alternative, but was introduced with considerable restraint, because of business interest in avoiding retaliatory measures by trading partners. As the fiscal deficits continued, an unprecedented dependence on Japanese purchases of U.S. government bonds became an additional constraint, more visible to the U.S. Treasury than to many of the legislators who were becoming responsible for Congressional activism on trade policy during the early 1990s. Any major trade measures directed against Japan could affect investor attitudes in that country toward the purchasing of U.S. government debt. U.S. industrial policy initiatives emphasizing support for technological progress under the Bush and Clinton administrations promised long-term improvements in the competitiveness of American firms, but trends in commerce during the early 1990s did not suggest that enhanced export performance would sufficiently counter the import-increasing effects of the fiscal deficits.[15]

The asymmetries in macromanagement interdependence have thus become extraordinary, especially because of the involvement of American problems of governance and the scale of competitive advantages associated with Japanese macromanagement. On each side the focus on bilateral issues has been intense, and there has been no question of constructive participation by other major industrialized democracies, as the European Community has on the whole failed to engage with issues in that relationship affecting its own interests in the stability of the world economy.[16] The industrializing East Asian states and other Pacific countries have lacked the cohesion that would be necessary to represent collective interests affected by the imbalances in U.S.-Japan economic relations.

American decision-making on the bilateral issues has been conflicted, short term and cybernetic rather than rational, leaving fundamental problems of macromanagement unresolved. Compromises to overcome distributional issues that have been necessary for the passage of budgets have perpetuated the heavy fiscal deficits. Executive and legislative choices on virtually all major policy questions have been directed at short-term solutions, with mainly reactive approaches to engagement, motivated by vote-maximizing concerns. Problems that have not attracted attention because of the prospects of difficult and low political rewards for the administration have been neglected, and among these has been the very high volume of overseas production by U.S. firms in relation to manufacturing in the U.S. for export, and in relation to foreign manufacturing in the United States.[17] Slack growth and strains in the U.S. economy, to which the corporate emphasis on overseas production has contributed, have given American enterprises stronger incentives to expand their transnational production operations, to increase foreign market shares and reduce risk exposure as well as tax and regulatory exposure at home.[18]

The U.S.'s fiscal deficits and the balance of payments effects of its trade deficits have become unsustainable, while strains in its financial system have indicated the danger of an economic crisis.[19] Predictions of dollar depreciation made several years ago have been validated, and falls in the currency are likely to continue. Attempts to increase growth and reduce trade imbalances by persuading the Japanese administration to undertake greatly increased domestic spending have resulted in only modest increases in U.S. exports. Higher consumer demand in Japan of course has mainly benefited that nation's own firms, strengthening their resources for international operations.

Altogether, the involvement of problems of governance in the macromanagement interdependence experienced by the U.S. has severely restricted the scope for constructive interaction in the relationship with Japan, while causing U.S. trade policy options to assume greater significance than industrial policy initiatives. If sufficiently constructive interaction had developed in the bilateral context, considerable industrial cooperation might have become possible, through complementary specializations agreed without forceful bargaining at conferences of Japanese industry groups and American consortia. In the absence of constructive interaction, U.S. leverage to secure some industrial cooperation has had very limited results, and accordingly there has been increasing reliance on pressures to secure market-opening concessions by Japan.[20]

For the industrializing East Asian states, the shifting asymmetries of interdependence in the U.S.-Japan relationship have facilitated a strengthening of the Japanese presence in the region while contributing to increases in U.S. restraints on imports of low, mature, and high technology products. Increased consideration of Japanese corporate interests has tended to become necessary because of both effects and also because of the probability that ASEAN will remain a rather loose association whose members will tend to compete against each other to attract Japanese direct investment.[21] This prospect, it must be stressed, has not encouraged South Korea and Taiwan to seek active cooperation with ASEAN, despite the needs of its larger members for diversification of their foreign economic relations.

Japanese Industrial Cooperation

A somewhat hierarchical pattern of industrial cooperation is developing in East Asia as Japanese--trade and investment--links with South Korea, Taiwan and the ASEAN states become larger. The links with South Korea have developed because of that country's capabilities for high-technology manufacturing, notably in the automobile and electronic sectors. Similar manufacturing on a narrower scale has been the basis for cooperation with Taiwan. In the larger ASEAN states collaboration has evolved principally through Japanese investment in assembly plants and resource-extraction ventures. Technocratic capacities in South Korea and Taiwan have been at levels appropriate for intensive industrial cooperation with Japanese economic ministries and firms. Lower levels of technocratic competence in the larger ASEAN members have tended to hinder Japanese quests for industrial cooperation, but the heavier investment and technological dependence of those members has in effect allowed Japanese economic ministries and firms wide scope for choice in shaping trade and investment connections in the ASEAN area.

South Korea's development of a relatively diversified high-technology manufacturing capacity has been strongly self-reliant. The intensifying competition associated with oligopolistic trends in the linking of high technology markets, however, has tended to obligate industrial cooperation with Japan on an increasing scale. Japanese corporate and technocratic interest has been very active because of South Korea's proximity and level of industrial development, and because the appreciation of the yen over the past decade has necessitated use of South Korea's capabilities for lower-cost research-intensive production, as well as access to the country's centers of innovation. South Korean corporate and technocratic interests been strong because the resources to support self-reliant internationally competitive high-technology manufacturing have been becoming inadequate. Very large Japanese and also U.S. firms investing heavily in advanced applied technology have been tending to force enterprises with less substantial resources into declines. Collaborative arrangements with U.S. firms have offered partial solutions, but Japanese proposals have held out prospects for more comprehensive and longer-term cooperation.[22] With the multiplication of trade and investment links between South Korea and Japan moreover there have been incentives to respond positively to Japanese proposals. Attitudes to these have been influenced by the protectionist shifts in American trade policy over the past decade. Heavy dependence on the U.S. market has obliged South Korean decision-makers to strive for greater penetration of that market through research-intensive production facilitated by links with Japanese firms. Such production has also been intended to aid diversification away from the U.S., especially through wider entries into the European market.

Asymmetries in the relationship with Japan tend to keep South Korea in a relatively subordinate position. Access to the Japanese market is restricted by its established patterns of relational contracting, which limit prospects for the development of balanced intra-industry trade at rising technological levels. The Japanese industry groups and networks remain exclusive, and their member firms tend to relate to South Korean enterprises at arm's length, with the advantages of superior bargaining power and technological leads, and with reservations about facilitating transfers of the results of very advanced research. At the policy level Japanese economic ministries also tend to relate to their South Korean counterparts at arm's length, with considerable potential leverage because of control of access to their market and influence on the strategies of Japanese firms.

Industrial cooperation develops mainly because of Japanese corporate initiatives, which account for the bulk of foreign direct investment in South Korea.[23] Investment dependence develops because of the pre-emptive effects of the integrated pattern of Japanese involvement, the increasing association of

South Korean suppliers with the incoming firms, the participation of those firms in joint ventures with host country enterprises, and strong reliance by South Korean corporations on imports of Japanese plant and machinery. Direct investment by U.S. firms is about half the volume from Japan, and has been tending to decline, while direct investment from the European Community is roughly 50% lower than the American level. South Korean direct investment in Japan is extremely low, and thus has very little significance for Japanese industrial policy. For that policy however the evolution of the large and diversified Japanese research-intensive manufacturing operations in South Korea has special significance because of its proximity and because it is the main component of what has become the largest Japanese share of foreign direct investment in an industrializing East Asian country.

Japanese industrial policy, closely aligned with the strategies of Japanese firms, fulfils broad coordinating functions based on consultations with those enterprises. The South Korean administration is not able to seek integrative industrial cooperation for the development of a more equal partnership in growth. Its situation tends to incline it toward the attraction of increased export-oriented Japanese direct investment, especially as a means of increasing exports to Japan. Such exports have to grow mainly as intrafirm shipments by Japanese corporations, because of their high degrees of control over access to their home market through industry group and network affiliations.[24]

Taiwan's strategy of self-reliant outward-oriented industrialization, in which large numbers of small firms have been active, with an emphasis on electronics, has also been obliged to accept strong commercial and investment links with Japan because of actual and threatened restrictions on access to the U.S. market, on which dependence has been heavy. American manufacturing investment in Taiwan for export had accounted for roughly half the total foreign inflow by the mid 1980s, and was about 10% higher than Japan's, but incoming Japanese direct investment has become increasingly larger than that from the U.S. during the current decade. This larger inflow has begun to assume special significance for reasons similar to those in South Korea.[25]

Taiwan's potential for moving into more advanced and wider-ranging high-volume high-technology manufacturing has been limited by the absence of large firms with research-intensive capabilities like those in South Korea, and by U.S. restrictions, over the past decade, on imports of mature- and low-technology manufactures that had been helping to finance Taiwan's industrial development. Export-led growth, moreover, has also become difficult since the late 1980s because of American pressure which forced appreciation of Taiwan's currency. To reduce the vulnerabilities of heavy dependence on the U.S. market Taiwan has sought to expand trade and investment links with Europe, but the main strategy has been to broaden economic ties with Japan. On the Japanese side interest has been strong because of the modest but increasing development of Taiwan's research-intensive manufacturing capabilities, which have been opening up opportunities for joint ventures and for subcontracting in support of Japanese production activities.[26] Politically the multiplication of commercial links between Taiwan and mainland China over the past half decade has tended to encourage some Japanese use of Taiwan as a base for the supply of the mainland market.

Dependence on Japan for high-technology plant and equipment and for technology transfers associated with Japanese research-intensive manufacturing is tending to increase, while Taiwan experiences the effects of a decline of U.S. direct investment in East Asia. Links with Japanese firms are bringing Taiwan into closer association with the integrated Japanese manufacturing and trading presence in the industrializing East Asian states. As in the South Korean case however it is difficult for Taiwan to expand exports to Japan, and there are few outflows of direct investment to Japan. Such outflows go mainly to the U.S., but a substantial volume goes into assembly-type manufacturing in the larger ASEAN members. Ties with overseas Chinese business groups in those ASEAN states have facilitated the outward direct investment. The resulting trade and production links help to offset the investment and technological dependence on Japan, and help also to strengthen Taiwan's bargaining power. That dependence, however, it must be stressed, has to be accepted because of the increasing difficulties of competition in the internationalizing markets for research-intensive manufactures. Revenues from commercial activities in the ASEAN area, mainland China, the U.S., and Europe, although increasing overall, are dispersed among numerous small enterprises and thus are not sufficient to finance internationally competitive ventures into advanced self-reliant manufacturing with a breadth approaching that in South Korea.[27]

Indonesia, Malaysia, and Thailand are the ASEAN members of major importance to Japan as trading partners. Indonesia has become very heavily dependent on exports to Japan--mainly primary products--and on Japanese direct investment in resource industries and assembly-type manufacturing. Malaysia has more diversified trade and direct investment links, but those with the U.S., Europe, and other Asian countries, although substantial, are not growing as fast as those with Japan. Thailand's external economic ties exhibit similar diversity and change, but with greater dependence on Japan. In both Malaysia and Thailand increasing dependence on Japanese direct investment is associated with high-volume imports from Japan--about 25% of each total. There are substantial deficits in commerce with Japan, mainly because Malaysian and Thai low-technology firms lack access to the Japanese market. Indonesia has relatively large surpluses because of energy exports, and because its domestic market is less developed and is sheltered by high protectionist barriers as well as by the effects of bureaucratic deficiencies.

Malaysian, Thai and Indonesian low-technology manufactures, because of cost advantages, may gradually replace exports of such products to Japan by South Korea and Taiwan, while those two states increase their sales to Japan of more technology-intensive products. Technological leads which Japanese firms have over their South Korean and Taiwan counterparts are likely to be maintained, while technological lags in Malaysian, Thai, and Indonesian industries will probably continue. Potentials for change in the pattern depend primarily on the evolution of each country's individual economic ties with Japan, and these are being determined mainly by the investment and trade decisions of Japanese firms.

Differing degrees of economic nationalism influence Malaysian, Thai and Indonesian policies. Malay communalism, antipathetic to Malaysia's Chinese community, welcomes foreign direct investment that can assist overall growth and weaken the economic power of that community. Dependence on foreign direct investment for industrial development has been increased in recent decades by Malay communal pressure on the Chinese business community, which has discouraged Chinese manufacturing entrepreneurship and contributed to a flight of Chinese capital. Dependence on Japanese technology and managerial skills, notably for the development of an automobile industry, has been growing more than reliance on other sources of foreign assistance. Because of the small size of the domestic economy the possibilities for self-reliant outward-oriented industrialization are quite limited. Various forms of cooperation with Japanese corporations have become necessary for aspiring Malaysian manufacturing firms on that account, and because association with the Japanese enterprises, although on a subordinate basis, can provide opportunities for entries into American, East Asian, and European markets. With technology transfers related to the operations of Japanese firms Malaysian enterprises can begin to compete against South Korean and Taiwan exports of low-technology manufactures to Japan. Technocratic capacities for the orchestration of export-oriented industrial growth however are likely to remain lower than those in South Korea and Taiwan. Hence the Malaysian dependence on Japanese industrial collaboration will probably become greater.[28] On the Japanese side, at the governmental and enterprise levels, dealings at arm's length are customary, as in relations with South Korea and Taiwan. There is evidently a perceived rationale for avoiding the build-up of a corporate presence large enough to provoke Malay resentments, although competitive displacement of American and European firms is clearly intended to continue.

Economic nationalism is a moderate force in Thailand, where there is much openness to Japanese direct investment but a relatively weaker technocratic capacity to promote and assist cooperation with incoming Japanese enterprises. The scope for Japanese exploitation of local business opportunities is wider because of a very liberal foreign direct investment policy, but use of these opportunities is limited by Thai administrative deficiencies, and by a fragmentation of authority in the present Thai government.[29] Those problems also limit what can be achieved through Japanese initiatives for cooperation in industrial policy measures. These could have special significance for Japanese firms because of a lack of coherence in the evolving Thai pattern of industrial development and serious shortcomings in the building of Thailand's industrial infrastructure.

The main incentives for incoming Japanese manufacturing enterprises are to undertake assembly-type operations with cost advantages for export but also for the relatively large expanding Thai market. Thai low -and mature-technology manufacturing enterprises, sheltered by high protectionist barriers and subjected to parasitic administrative attention during long periods of military rule, lack capacities for efficient cooperation with Japanese corporations. There is little host government pressure to collaborate with them and Japanese managements can concentrate on extending their own corporate structures for operations in the Thai economy. These operations tend to restrict opportunities for American and European firms, while giving Thai and local Chinese firms incentives to develop links with the expanding Japanese presence.[30]

Economic nationalism in Indonesia is a strong force, and can be given firm expression by the ruling military elite, which implements its policies in an authoritarian manner, through Western-trained technocrats. These influence and are responsive to the idiosyncratic preferences of the military leadership, and have to live with its neopatrimonial practices, which retain the loyalties of prominent figures in the armed forces. There is a high-level technocratic capability to promote significantly self-reliant outward-oriented industrialization, but the use of revenues from large energy exports for this purpose has been inadequate, because of much corruption and incompetence. Low technology manufacturing under a heavily protected import substituting industrialization strategy has had to cope with serious administrative failings, and has not been able to support advances into internationally competitive production at higher technological levels. There has been increasing openness to Japanese direct investment in resource extraction and manufacturing assembly plants producing for export.[31]

Politically the relationship has to be managed skilfully by the Japanese side because the military leadership is capable of changing policy arbitrarily, can impose its wishes on its technocrats, and is not very open to representations from the business community. Assertions of economic nationalism can help to strengthen the domestic strength of the leadership, which rests on popular submission to the army's monopoly of power. Politicized urban populations may challenge that power, as happened in Thailand during 1992. The dimensions of the Japanese economic presence could become an issue in such a context, or in the equally unstable setting of factional rivalries for control of the military establishment and the regime. Japanese firms accordingly have interests in developing joint ventures and linkages with Indonesian firms, especially those with which military leaders have special bonds, while preserving the distinctive managerial cultures which can ensure efficient management of those relationships.

Japan's industrial policy, cooperating with the strategies of its firms, appears to be working at arm's length toward a widening interdependence with asymmetries acceptable to the military regime because of the growth processes to which they contribute. Indonesia is the principal source of Japan's energy imports, and the large size of its developing economy clearly merits high priority in long-term planning for the marketing of Japanese manufactured products. Indonesia's imports from Japan have been roughly double those from the U.S. over the past decade and have been much larger than those from Europe. Issues about Indonesian access to the Japanese market for -low and mature-technology products have not become prominent in the relationship because Indonesia's energy exports account for a large surplus in its favor, and because the Japanese investment in assembly plants is building up a capability for exporting to the U.S. and Europe. A decline in U.S. direct investment, relative to that from Japan, is a well-established trend. The acceptability of a large Japanese corporate presence moreover is apparently influenced by antipathies toward the U.S. because of its criticisms of the military regime's human rights violations and its suppression of the independence movement in Timor.[32] Japanese economic diplomacy has avoided comments on the Indonesian regime's hard authoritarianism.

American Regional Involvement

The U.S.'s market-opening trade policy, together with a market-opening thrust in its foreign direct investment policy, is the main regional challenge at the macromanagement level to Japanese economic expansion. American international high-technology firms, while tending to lose their national identities, have been showing less active interest than their Japanese counterparts in the industrializing East Asian states because of difficulties of operating in those environments. These have included high transaction costs, high information costs, frequently low levels of administrative cooperation, and the informal entry barriers maintained by local business groups.[33] American enterprises have to function without the industry group and network affiliations which enable Japanese firms to cope with those problems in the industrializing East Asian states. While relating to each other almost exclusively as competitors, moreover, the American enterprises are not indirectly aided by U.S. official assistance for infrastructure development in East Asian host countries on a scale that would compare with Japanese developmental aid. The U.S. administration's market-opening policy tends to discourage positive responses because of the manifestations of less active U.S. corporate interest in direct investment, and also because of the reluctance of U.S. managements to enter joint ventures with host country partners. Japanese corporate and official involvement does not have an explicit market-opening thrust, and tends to gain acceptance because of its larger contributions to the development of export potentials.

The U.S. market-opening policy, demanding reduction of the protectionist barriers sheltering East Asian economies, affirms interest in balanced trade without showing appreciation of concerns in the industrializing East Asian states about the vulnerabilities of their domestic firms and about the American capacity for leverage on trade issues. For the East Asian decision-makers the development of unequal but growth-enhancing links with the Japanese corporate presence is thus an appropriate means of coping with the American pressure and limiting the costs of yielding incrementally to U.S. requests. The absence of a developmentally significant industrial policy dimension in American economic diplomacy tends to increase the significance of the more comprehensive forms of cooperation offered on a long-term basis from the Japanese side.[34]

Regional perceptions of reduced American interest in political bonds with the industrializing East Asian states and stronger focus on the pursuit of market opportunities for U.S. firms have influenced perspectives on the American market-opening demands. It has evidently been clear, moreover, that U.S. pressures could be applied against South Korea, Taiwan, and the ASEAN members more readily than against Japan, because of the constraints of interdependence in that relationship. The American endeavor to establish a North American Free Trade Area, while signalling a reorientation of foreign economic policy, has been viewed with fears that U.S. links with East Asia would be managed more distantly, and that American corporations would give more attention to Mexico's location advantages than to those in developing East Asian states. The development of an East Asian Economic Caucus has become an ASEAN objective, to balance the North American Free Trade Area, but as it promises to be a loose association, each industrializing East Asian state tends to be drawn individually toward accommodation with Japanese regional interests.[35]

While American manufacturing firms are undertaking production and trading activities in the industrializing East Asian states on a relatively smaller scale than the Japanese--and losing home country identities--the regional involvement of U.S. financial enterprises is tending to decrease relative to the Japanese financial presence. Impetus is being given to this process by the strength of the yen and the volume of transactions in yen, as well as by an expansion of Japanese financial institutions. Reports of stresses and fragility in the American financial sector evidently contribute to the trend. A regional network of Japanese financial enterprises provides multiple sources of support for operations by manufacturing firms in related industry groups and consortia, with competitive advantages over U.S. financial corporations because of lower cost and longer-term relational lending. The Japanese financial network is well placed to assist local firms in the industrializing East Asian states, and can do so with wide spreading of risk because of the incentives of assisted enterprises to contract with manufacturing and trading firms in industry groups with which the Japanese financial corporations are affiliated.[36]

American policy in the area is overshadowed by problems in asymmetrical structural interdependence with Japan. A strong focus on the bilateral issues limits U.S. attention to relationships with the industrializing East Asian states. In the interactions with Japan, industrial policy objectives have been introduced into trade policy, and interest in those objectives has been tending to assume wider dimensions. American market-opening demands over the past few years have secured some shares of the Japanese market for semiconductors, communications equipment and automobile parts. Efficiencies hopefully made possible for the assisted U.S. enterprises have been expected to help them operate with greater international competitiveness, in trade with Japan and the rest of the world. The intended benefits for American firms however have become elusive because of continuing Japanese advances in applied technology that cause items designated for managed trade to become obsolete and that result in market gains in the U.S. itself and in Europe. Meanwhile Japanese progress in related areas of applied technology also ensures market gains that provoke U.S. pressures for managed trade on a wider scale.[37]

The governmental interactions have been competitive and conflicted and have not led to any linking of policy communities on the basis of shared perceptions of compatible interests that could be served through integrative cooperation. On the Japanese side coping with U.S. demands has evidently tended to increase emphasis on maintaining the exclusive quality of the national culture and the high degree of integration in the political economy. Hence the relationship has been managed distantly, without initiatives to promote rapport. Intense long-established awareness of resource deficiencies has been a fundamental source of Japanese motivation, because an acute sense of vulnerability has been felt to obligate striving for comprehensive economic security, through maximizing competitive penetration of foreign markets.

The U.S.'s problems of governance, due to institutional weaknesses, distributional pressures, and strong pluralism, have been seen as hindrances to the development of a stable and constructive policy consensus to which Japanese policymakers could relate. American bargaining for greater market access, with threats of increased protectionism, has accordingly been countered by delaying tactics and minimal concessions. This diplomacy has been implemented with apparently broad consensus in Japan's business and political elites. Its feasibility has clearly been influenced by the growth of Japanese exports to industrializing East Asian states, which exceed exports to the U.S. and are increasing much faster, and also by increases in Japanese exports to the European Community, which have been rising at about the same pace over the past half decade and which could soon equal or surpass those to the United States. The expansion of Japanese exports to the U.S. has been slowed over the past decade by increasing export substitution through manufacturing in the United States.[38] At the same time continuing U.S. financial dependence on Japanese investors for the sale of government debt, while potentially destabilizing strains in the American financial system remain serious, is evidently recognized to be a constraint on U.S. trade leverage. That leverage of course could be more potent if the U.S. had strong rapport with the European Community, but stresses in that relationship, notably over agricultural protectionism, have in effect been advantageous for Japan.

The structural interdependence increased by market-opening demands has been largely unrelated to the interdependence resulting from strategic alliances between U.S. and Japanese high-technology manufacturing firms through spontaneous initiatives for technology sharing and market sharing. These have complicated industrial policy concerns in American trade policy, as they have been increasing in line with the general multiplication of strategic alliances between American, Japanese and European high-technology firms.[39] These have facilitated wider Japanese exploitation of the advantages of industry group and network affiliations, which have made possible more extensive technological and market gains, while increasing incentives for U.S. firms to participate in such alliances.

The American market-opening endeavors have caused Japanese corporations to become more aware of the value of their industry group and network ties. With those ties Japanese managements have been able to undertake strategic alliances with U.S. and European firms at their discretion. As these have developed the context in which the U.S. administration has been able to push for shares of Japan's high-technology product markets has been altered. U.S. corporate interest in strategic alliances with Japanese firms has in some respects moderated American business pressure for increases in the managed trade. Many of the benefits of the strategic alliances have been secured by U.S. enterprises in the course of overseas production and intrafirm trade, without major effects on the bilateral trade balance, while the shares of those enterprises in Japanese markets have been obscured by the distribution functions of the Japanese partners.[40] Tracking and assessing the results of the strategic alliances has been more feasible for the management of Japanese industrial policy, because of pervasive relational information sharing, than it has been for the diverse agencies involved in American trade policy.

Collective Management Issues

Trends in the evolution of regional structural and policy interdependencies, as they are being shaped mainly from the Japanese side at the corporate and government levels, are presenting issues for the U.S. and the industrializing East Asian states, but there is little recognition of these as problems requiring *collective* management. The industrializing East Asian states have to accept status inferiority in the external relations of Japan and the U.S., and the preferences of those two major economic powers are to manage their mutual concerns bilaterally. In that relationship the U.S. initiatives for the advancement of industrial-policy concerns through trade policy are in part endeavors to use scope for executive discretion that does not depend on legislative support. To engage with fundamentals affecting the trading relationship however, that administration seeks legislative authorizations for a technology-enhancement program.[41] Depending on its scale and the ways in which it is administered it may become a source of change in the regional pattern. While it may gradually contribute to the development of more balanced trade with Japan, however, it may not significantly affect the strengthening of economic bonds between the industrializing East Asian states and Japan. The external reach of Japanese industrial policy may thus continue to expand.

If the structural interdependence between the U.S. and Japan became more balanced, with commitments at the policy level to maintain a relatively even spread of gains from trade and transnational production links, some collaboration for the promotion of regional economic cooperation could evolve. Japanese political and corporate elites however have intense motivations to strengthen their nation's structural competitiveness and thus secure an increasingly powerful position in the world economy. The less-integrated policy communities and corporate associations in the U.S. are working mainly for a balanced relationship, to be attained hopefully by enhancing the competitiveness of American firms and inducing the Japanese administration to adopt more liberal policies. A reorientation of American perspectives toward regional economic cooperation at an elementary level would be feasible, as an extension of the concept of a North American Free Trade Area. The reorientation that would be necessary in Japan however would be very difficult because of the intensity and duration of the socializing processes that have sustained the nation's entire system of normative integration and relational contracting for superior structural competitiveness.

The elementary level of regional economic cooperation acceptable to American political and corporate elites would be the formation of a liberalized Pacific trade area, on terms that would promise the continued evolution of balanced commerce with Japan, and substantial reductions of the high levels of effective protection maintained by many of the industrializing East Asian states. Regional trade liberalization is a stated objective of the Asia Pacific Economic Cooperation forum, in which the U.S. and Japan are the principal members, and negotiations for general reductions of trade barriers could develop under the auspices of that forum. The United States has more regional scope for initiative than Japan, because of dissatisfactions in the industrializing East Asian states with their lack of access to the Japanese market, and because culturally the Japanese political economy is a relatively closed system.[42] Aggressive American unilateralism, however, could antagonize the industrializing East Asian states as well as Japan. This could happen because an American effort to promote free trade would be an endeavor keyed to the administration's short-term political interests, and would tend to evoke cautious and delayed East Asian responses.

Because of the increasing significance of transnational production in the regional pattern of structural interdependencies, liberalized Pacific trade would have to be accompanied by a liberalization of regional foreign direct investment policies. This would be necessary to meet American concerns about the potent informal restrictions on U.S. direct investment in Japan, which contrast with the wide scope for operations by Japanese manufacturing and trading firms in the U.S. Formal commitments by the Japanese administration would have to be given sufficient significance by changes in the behavior of Japanese firms to allow more freedom for foreign enterprises. Yet for the Japanese this would be a difficult and unwelcome solution, as it would disturb the relational contracting which sustains solidarity in the national business community.[43]

The problems to be considered in the dominant economic relationship of the region can thus be seen to demand more attention than would appear after initial recognition of the potential benefits of lowering barriers to Pacific trade. Questions about the spread of gains which would arise in any regional setting become especially complex in the Pacific because of asymmetries in the operations of Japanese and American firms which relate to the dimensions of entry barriers and the scales on which those enterprises internalize market segments. The asymmetries are becoming more significant, with advantages mainly for the Japanese side, and, while causing intensifications of pressure for change in the U.S., are tending to make quests for a cooperative solution more difficult.

Change in Japanese industrial policy could assist the development of a more balanced transnational production and distribution pattern which would benefit the bilateral relationship and the regional system of economic relations. Politically it may well be possible to effect changes without seriously weakening the solidarity-based technocratic-managerial consultative links which ensure structural competitiveness. The most important options that appear to be open are an expansion of the industrial policy community, to facilitate U.S. inputs, and a reorientation of administrative guidance toward increased industrial cooperation in the bilateral relationship.

The higher levels of the Japanese industrial policy community could be brought into close and continuous contact with officials shaping U.S. technology policy through the establishment of a joint long-range planning group by the Ministry of International Trade and Industry and the main technology bureau in the U.S. Department of Commerce. A Japanese initiative for this could be explained domestically as an endeavor to develop continuing rapport with U.S. decision makers about fundamental long-term complementarities of interest relating to Japanese industrial capacity in the U.S. and U.S. industrial capacity in Japan. Positive responses from the U.S. Department of Commerce could be hoped for because of the improved prospects of working toward a more balanced trading relationship and a more symmetrical transnational production relationship. Participation in the joint policy planning moreover could enable the Department of Commerce to encourage many of the business groups in the U.S. to unite for the formation of strong peak industrial associations, thus overcoming a fragmentation of producers' interests which contributes to pluralistic stagnation at the legislative level.

Deep-seated American corporate distrust of government would limit the cooperation needed for a suitably functional U.S. technology policy, while business lobbying and legislative opportunism would tend to distort public-goods objectives in that policy. U.S. officials in the joint-planning group moreover would be inclined to see the Japanese participants as representatives of a very exclusive and quite alien policy community, cooperating with many reservations about information to be shared and interests to be identified. To help overcome these problems the Japanese members of the joint-planning group could develop supplementary skills for relating to U.S. business groups, while giving their U.S. counterparts opportunities to do the same in Japan. The dysfunctional effects of lobbying and legislative opportunism on U.S. technology policy would remain serious, but could be moderated by firm executive restraints on the use of subsidies and emphasis on guidance functions in the promotion of cooperative private sector research.[44]

The Japanese option of reorienting the Ministry of International Trade and Industry's administrative guidance would require a sustained educative effort to increase corporate awareness of problems regarding the political acceptability of production and trading activities in the U.S. The increasing importance of concerting corporate strategies toward the development of more balanced interdependence would have to be given much stress. The integrated complex of Japanese manufacturing firms, suppliers, trading enterprises and financial organizations in the U.S. could be urged to become open to the development of long-term collaborative arrangements with selected U.S. enterprises. In the home economy Japanese industry groups and networks could also be encouraged to seek enduring links with American firms in Japan, on the basis of informal affiliations.

The established tradition of administrative responsiveness to corporate interests, together with pressures exerted in the expression of those interests, could hinder the development of an elite consensus for change in administrative guidance. Politically however the building of such a consensus could be helped by the setting up of the proposed joint long-range planning group through which the Ministry of International Trade and Industry would relate to the U.S. Department of Commerce. A shift in American foreign economic policy away from aggressive unilateralism would also help, that is if leadership could be provided to counter domestic pressures activated by perceptions of unequal gains in the trading relationship. Increased cooperation between U.S. firms, to reduce

X inefficiencies due to totally competitive behavior, would meanwhile increase the U.S.'s structural competitiveness, thus changing fundamentals in a way that would make the relationship more balanced.[45]

The increased collaboration in areas of industrial policy according with the American tradition of limited government could have policy-learning effects conducive to wider cooperation. This could happen because of increases in understanding and trust, and greater awareness of potentials for technology sharing. In the U.S., corporate contributions to policy and Commerce Department attitudes could be influenced by the moderation of bilateral trade conflicts. Similar effects would be possible in Japan. Meanwhile increased and more stable trade-assisted growth in the U.S. could help reduction of its fiscal imbalance. In both Japan and the U.S., then, policies could be managed with greater attention to Japanese needs for access to basic research in the U.S. and American needs for Japanese cooperation in commercial applications of advanced technology.

Regionally, the increased bilateral cooperation could encourage industrializing East Asian states to show more active interest in collective management of their economic links with Japan and the U.S. The possibility of a joint U.S.-Japan approach to trade and investment dealings with the industrializing East Asian states would be evident. This would offer a wider range of choices for those states than would be possible if they had to anticipate only a strengthening of the Japanese presence in their area. To make appropriate choices in their common interest however they would have to concert their policies. This would be difficult, but the Association of South East Asian Nations, to which several of them belong, could become a more cohesive and more active grouping. Change of that kind could be aided by U.S. initiatives to promote industrial cooperation with the Association, on terms suited to the special needs of ASEAN firms as enterprises adjusting to the gradual integration of their market and to imperatives for greater openness in the Pacific economy.

Notes

1. For a review of APEC see Donald Crone, "Does Hegemony Matter? The Reorganization of the Pacific Political Economy," *World Politics*, 45 (July 1993) 4: 501-525.

2. John H. Dunning, and Peter Robson, "Multinational Corporate Integration and Regional Economic Integration," in John H. Dunning and Peter Robson (eds.), *Multinationals and the European Community* (Oxford: Blackwell, 1988), 1-24.

3. On the efficiencies of interactions within industry groups, see W. Carl Kester, "Industrial Groups as Systems of Contractual Governance," *Oxford Review of Economic Policy*, 8 (Autumn 1992) 3: 24-44.
4. On the network of Japanese firms in East Asia, see *World Investment Report*, 1991 (New York: United Nations Centre on Transnational Corporations, 1991), 44-52, and *Foreign Direct Investment Relations between the OECD and the Dynamic Asian Economies* (Paris: OECD, 1993), 31-60.
5. Linda Lim, "Explaining the Decline of U.S. Investment in Southeast Asia," *Journal of Southeast Asian Business*, 7 (Spring 1991) 2: 90-93.
6. See observations on Japanese firms in World Investment Report, 1991..., and in Dennis J. Encarnation, "A Common Evolution? A Comparison of United States and Japanese Transnational Corporations," *Transnational Corporations*, 2 (February 1993) 1: 7-32.
7. See symposium in *ASEAN Economic Bulletin*, 8 (March 1992) 3; Somrudee Nicro, "Thailand's NIC Democracy: Studying from General Elections," and William Case, "Semi-Democracy in Malaysia: Withstanding the Pressures for Regime Change," *Pacific Affairs*, 66 (Summer 1993) 2: 167-182, 183-205; and Michael Leifer, "Uncertainty in Indonesia," *World Policy Journal*, VIII (Winter 1990/91) 1: 137-158.
8. *ASEAN Economic Bulletin...*
9. On the orientation of U.S. trade policy, see I.M. Destler, *American Trade Politics* (Second edition) (Washington: Institute for International Economics, 1992).
10. Lim, "Explaining the Decline of U.S. Investment..."
11. See discussion of Japanese firms in the U.S., in Dennis J. Encarnation, *Rivals beyond Trade: America versus Japan in Global Competition* (Ithaca: Cornell University Press, 1992), ch. 3.
12. Ibid.; and Encarnation, "A Common Evolution? A Comparison..."
13. On Japanese technological strengths, see Nathan Rosenberg, Ralph Landau, and David C. Mowery (eds.), *Technology and the Wealth of Nations* (Stanford: Stanford University Press, 1992); David C. Mowery, and David J. Teece, "Japan's Growing Capabilities in Industrial Technology: Implications for U.S. Managers and Policymakers," *California Management Review*, 35 (Winter 1993) 2: 9-34.
14. On the sourcing of foreign products by U.S. firms, see Masaaki Kotabe, *Global Sourcing Strategy* (New York: Quorum Books, 1992), part II; and Encarnation, *Rivals beyond Trade...*, ch. 2.
15. Destler, *American Trade Politics...*, ch. 9.
16. On the Community's external economic relations, see William James Adams (ed.), *Singular Europe: Economy and Polity of the European Community after 1992* (Ann Arbor: University of Michigan Press, 1992), part 3.

17. The scale of the overseas operations is reviewed in Raymond J. Mataloni, "U.S. Multinational Companies: Operations in 1991," *Survey of Current Business*, 77 (July 1993) 7: 40-49.
18. Profits reinvested abroad are not subject to U.S. tax. James Hines, and Glenn Hubbard, *Coming Home to America: Dividend Repatriations by U.S. Multinationals* (Cambridge: National Bureau of Economic Research, Working Paper No. 2931, 1989).
19. Martin Feldstein (ed.), *The Risk of Economic Crisis* (Chicago: University of Chicago Press, 1991).
20. Laura D'Andrea Tyson, *Who's Bashing Whom? Trade Conflict in High Technology Industries* (Washington: Institute for International Economics, 1993).
21. On the spread of this investment in ASEAN, see *Foreign Direct Investment Relations between OECD...*; and Encarnation, *Rivals beyond Trade...*, ch. 4.
22. Shujiro Urata, "Japanese Foreign Direct Investment and its Effect on Foreign Trade in Asia," in Takatoshi Ito and Anne O. Krueger (eds.), *Trade and Protectionism* (Chicago: University of Chicago Press, 1993), 273-306.
23. See *Foreign Direct Investment Relations between OECD...*
24. Encarnation, *Rivals beyond Trade...*, ch. 5.
25. See *Foreign Direct Investment Relations between OECD...*; and Tun-jen Cheng, "Political Regimes and Development Strategies: South Korea and Taiwan," and Chi Schive, "The Next Stage of Industrialization in Taiwan and South Korea," in Gary Gereffi and Donald L. Wyman (eds.), *Manufacturing Miracles: Paths of Industrialization in Latin America and East Asia* (Princeton: Princeton University Press, 1990), 139-178, 267-291.
26. Urata, "Japanese Foreign Direct Investment..."
27. Cheng, "Political Regimes and Development..."; and Schive, "The Next Stage of Industrialization..."
28. Gavin Boyd, *Corporate Planning and Policy Planning in the Pacific* (London: Pinter, 1993), 129-132.
29. Nicro, "Thailand's NIC Democracy: Studying..."
30. This presence is growing rapidly. See *Foreign Direct Investment Relations between OECD...*
31. Urata, "Japanese Foreign Direct Investment and..."
32. *Far Eastern Economic Review*, 13 May 1993, 13.
33. The difficulties are more serious in the ASEAN area (excluding Singapore) than in South Korea and Taiwan. Boyd, *Corporate Planning and Policy...*, ch. 6.
34. Vigorous export promotion is the main emphasis in U.S. foreign economic policy. See *New York Times*, September 30, 1993, Dl. On the potential advantages of cooperating with Japanese firms, see references to their capabilities for global management, in Allen J. Morrison and Kendall Roth,

"The Regional Solution: an Alternative to Globalization," *Transnational Corporations*, 1 (August 1992) 2: 37-56.

35. See review of ASEAN in *ASEAN Economic Bulletin...*

36. See references to Japanese core networks in *World Investment Report, 1991...*

37. Mowery and Teece, "Japan's Growing Capabilities in Industrial..."

38. Encarnation, *Rivals beyond Trade...*

39. Dileep Hurry, "Restructuring in the Global Economy: The Consequences of Strategic Linkages between Japanese and U.S. Firms," *Strategic Management Journal*, Special Issue, 14 (Summer 1993): 69-82.

40. Encarnation, *Rivals beyond Trade...*, ch. 2.

41. President William J. Clinton and Vice President Albert Gore, *Technology for America's Economic Growth, a New Direction to Build Economic Strength* (Washington: U.S. Government Printing Office, 1993).

42. Shumpei Kumon, and Henry Rosovsky (eds.), *The Political Economy of Japan* (Stanford: Stanford University Press, 1992) Vol. 3.

43. Kester, "Industrial Groups as Systems of Contractual..."

44. On the effects of lobbying and legislative opportunism, see Linda R. Cohen and Roger G. Noll, *The Technology Pork Barrel*, (Washington: Brookings Institution, 1991); and Roger G. Noll, "Structural Policies in the United States," in Samuel Kernell (ed.), *Parallel Politics: Economic Policy-making in Japan and the United States* (Washington: Brookings Institution, 1991), 230-280.

45. Kester, "Industrial Groups as Systems..."

About the Book and Editors

In GATT negotiations over the past several years the United States, a founding member of the Asia Pacific Economic Cooperation Forum, has been pushing hard for a global liberalization of trade in services. This development would have special significance for the Pacific because of the intensifying competition between the United States and Japan for market shares. A comprehensive analysis of the service sector's role in that dynamic region is offered in this timely volume.

Leading experts explore how service enterprises have affected trade in goods and transnational manufacturing, forming a regional pattern of interdependence. The authors assess each service sector from a regional perspective and offer detailed individual country studies as well. The concluding chapters provide a broad overview of corporate strategies, discuss questions of regional cooperation, and identify opportunities for new regional service enterprises.

Gunnar K. Sletmo is Omer DeSerres Professor of Commerce at l'École des Hautes Études Commerciales, Montreal. He has academic degrees from the University of Oslo, the Norwegian School of Economics and Business Administration, and the Graduate School of Business, Columbia University.

Professor Sletmo has held academic appointments in economics, distribution and transportation at the Norwegian School of Economics and Business Administration (1960-1967) and the Graduate School of Business, Columbia University (1969-1977). He has been at HEC since 1977, where he was appointed to the Omer DeSerres Chair of Commerce in 1989.

He has held visiting professorships at the London School of Economics, Maritime College (SUNY), the University of Cape Town, and the University of Tianjin, People's Republic of China.

He was Chairman of the Federal Task Force on Deep-Sea Shipping Canada (1984-1985) and has been consultant to business and governments in Asia, North America and Europe. He authored *Conferences in the Container Age — U.S. Policy at Sea* (with Ernest W. Williams, Jr.) with a foreword by Karl E. Bakke, former Chairman of the U.S. Federal Maritime Commission, and he has published extensively on distribution, trade and transport. He has served as consultant to a number of international organizations, government agencies and large corporations. Since 1985, he has worked regularly in China on projects related to management education, infrastructure investment and the open cities program.

Gavin Boyd is a research associate at the Centre for International Business Studies (CETAI), l'École des Hautes Études Commerciales, affiliated with the University of Montreal, and Honorary Professor, Political Science Deparment, Rutgers University, Newark, New Jersey, where he was a Visiting Professor for the 1989-1990 academic year after retiring from Saint Mary's University, Halifax, Nova Scotia. Previously he had held visiting professorships, during sabbaticals, at the University of Louisville, Arizona State University and the State University of New York, Brockport. During the 1970s and 1980s he was a consultant to the Defence Department, Ottawa, on projects relating to Pacific security. He is now working on a project relating to Canada's foreign economic policy for the Department of External Affairs, Ottawa. In the 1950s and 1960s he held research posts in the Australian Defence Department, the Southeast Asian Treaty Organization, and the Department of International Relations at the Australian National University.

His current research interests cover regional integration in the Pacific, global economic organizations, political change, and advanced political development. His recent books include *Corporate Planning and Policy Planning in the Pacific* (1993); *Structuring International Economic Cooperation* (1991); and *Pacific Trade, Investment, and Politics* (1987).

About the Contributors

Tun-jen Cheng is an associate professor in the Department of Government at the College of William and Mary, Williamsburg, Virginia. He has written extensively on the growth strategies of the East Asian newly industrializing countries.

Donald Crone is professor and chair of Politics and International Relations at Scripps College, Claremont, California. He has published on Southeast Asian political economy issues in *World Politics*, *Pacific Affairs*, *World Development*, the *ASEAN Economic Bulletin*, the Harvard *International Review*, and several edited volumes. He is completing a volume on *Stability and Social Welfare in Southeast Asia*.

J. Colin Dodds is academic vice-president at Saint Mary's University, Halifax, Canada. He has published extensively on international financial issues and has been vice chair of the Canadian Consortium of Management Schools and a governor of the Canadian Institute of Bankers. He has also served as a consultant to a number of international firms and international agencies.

Edward M. Graham is a senior fellow of the Institute for International Economics, Washington, D.C. He has specialized extensively on international trade and technology policies and on the strategies of international firms. With colleagues at the Institute for International Economics he is working on several forthcoming studies of interdependent growth in the industrialized democracies.

Michael P. Ryan is a visiting assistant professor in the Landegger Program in International Business Diplomacy at the Georgetown University School of Foreign Service. He has published on U.S. foreign trade policy and is the author of *Playing by the Rules: USTR, GATT, and American Trade Power in the Pacific* (forthcoming). His current research is on international intellectual property issues.

Yoko Sazanami is professor of economics at Keio University, Tokyo. Her research deals with trade and investment flows between Japan and the U.S. She contributed a chapter on "Japanese Service Enterprises in the Pacific" to *Pacific Service Enterprises and Pacific Cooperation* (1993, Gunnar K. Sletmo and Gavin Boyd, eds.).

Alain Van Peeterssen is professor at the Institute of Applied Economics at l'École des Hautes Études Commerciales, a member of CETAI and director of the Canada-China Management Program linking the HEC, Concordia and Tianjin business schools.

Index